Ordinarily Well

Ordinarily Well

The Case for Antidepressants

Peter D. Kramer

FARRAR, STRAUS AND GIROUX   NEW YORK

Farrar, Straus and Giroux
18 West 18th Street, New York 10011

Library of Congress Cataloging-in-Publication Data
Names: Kramer, Peter D., author.
Title: Ordinarily well : the case for antidepressants / Peter D. Kramer.
Description: First edition. | New York : Farrar, Straus and Giroux, 2016. |
    Includes index.
Identifiers: LCCN 2015036472 | ISBN 9780374280673 (hardback) |
    ISBN 9780374708962 (e-book)
Subjects: LCSH: Antidepressants—History. | Antidepressants—Effectiveness. |
    Psychotropic drugs. | BISAC: PSYCHOLOGY / Mental Health. | PSYCHOLOGY /
    Psychopathology / Depression.
Classification: LCC RM332 .K73 2016 | DDC 615.7/8—dc23
LC record available at http://lccn.loc.gov/2015036472

Designed by Jo Anne Metsch

Our books may be purchased in bulk for promotional, educational, or business
use. Please contact your local bookseller or the Macmillan Corporate and
Premium Sales Department at 1-800-221-7945, extension 5442,
or by e-mail at MacmillanSpecialMarkets@macmillan.com.

www.fsgbooks.com
www.twitter.com/fsgbooks • www.facebook.com/fsgbooks

1   3   5   7   9   10   8   6   4   2

For Eric and Lore, sorely missed,
and, as always,
for Rachel

No one dares any more to say or to acknowledge that he sees what he sees, what is quite simply there, perhaps unspoken or almost unsaid, but readily apparent.

—JAVIER MARÍAS, *Your Face Tomorrow*

Sweet Analytics, 'tis thou hast ravished me.

—CHRISTOPHER MARLOWE, *Doctor Faustus*

Contents

Preface

TOWARD THE START of 2011, I learned that a good friend, Alan, had suffered a stroke. I had met Alan more than forty years before, when we lived on the same small floor of a freshman dormitory at Harvard. In an era when kids from Andover and Exeter seemed to rule the college, we had come from public schools near New York City. We chose the same small field of study, a combined major called History and Literature. We both joined the staff of the college newspaper.

Six years after graduation, we were reunited when, on completing medical school, I entered a psychiatry residency at Yale. I trained at the mental health center where Alan had just finished his psychology internship. We discussed psychotherapy. We supported each other as aspiring writers. Most importantly—this favor bound us forever—Alan introduced me to my future wife. When Rachel and I had children, Alan became an honorary uncle.

Nor was it a matter of shared history, common interests, and gratitude only. Alan was kind, generous, funny, and wise. I loved him dearly.

If patients get to the hospital soon after the first symptom of a stroke appears, they can benefit from clot-busting drugs that limit the damage to the brain. Alan had not gotten that treatment. He was paralyzed on the right side of his body. His speech was severely impaired.

The news reached me days after the event, once Alan asked his cousin, a doctor, to fill me in. The cousin was worried because Alan was not recovering his capacity to move or to speak fluently. It was uncertain that he would be able to practice psychotherapy or to live outside a nursing home.

Desperate to be of use, I searched the medical literature for a research result that I recalled only vaguely. I found it in a respected journal, *The Lancet: Neurology*. A group in France had tested an intervention on more than one hundred patients with the sort of stroke Alan had suffered, where an interruption of blood flow to the brain causes paralysis in one side of the body. In the study, all the patients received physical therapy. In addition, half were put on the antidepressant Prozac and half on a placebo.

Three months down the road, the patients on Prozac had recovered much more of their arm and leg movement than had the patients on placebo. Those given the antidepressant were more likely to be living independently. The benefits extended to those who had not been treated with clot-busters.

The study answered my question about what more could be done for Alan. This congruence—a dilemma in patient care and a high-quality trial that is directly on point—is rarer than you might imagine.

The findings meshed well with a strong, consistent body of research. Stroke survivors commonly suffer depression, for the evident psychological reasons but also because the injury to the brain can involve regions that sustain mood. In the wake of stroke, antidepressants prevent depression and preserve the ability to think clearly. In one study with a nine-year follow-up, patients given an antidepressant in the early going were almost twice as likely to survive in the long term. The decision, prescribe or not, might be a matter of life and death.

Alan had yet to be offered an antidepressant. I urged him to raise the issue with the treatment team and forwarded relevant publications to his physicians. They added antidepressants to Alan's regimen of physical therapy. Within weeks, he began to regain movement in his right leg, progress I observed, as I had been traveling to visit him in the rehabilitation center where he was recovering. Soon he was able to talk to me by phone.

Meanwhile, I'd had a disturbing interchange with a neurologist involved in Alan's care. In prescribing, he said, he was making an exception, based on the preferences that Alan's cousin and I had expressed. In his practice, the neurologist had pulled back on his use of antidepressants since he understood that they were little better than placebos. He mentioned a news report that claimed that medication was effective only in very severe depression.

Later, I spoke with an authority on stroke and mood disorders, Robert Robinson, a psychiatrist at the University of Iowa. Robinson said, "Neurologists tell me they don't use an antidepressant unless a patient is suffering very serious depression. They're influenced by reports that say that's all antidepressants are good for."

I found these conversations distressing.

I had read the news stories. In 2010, *Newsweek* had run a cover piece whose subhead read, "Studies suggest that the popular drugs are no more effective than a placebo." The same year, an analysis of different outcome trials had led to a *USA Today* feature under the banner "Antidepressant Lift May Be All in Your Head." That article had included the claim that the medications work only for very severe depression. "On average," the lead said, "antidepressants may be little more effective than a sugar pill in most patients who take them."

Attacks on antidepressants are not new. Skeptical essays appeared as soon as the class of medication did, over half a century ago. Generally, they constituted elements in a rearguard campaign, an indirect defense of psychotherapy. Because the critiques arose in the context of a partisan dispute, they had little impact. Now, it seemed, colleagues found the arguments so persuasive that they cast a shadow even on the neurology literature, which shows consistent benefits from antidepressants.

To me, the debunking reports were misleading, and it seemed urgent to say so. I was in an uncomfortable mental state, laid low by grief but also agitated. Should I have noticed early warnings of Alan's failing health? One self-indictment led to another, until I began to ask whether I might bear some responsibility for the neurologist's misapprehension.

In 1993, I had written *Listening to Prozac*, a book about the social and ethical implications of certain incidental effects I had observed when prescribing the new antidepressants. Some patients became more assertive. If doctors gained the capacity to tweak personality, how should they use it? The book's success led news editors to ask me to comment on more mainstream questions—lately, this matter of anti-depressants' ability to treat depression. I had declined.

It's not that my words would have borne great weight, but that I had not done what I could. I had known that mistrust of antidepressants was gaining ground. My patients were telling me.

Not long before learning of Alan's stroke, I had been in session with Nora, who had suffered repeated bouts of depression. Although it brought relief in the early going, finally psychotherapy had not kept pace with Nora's worsening episodes. When she moved to Providence, Nora sought me out. In our early discussions, it became apparent that her strengths, which included large measures of creativity, had masked the gravity of her mood disorder. It blighted every aspect of her life. I suggested a trial of antidepressants.

By now, they had held her steady for four years, the longest period since adolescence that Nora had been free of symptoms. Antidepressants had allowed Nora to remake her life. They had saved her marriage, kept her on track in her career, and helped her to function as a mother. But in a recent session with me, she had asked whether the medication was really helping. "Perhaps I'm only experiencing a placebo effect." She had heard a radio news segment. Was it true that antidepressants did nothing, that her faith in them made all the difference?

Nora and I could consider—continually, we did consider—whether it was time to taper the medication. In the past, after efforts to cut back, she had returned to full doses because they were stabilizing. Now, it was the cause for reevaluation that I found striking, the notion that the medicines had acted as mere symbols, stimulating the imagination.

I have worked with patients on antidepressants for four decades, so I had encountered the placebo question repeatedly. In what period have psychotherapeutic medicines been comfortably embraced? But lately, the expressions of doubt had turned more frequent.

Reviewing this trend in my practice, I thought, It should not have taken Alan's stroke to impel me to action. My patients' circumstances should have sufficed. Depression, in its insidious way, acts as a degenerative disease, harming nerve cells. Like Alan's, my patients' brains were under attack. As with Alan, so with my patients: if decisive action was not taken early, the long-term prognosis was grim.

I knew as much. In *Against Depression*, I had discussed the harm depression does. The World Health Organization had found that in developed countries—and everywhere for adult women—mood disorders cause more disability than any other illness. In the United States, only a third of severely depressed patients are on medication. But then, in a given month one in eight American adults takes an antidepressant, with rates for women in their forties and fifties running almost double that. If the drugs don't work, we need to know. If they do work, that truth should not be cast in doubt.

Why had I not entered the fray?

The contemporary antidepressant controversy began with an essay, published in 1998, whose title, "Listening to Prozac but Hearing Placebo," referenced my work. I considered "Hearing Placebo" an act of provocation. It used an idiosyncratic selection of data to argue that antidepressants were less effective than doctors imagined. Never mind. If the piece sometimes read like a satire on research into treatment outcomes, well, that puffed-up enterprise could stand twitting. So could the pharmaceutical industry. I respected "Hearing" as street theater. I saw no need to respond.

I had held back for another reason. With the publication of my Prozac book, I had become a public figure. Reporters interviewed me on national TV news broadcasts, morning and evening. Roz Chast drew "Listening to" cartoons for *The New Yorker*. In a year-end retrospective, *The New York Times* ran a headline, "Listening to 1993," and led with the observation "Prozac had its say."

As much as the next guy, I liked riding the wave, but what was the point of success if I could not pursue my own interests—which were diverse?

Mostly, I held my own. I wrote about intimacy, in *Should You Leave?* Scribner published my novel.

In other media, I tried to broaden my range. For a TED talk, I discussed psychotherapy as a technology. On radio, I hosted programs on domestic violence and mental health care for immigrants. When I contributed to publications such as *The New York Times*, *The Washington Post*, and *Slate*, the topics varied: neuroscience, yes, but also literary fiction, theater, television, politics, and religion.

Viewing my uncomfortable efforts at independence, a friend sent along Norman Mailer's self-report about the impossibility of escaping

one's public persona: "He had, in fact, learned to live in the sarcophagus of his image—at night, in his sleep, he might dart out, and paint
improvements on the sarcophagus." Reviewers of downstream books
called me "that Prozac man" and "Dr. Prozac." Against all indications,
I remained hopeful that I might walk free by day, alter my obituary.

I skirted the antidepressant debate. In *Against Depression*—the
book is about the tension between romantic views of melancholy and
the modern neuroscientific perspective—it's clear that I consider medication a tool for treatment. In my blog entries and book reviews, too,
that opinion was apparent. But I understood that if I took on the larger
issue, the design of the sarcophagus would be complete.

I worried, too, that as a doctor and a writer I might become tainted
by association. In the post-Prozac years, Big Pharma had crossed any
number of lines, corrupting the scientific literature, subsidizing influential physicians, and hiding bad outcomes. I saw no upside in joining
a controversy on the drug companies' side.

Now, those reasons for holding back seemed insubstantial. I was
ready to engage.

Providentially, the opportunity arrived right then. In late April of
2011, Trish Hall, an editor at *The New York Times*, invited me to write
about antidepressants. The *Times* was launching a new section, the
Sunday Review, that would feature opinion pieces by nonstaffers. At a
dinner party, a fellow guest had surprised Hall by insisting that the
medications don't work. Checking magazine articles, Hall found reports of studies that judged Prozac, Zoloft, Lexapro, and the rest to act
only through hopeful expectancy. She wondered whether I would comment on the claim that the drugs are inherently ineffective.

I said that I was eager to contribute a corrective essay—but I wondered, would she run it? Aware that the story lacked a news peg, I
opted to "write long," discussing research in detail. My hope was to
confirm for Hall that the topic mattered. When relevant news arose, I
would tailor my content to the event.

In early June, *The New York Review of Books* posted online the first
part of a roundup review, critical of psychiatry, by Marcia Angell, a
formidable figure. Angell had served as interim editor of *The New
England Journal of Medicine*, the profession's best-respected publica-

tion. She was an advocate of evidence-based medicine, a two-decade-old movement that, in its extreme form, foresaw a future in which doctors would dispense with clinical wisdom and rely almost exclusively on the results of highly structured experiments.

Discussing antidepressants, Angell drew on a book that equated them with placebos. She bought its conclusions. Angell ended her consideration of psychotherapeutic medication by entertaining the premise—it might be fair to say that she endorsed it—that "psychoactive drugs are useless . . . or worse than useless."

My Sunday Review piece sped toward publication. I decided that, for my purposes, the particulars of Angell's argument were a distraction. Beyond inserting a reference to her *New York Review* piece, I did not change my essay except by tightening it. I engaged the debunking analyses directly.

"In Defense of Antidepressants" ran in July of 2011. In the piece, I reviewed research studies and concluded, based on their findings, that antidepressants were as beneficial as most treatments that doctors are content to use. The importance of the essay was less in the points I had fussed over than in its having been well published, filling most of the front page of the new section. The lead placement said, The story has two sides. There was the view that antidepressants do not work at all and (now, again) the view that they work ordinarily well.

Responding to my essay with a letter to the editor, Angell restated her position. One sentence struck me as misdirected. Angell had written, "Anecdotes of effectiveness are no substitute for clinical trials, since they can't take into account the placebo effect or how often a drug is ineffective or harmful."

What anecdotes might Angell have had in mind? I had included only one. To illustrate my topic's urgency, I had described Alan's progress, but then said, "As is true with much that we see in clinical medicine, the cause of this change is unknowable." It was controlled trials such as the one in *The Lancet: Neurology*—studies in which antidepressants are contrasted to dummy pills—that had justified prescribing for Alan. In citing the research literature, had I not shown myself to be Angell's colleague—like her, a doctor obsessed with scrupulous experiments?

There, with fast-fading annoyance, the matter might have rested had not Angell come at me again. Within days, Alex Beam, a columnist for *The Boston Globe*, contacted me. Beam asked whether I was in a boxing match with Angell.

No, I said, no fight was in progress. This correction was easy to make. I had composed the *Times* essay unaware of Angell's misgivings about antidepressants.

Undeterred, Beam led his column with boxing and tug-of-war metaphors. He described a contest between local New England doctors, Angell and Kramer, an impression that Angell had done nothing to dispel. According to the column, when Beam interviewed Angell, she had complained, "You can't base judgments on anecdotes from clinical experience, because that can be very misleading . . . I have faith in the evidence—in rigorous, randomized, double blind controlled clinical trials, and that's the only way we can get at the facts. Medical history is filled with storytelling, and it is often wrong." How exasperating! Did Angell imagine that psychiatrists ignore those rigorous, randomized, and on-and-on trials? I was on my high horse. And then I paused.

I took it as likely that Angell and I were in agreement on important points. We would both say that the antidepressant controversy matters, that doctors and patients should know whether drugs work. I imagined that we would agree, too, that some psychiatric research—including studies that are exemplary in design, incorporating randomization and the other virtues—can in practice be pretty bad, flawed in execution. Certainly, we both believed that drug companies had a lot to answer for and that, finally, it would be better if assessments of medication were performed by neutral experts. Angell was famously critical of Pharma.

At the same time, I saw that, however imprecisely, Angell was pointing to a difference of viewpoint. She was a pathologist and an editor. She believed—this point was the one she reiterated—in objective evidence as the be-all and end-all. I treated patients. Like most doctors, I kept abreast of research results, but I read them in the context of what I saw in my daily work.

I had made no secret of my perspective. Once before, I had crossed paths with Angell. In 1994, we had shared a dais at a medical meeting, convened by epidemiologists, at the University of Iowa. I had begun my talk—about biological perspectives on the self, the material of *Listening to Prozac*—by facing the audience and confessing, "I stand before you as a clinician."

I'd had in mind Bill Clinton's recent presidential campaign and the way that errant politicians open their sermons on visits to churches. When I said *clinician*, I had wanted my listeners to hear *sinner*. The Iowa doctors laughed in response. Academics had their doubts about practitioners.

When I returned to my seat, Angell had a question for me: How much of what I had discussed was supported by randomized trials?

Now as then, she was affirming her faith in careful experiments that stand as bulwarks against unreliable informal impressions. What I subscribed to was harder to name, although, as a one-word summary, pragmatism might do. Clinicians need to act. They bring to bear whatever they can lay their hands on. I believed that incontrovertible truths are rare and doubt is a constant. In psychiatry, it seemed to me that decision making requires poking and prodding all sorts of material.

Nor was my confession, *clinician*, a full one. Most doctors come to the profession through the sciences. I had studied the humanities, and the training had left its mark. I approached research monographs as texts to be interpreted in light of their genre. Some were high literature; others, potboilers. Other papers were, to my reading, polemics or tall tales. A few analyses struck me as transgressive and witty. I loved quirky small studies.

Where Angell proposed a dichotomy—refined research, which gets at the facts, versus anecdotes, which are often misleading—I saw a spectrum on which sit flawed efforts at objectivity. I respected clinical experience. Why else would I ask colleagues for advice? I wanted my own doctor to have seen a thing or two.

Are clinicians sinners? More and more. As a society, we don't trust doctors as we once did. Ours is an era of fascination with medical error. Atul Gawande's writing on surgical complications and Jerome Groopman's on ways that physicians fool themselves—admirable books—have earned places on bestseller lists. Doctors are human. The human mind is fallible, a truth that forms the basis for broad swaths of contemporary psychology: studies of how we overgeneralize based on the last event we've seen, how we savor cheap wine presented in fancy bottles. And then, there's the vogue for placebo—an upswing in the belief that expectancy aroused by dummy pills can do great things. If so, doctors will often be deceived about the cause of their patients' progress.

To grant doctorly judgment a role is to oppose the zeitgeist, never a wise move. And then, I have always been subject to self-doubt—out ahead of the trend in that regard. Patient care is humbling.

That said, after Alan's stroke, engaging the antidepressant controversy seemed unavoidable. Angell's response to my piece made me understand that the task had two elements: answering the do-they-work question and showing what a practicing doctor brings to the moment of decision making.

This book is about two influences on medical practice: rigorous trials and clinical encounters. In an attempt to keep the strands separate, I will use the title "Interlude" for chapters that, more than others, discuss time spent with patients. But the distinction holds up poorly. Observations from my own experience intrude on scientific sections, and case vignettes introduce technical points. This mingling reflects a dialectic that shapes practice. Doctors interrogate the literature, try new approaches, note results, revise their sense of what's plausible, and read further.

I begin the narrative by reviewing the development of antidepressants and the research that tests their worth. At the start of my career, I happened into a glancing acquaintance with pioneers from the early generations of psychopharmacologists. Their history sets the context in which I, and colleagues like me, view questions of treatment efficacy.

Since they inform the interpretation of the scientific narrative, I will need to say something about statistics, the "inside baseball" of psychiatry. I'm hoping that there's some fun, some fascination, in the details. I read the literature with a clinician's eye, read it, as I have confessed, as "literature." Still, my critique involves attending to how trials are constructed, asking whether one or another design compromise or analytic method opens the door to the systematic bias that formal studies are meant to avoid. The more liable it is to error of this sort, the more like subjective commentary a contribution becomes, never mind that the opinion is expressed in numbers.

For the most part, I will not discuss brain biology—neurons or synapses, mice or monkeys. Our narrow topic is complex enough, and besides, I reviewed that other material in *Listening to Prozac* and *Against Depression*; in broad strokes the theories of illness and recovery remain unchanged.

This book does look at patients, however: patients as their stories play out in doctors' offices and patients as their progress is captured in data. Throughout, I will raise questions about evidence: what it is, where it is gathered, how it is processed, what forces might distort it, and how a clinician incorporates it in practice. I will try never to lose sight of our main question, whether antidepressants work. We're talking about a major scourge of humankind, depression. We're thinking about many millions of people, those on medication and those not yet offered care. We need to know.

Weekday afternoons, I sit with patients. They are failing, they are suffering, they are at risk of further injury. I can recommend medication or hold off. How to proceed? How best to address Alan's crisis or Nora's doubts? This book is a clinician's, a sinner's—my—idiosyncratic attempt at an answer.

This, the most technical of my books, may also be the most personal, and the act of its composition, the most solitary. I have tried to query my behavior as a physician, to ask why I act as I do, and to bring my decisions and the grounds for them to the page. At the same time, the research has thrust me into a field, statistics, about which I know only the little that clinicians rely on as readers. For that reason, it also is the book for which I have leaned the most on others for guidance.

As always, I want to thank my patients, who entrust so much to me while tolerating my shortcomings.

To preserve privacy—for my patients and for drug trial participants—in vignettes I have altered names, ages, eras, genders, and the circumstances of love and work. Sometimes I have combined aspects or histories of different people to create a single character. Always, I have aimed to retain the nub of salient encounters: a person and her response to adversity, an illness and its response to treatment. I hope that this method accords with a theme of the book, that while they cannot force particular conclusions, anecdotes that convey clinical experience can, together, form a useful perspective from which to view a scientific literature in need of interpretation.

In the care of my (real) patients, I have often relied on the wisdom of colleagues. They have my gratitude.

My agent, Andrew Wylie, and my editors, Jonathan Galassi and Alex Star, have shepherded this project (and me) along with understanding and forbearance.

Without the support of my wife, Rachel, there would be no books.

But, especially for this project, I would be remiss if I did not thank the many doctors, scholars, and other experts who, in response to my questions, have been generous with their time, instruction, research results, stories, theories, advice, and opinion. With deep gratitude, I want to acknowledge the contributions of Scott Aaronson, Goldie Alfasi, Per Bech, Harold Bursztajn, Linda Carpenter, Rachel Churchill, Philip Cowen, James Coyne, Pim Cuijpers, John Davis, Carl Elliott, Yiru Fang, James Faucett, Maurizio Fava, Jan Fawcett, Anna Fels, Robert Fenster, Murray Finkelstein, Konstantinos Fountoulakis, Ellen Frank, Richard Friedman, Nassir Ghaemi, Pedro Gozalo, Alan Gruenberg, Ralitza Gueorguieva, David Hellerstein, Verena Henkel, Jamie Horder, Asbjørn Hróbjartsson, Thomas Insel, John Ioannidis, Blair Johnson, Ronald Kessler, Arifula Khan, Donald Klein, Helena Kraemer, Thomas Laughren, Stephan Leucht, Robert Liberman, Michael Liebowitz, Scott Lilienfeld, Mauricio Silva de Lima, Richard Metzner, Andrew Nierenberg, Mark Olfson, Raymond Osheroff, Ronald Pies, Alan Pollack, Walter Reich, Robert Robinson, Norman Rosenthal, Anthony Rothschild, Bret Rutherford, Timothy Ryan, M. Tracie Shea, Richard Shelton, Charles Silberstein, David Solomon, Michael Stein, Jonathan Stewart, Michael Thase, Thomas Trikalinos, Erick Turner, Bruce Wampold, and the administration and staff of the clinical research center where I observed antidepressant assessment in progress.

I list these colleagues without meaning to implicate them in the work at hand. Many of them will disagree with my conclusions. To their great credit, many have cooperated while knowing that we differ in our views. We had fun, I think, batting around ideas, and when it came to instruction, I hope that I proved a willing, if not always an apt, pupil.

Ordinarily Well

1

The Birth of the Modern

A SWISS PSYCHIATRIST, Roland Kuhn, invented the modern antidepressant. He didn't synthesize a chemical. He created the concept.

Kuhn gave the antidepressant era a birth date, January 18, 1956. Six days earlier, under his care, a forty-nine-year-old hospitalized woman had begun taking 100 milligrams daily of G22355, a substance supplied by the Swiss pharmaceutical firm Geigy. On the eighteenth, Paula J.F. was markedly better—less afflicted by what Kuhn called her "vital depression." By the twenty-first, the ward staff noted that the patient was "totally changed." An entry in the medical record read, "For three days now, it is as if the patient had undergone a transformation."

Kuhn was aware that spontaneous remissions occur, but he knew his patients well. Paula J.F. was different, even from how she had been before the depressive episode. Characteristically aggressive and quarrelsome, now she was friendly. For the first time in years, Paula J.F. enjoyed work and reading. She thought more clearly. Her sleep had improved as well.

Kuhn bridged the old and the new in psychiatry: psychoanalysis and psychopharmacology. Born in Biel, Switzerland, in 1912, he studied medicine in Bern and Paris. In 1939, he took a post at the psychiatric hospital in Münsterlingen, a hundred-odd miles from his birthplace. Kuhn had chosen the assignment in hopes of learning from the psychoanalyst and existential philosopher Ludwig Binswanger, who worked nearby and whom Kuhn considered a genius in his understanding of mood disorder. At the core of Binswanger's practice was attention to Martin Heidegger's concept *Dasein*—personhood or presence, the reality of being here. Kuhn practiced *Daseinsanalyse*, receiving supervision from Binswanger and interacting with philosophers, including Heidegger. Kuhn treated inpatients and clinic patients both. Thus far, nothing unusual: the psychiatry of midcentury was psychoanalytic. Kuhn was a generalist, working in obscurity.

But Kuhn was a polymath. Interested in psychiatric classification, he developed his own diagnostic approach. He also employed the direct biological interventions of the time, including insulin shock therapy, where, via a rapid lowering of their blood sugar, patients were thrown into epileptic seizures. Kuhn prescribed drugs like morphine and amphetamine. Opiates and stimulants were what passed for psychotherapeutic medications. They might calm or arouse patients, but nothing targeted schizophrenia, depression, or mania directly.

The breakthrough came in the early 1950s with the development of Thorazine—called Largactil in Europe—the first effective drug for psychosis. Kuhn requested a supply for his hospital. For six months, the manufacturer offered Largactil gratis: "The whole clinic was swallowing Largactil, as one could imagine." The drug replaced the life-threatening therapies, and it worked. But at the end of the trial phase, the company began to charge for Largactil.

Kuhn understood—the whole small society of psychiatrists who dealt with pharmaceuticals understood—that the world had changed. For the first time in history, doctors could offer medication to schizophrenic patients and have a fair hope of making a difference.

With depressed patients, Kuhn observed, Largactil might calm agitation, but it left the core symptoms untouched. In any event, the hospital could not afford Largactil. But Kuhn had a relationship with Geigy. He asked whether the company had similar chemicals.

The first preparation that Geigy delivered helped relieve schizophrenia, but poorly, and it had unpleasant side effects. Kuhn then asked for a chemical like the one he had previewed but with a molecular structure more like Largactil's. As it happened, Geigy had synthesized that substance, G22355.

In retrospect, after decades' more progress in molecular biochemistry, Kuhn's request looks to be a shot in the dark. Even with sophisticated imaging capabilities, scientists cannot readily predict function from structure. And other accounts differ from Kuhn's. Alan Broadhurst, a chemist in charge of pharmaceuticals for Geigy in Britain, was one of the first people to ingest G22355, in a test of its safety. He said that once Largactil had shown its worth, Geigy took an interest in G22355. The company, Broadhurst recalled, had proposed a meeting with Kuhn, despite his known allegiance to "the old, strictly nonbiological school of psychiatry, with a strong psychodynamic and psychotherapeutic component."

One way or another, Kuhn obtained a supply of G22355, later christened imipramine. He tried the medication on three hundred patients. It was a weak antipsychotic. But Kuhn noticed that on G22355 some schizophrenic patients got less depressed. He wondered whether the medication might be useful for depression.

At the distance of sixty years, it is difficult to appreciate how original Kuhn's thinking was. Psychoanalysts addressed depression piecemeal. A neurotic man might lose his energy because it remained bound in feelings for his dead mother and, separately, feel suicidal because anger toward his father had been deflected to the self. Kuhn saw depression as a syndrome composed of symptoms that wax and wane in concert and that might be responsive to direct effects on the brain.

Once there was glory to be claimed, Geigy scientists recalled that they, too, had considered approaching depression as a medical disorder, but the bigger truth seems clear: Geigy had little interest in inventing or marketing an antidepressant.

Most practicing doctors were unprepared to accept the concept. Some schools of thought understood schizophrenia to be "extrapsychic," a result of an organic disease whose cause had not been identified. To approach it with medication was not unthinkable. Depression was another matter. Freud had defined the field with "Mourning and Melancholia," the essay that located the source of even severe depression in ambivalent feelings about loved ones. If Freud had also been open to ideas of biological causation, his followers dropped that consideration.

They focused on meaning, depression as unresolved emotional attachment. Depressive neuroses were at the heart of psychoanalytic practice.

Kuhn knew that depression often responded to electroconvulsive therapy, or ECT, where current is applied to the scalp, causing the equivalent of a seizure in the brain. He reasoned the disorder must also have an organic basis. When he saw that patients' mood states, more than their psychoses, were altered by G22355, he tried using the drug to treat depression in nonpsychotic patients.

He began with the condition that he considered most biological, "vital depression." Patients with vital depression suffered "feelings of fatigue, lethargy, confinement, oppression, and inhibition, accompanied by a slowing-down of thinking, acting, and decision." The disturbance was worse in the morning. In contrast, "reactive depression" was triggered by a psychological cause and worsened as the day progressed.

Kuhn considered vital depression difficult to identify. Patients might reveal the nature of their affliction only in the course of a long relationship with a doctor. In his practice outside the hospital, Kuhn diagnosed vital depression in patients with gastrointestinal distress whose cause had been hard to pin down. Overall, Kuhn's notion of depression corresponded to an informal understanding we might have today, a substantial psychological impairment with despondency at the core.

After administering G22355 to three depressed patients, Kuhn concluded that it was likely an antidepressant—the first specific medication treatment for mood disorders ever discovered. The drug reversed the fatigue, oppression, and impaired thinking all at once. It resolved the syndrome—the cluster of symptoms—of depression.

Kuhn notified Geigy and went on to study the effects of G22355 on forty patients whom he could observe closely over time. Most were seriously ill inpatients, but Kuhn also medicated outpatients whose depression was not immediately apparent. The medicine worked even for patients whose black mood had an obvious cause. Kuhn mentioned a young woman who had developed depression in the face of "a criminal abortion under difficult circumstances" and an older woman who had faltered in response to paralysis from polio.

In August of 1957, Kuhn reported his findings in a Swiss medical weekly. The short paper is a classic in the psychiatric literature. Kuhn got many points right. He characterized imipramine's side effects: dry mouth, rapid heartbeat, and constipation. He estimated the dosage needed for efficacy, often up to 200 or 250 milligrams. He described the drug's course of action. Some patients responded within days, but many took one to four weeks to improve. Kuhn had not seen enough patients to be confident of his estimates, but he believed that on imipramine a quarter to a half of patients would achieve full remission directly. Another group would gain enough relief to make their condition bearable while they awaited a natural remission. In all, three-quarters to four-fifths of patients would benefit.

On imipramine, Kuhn explained, patients did not regain one faculty only—energy, say, as on amphetamine. They woke in the morning without the discouragement that had dogged them. They took renewed interest in family life. They slept without the aid of a sleeping pill. Their suicidal impulses disappeared. The nurses reported fluent conversations, free of whines and sighs.

Stories of medical priority tend to have asterisks. In the early 1950s, a medication for tuberculosis was noted to rev up and remoralize patients. Later, simultaneously with Kuhn's paper, a drug related to the antituberculars was promoted as a "psychic energizer." The word *antidepressant* was first applied to this class of substances, the monoamine oxidase inhibitors, or MAOIs, drugs that interfere broadly with the breakdown of transmitter chemicals in the brain, the monoamines. (Imipramine, and medications like it, would be called tricyclics, a reference to their three-ring chemical structure.) I tell the MAOIs' story briefly in *Listening to Prozac*.

Because the MAOIs presented medical risks, they did not achieve the popularity of tricyclics. Also, conceptually the MAOIs were unsurprising. Often, they acted as stimulants first, before moderating patients' depression. In contrast, imipramine had calming properties and lifted mood nonetheless. Remarkably, Kuhn had taken a drug that was not energizing and employed it as a specific for melancholy.

Kuhn's discovery of the therapeutic powers of imipramine illustrates one way of coming to know, scientifically: seeing a medicine do something that no substance has done before. Kuhn's assessment of imipramine had virtues that formal drug trials rarely duplicate. He knew his patients well and interviewed them extensively. He could be confident of their diagnoses. He gave imipramine when it became available—at an arbitrary moment—and so avoided the confusion that can arise when volunteers sign on for treatment, perhaps in an interval of optimism, when their depression is waning. Kuhn tested imipramine for eighteen months, without deviating from his customary administration of care.

And Kuhn had a good sense of what placebo aficionados call the counterfactual condition, how his patients would have fared had the new treatment not been given. The ward had observed Largactil work wonders for psychosis, yet depressed patients did only so well with it. Other Geigy drugs had proved disappointing. Neither pill taking nor psychotherapy, the best-supported treatment of the time, did what imipramine did. The new medication produced unprecedented levels of change.

Kuhn tested imipramine at a moment that can arrive only once, when an antidepressant is available but no one has been treated with one. Today, trials of new drugs attract people who have failed on readily available medications or people outside the medical system, not diagnosed in the ordinary course of practice—an unrepresentative sample. Kuhn had access to a population "naïve," that is, never before exposed, to antidepressants. Although it lacked rigor, Kuhn's experiment was of singular evidentiary value. Kuhn would say as much. He had witnessed the full power of an antidepressant.

In September of 1957, Kuhn discussed his results at an international psychiatric congress in Zurich. A dozen participants attended the talk, and the reception was mixed. Looking back, one attendee compared the presentation to the Gettysburg Address. He was referring to the high quality of expression and the audience's belated appreciation of the message.

Only after an important Geigy shareholder tried the pills on his wife to good effect did the company push imipramine forward.

Kuhn understood that imipramine represented a new category of medication. His discovery helped to redefine the disorder, depression, and to invigorate a branch of psychiatry, psychopharmacology. Robert Domenjoz, who oversaw all pharmacological research at Geigy, later emphasized the uniqueness of Kuhn's contribution: "One thing is certain, Roland Kuhn was the person who discovered the antidepressant effect, without a shadow of a doubt. No-one else realized this."

2

Interlude
Anecdote

IF KUHN'S STORY plays an important role in my imagination, it is because all psychiatrists of my generation were discoverers. Each of us came upon antidepressants for the first time—the first in our own careers, anyway.

I saw imipramine in action in my freshman year of medical school, at Harvard. When I arrived, in 1972, the medical school was a Brigadoon, caught in the psychiatry of fifteen or even fifty years earlier. Other programs had moved on. Harvard remained a bastion of Freudianism.

I liked the outdated orthodoxy. After college, while studying literature and philosophy in London, I had undergone psychoanalysis and decided to become a psychiatrist. I entered medical school not knowing the location of the liver or the cause of measles. To maintain my sanity in the early going, I signed on to spend spare hours interviewing psychiatric patients at Boston's Beth Israel Hospital, steps from the academic campus.

The clinic was my haven from anatomy and biochemistry. One chief resident, a tall woman, called me the departmental mascot, although perhaps that was because I ventured upward glances at her with puppy-dog eyes. At twenty-three, I could scarcely have been greener. Still, by

the second semester I had achieved the privilege of conducting psychotherapy.

One of my first patients was a twenty-six-year-old elementary-
school teacher, Adele. Since her teens, Adele had suffered intervals of
moodiness in which she had functioned poorly. In the months before
her visit to the clinic, a down period had deepened. She was distraught.
She considered suicide.

Adele had her reasons. A two-year romantic relationship had ended.
When her fiancé moved on, Adele had returned home to a disorganized mother. Adele's younger sister was involved with an abusive older
man, and Adele had attempted a futile rescue effort. Meanwhile, she
was under pressure from a rigid school principal who seemed jealous of
Adele's youth and idealism.

I gave what I had from my time on the couch. I listened. I inquired.
Suicide?

Adele was half-Irish, half-Italian, a Boston type, the sober member
of a loud, impulsive family. Her only dramatic act had been cutting
herself, in high school. Then, she felt dejection. Now, she was coming
out of her skin.

That last remark made me curious. For a first-year adviser, Harvard
had assigned me an endocrinologist, another Boston type, the lone professional in a working-class, left-wing family from the North End. Psychiatry was on the list of indulgences she disdained. If I wanted to
understand mood disorders, I should learn about glands. I knew that
thyroid abnormalities could produce the psychic and bodily discomfort
that Adele described.

Because my adviser had half my loyalty (psychotherapy had the
rest) and because Adele was convincing when she called her agitation
unfamiliar, I tested her thyroid. When initial blood results came back
normal, I had vials run for a second form of thyroid hormone, one that
had only lately been implicated in disease.

Adele did have an overactive gland. News of my "catch" sped through
the psychiatry department. The holdout from the circle of admiration
was my supervisor for the prolonged elective, Theodore Nadelson.

A skilled therapist, Ted would become known for work in psychosomatics, the overlap of psychiatry and general medicine. He warned me
to keep track of Adele as she moved to the endocrine and later (after a

radioactive-iodine swallow failed to destroy the gland) the surgical service. He predicted that Adele would emerge from her thyroid treatment still in need of psychotherapy, as she did. We gave the replacement
hormone time to reach the proper level. If anything, Adele's despondency deepened.

Ted never explained why he considered antidepressants for Adele.
In Boston, recourse to psychiatric medication was thought to signal a
failure of imagination on the part of the doctor. The therapist's goal
was not to mute symptoms but to understand them and allow them to
act as spurs to self-examination. A patient offered antidepressants might
sit back and wait for the drugs to take effect. She would get a read on
her doctor's anxiety as he adjusted the dosage. Because the patient was
on medication, the real treatment, based on the doctor's neutral presentation of self and resulting in the patient's increased tolerance for
feelings, would bog down.

Freud had compared the setting for psychoanalysis to the surgeon's
sterile field. In this clean work space, unsullied by the therapist's intrusions, insights into the patient's mental makeup might emerge. But for
Adele, the treatment relationship was already contaminated. With
other doctors, I had held forth a promise of a cure through powerful
interventions: radiation and surgery. Now Adele required adjustments
of the hormone she took in pill form, so she got repeated indications of
her doctors' assessment of her well-being. How much confusion would
an antidepressant add?

Perhaps a bigger factor in Ted's decision to consider antidepressants
was a change in Adele. With the thyroid under control, she appeared
more purely despairing. There was so much she could not save: job,
romance, sister. By Adele's new account, she had always seen life as
bleak, always wanted death to come to her young.

Doubtless Ted was uncomfortable with the idea of a first-year
trainee's mucking about in the unconscious of a morbid young woman.
Ted arranged for the chief resident to assess Adele for treatment with
medication. The resident prescribed imipramine. The dose was raised
until Adele complained of constipation. She was offered a stool soft-
ener and a dose decrease.

I wanted Adele out of pain and danger, but more, I wanted her better, which was a different matter, involving self-understanding.

Imipramine acted in a fashion I later came to call courteous. It afforded modest but invaluable relief. Imipramine quieted ruminations, damped impulsivity, and restored concentration. This quick improvement, however partial, was arresting.

In twice-weekly meetings, Adele had discussed her emotional responses to neglect by her mother, intrusion from her stepfather, and rejections by men. She had gone in circles, turning from blame to self-recrimination. On medication, Adele became reflective, arriving at a stable assessment of her background. Her distress seemed proportionate to her practical frustrations. She found allies at school. If she continued to seek out unreliable lovers, she handled them more prudently.

Antidepressants were short-term treatments. After four months, the resident tapered the drug. Adele and I were at work on our project, confronting masochistic drives, when a job offer drew her to another city and I lost contact.

Later, prescribing antidepressants to other patients, I witnessed dramatic remissions of the sort that had set Kuhn on his way. Adele's subtler improvement had its own special impact: imipramine had made me a more competent therapist.

Only once have I had a similar experience, and that was on the ski slopes. In 1996, a magazine commissioned me to write a first-person piece about whether expert lessons could lift an unathletic, uncoordinated skier above the intermediate plateau. Midway through the experiment, an instructor put me on the new, shaped—parabolic—skis. The technology trumped the teaching. With no further learning, I had more control and more courage on the steeps.

In the work with Adele, imipramine made my level of skill suffice.

As an acolyte, I retained my teachers' misgivings about drug treatment. If medication made therapy more productive, still perhaps Adele had skipped some necessary step. What I did not doubt was imipramine's ability to moderate symptoms in short order.

I gave little thought to placebo effects. If Adele had been a placebo responder, her low mood would have disappeared in the face of radiation or surgery.

Because my teachers at Harvard considered pharmacotherapy only in medically complex cases, I had this sort of experience repeatedly—

seeing antidepressants work for patients who had not responded to a host of prior treatments.

Adele was the first in a private series, patients I worked with in psychotherapy and then followed as they began antidepressants. The library of cases is what we have in mind when we speak of experience. We like doctors to have firsthand familiarity with treatments they offer.

But then, experience does not arise in isolation. Ted read the journals. It was because imipramine tested out well in formal studies that I got to see Adele's new openness to change.

3

Random Thoughts

BECAUSE RANDOMIZED TRIALS have become essential to medical practice, we may forget that they are of recent origin. Developed in agriculture, where farming methods were tested through being applied to random sections of fields, the approach entered medicine in the late 1940s, after the discovery of the first antibiotics. The pioneering work concerned a treatment for tuberculosis.

Tuberculosis that reaches into the nervous system, tuberculous meningitis, was almost always fatal. When meningitis responded to streptomycin, it was clear, without recourse to sophisticated evaluation methods, that the drug worked.

Tuberculosis in its more frequent location, the lung, behaved differently. Some infected patients recovered on their own. The question of whom to treat was critical, since pulmonary tuberculosis was common and streptomycin was in short supply. In 1946, the British Medical Research Council, guided by the pioneering statistician Sir Austin Bradford Hill, planned a trial with a new design. Participants would be randomly assigned to receive the usual treatment, strict bed rest, or the experimental treatment, bed rest supplemented by injections of the antibiotic.

The study's main outcome measure was progress of the disease as it appeared in chest X-rays. Streptomycin performed well. In the first weeks, patients on streptomycin were much likelier to see marked radiologic improvement—and fewer died. Looking more broadly, twice as many patients on streptomycin (69 percent, versus 33 percent of those on bed rest only) showed some clearing on their chest films.

Antibiotic treatment rarely eliminated infections. By the four-month mark, new strains of the bacillus emerged. In the following two months, bed rest matched the antibiotic. Using unsystematic observation, doctors had already reached the right conclusion: streptomycin helps in the early going. Even though the experiment only confirmed clinical wisdom, the research design was seen to enact the scientific spirit of the age. The study established the randomized trial as a standard in medicine, especially to evaluate treatments for conditions like pulmonary tuberculosis, which wax and wane on their own, with remedies like streptomycin, whose reach is limited.

Because the antidepressant controversy turns on the interpretation of randomized trials, we will need to gain comfort with them. The design has three elements intended to keep assessments objective: a *control condition, randomization*, and *blinding*.

In an outcome trial, a promising intervention is contrasted to a comparison intervention, the control, in which participants receive all the elements of patient care except the active treatment under study—in this case, streptomycin. The testing setups are called *arms*. The streptomycin trial had a medication-plus-bed-rest arm and, as a control, a bed-rest-only arm. Sometimes, the control condition will include a *placebo*, or sham treatment.

In patient care, lots of things happen at once. Doctors prescribe, but they also offer support and attention. Time passes, allowing for what commentators on the streptomycin trial called *vis medicatrix naturae*, the healing power of Mother Nature.

Including a control arm helps researchers to estimate the *inherent efficacy* of an intervention, the contribution that it makes through its special properties—with streptomycin, the ability to inhibit the growth of bacteria. When we ask whether a medicine is inherently effective, we are asking whether it offers benefits beyond those of time, circumstance, and the doctorly encounter. A simple assumption—not always justified, but a fair starting point—is that if we subtract the progress patients make in the control arm from the greater progress their counterparts make in the treatment arm, the remainder will be the contribution made by the active ingredient, the treatment's inherent efficacy.

A placebo is a treatment that has the same form as the active intervention but lacks the ingredient understood to be effective. In a test of acupuncture, a sham version, with needles stuck in the wrong spots, where they ought not to promote healing, will serve as a placebo. In tests of antidepressants, inert pills, containing, say, sugar, act as placebos.

Hearing *placebos*, people may think of the magic feather that lends Dumbo confidence and so allows him to fly—talismans that work through inspiring hopeful expectancy. As we shall see, scientists disagree about how commonly this specific phenomenon, the *classic placebo effect*, operates in clinical medicine. In practice, the placebo arm of a trial covers a host of sins and virtues. Some patients will recover naturally, over time. Others will, on entering the trial, have been misdiagnosed; later, when diagnosed correctly, they will be counted as free of the disease under study. These recoveries, real or apparent, are not due to the inherent efficacy of the treatment.

The control condition packages what statisticians call *nuisance variables*: the noise that researchers want to filter out—as with noise-canceling headphones a passenger might use during an air flight—so that they can hear the pure music of the active treatment. Placebo is the equivalent of static, engine hum, and murmured conversation—everything other than the signal we're listening for.

The statisticians who designed the streptomycin trial were unconcerned about classic placebo effects. The antibiotic was given by injection into a muscle, four times a day; participants in the control arm were not subjected to that pain. The control arm took into account improvement due to bed rest, nursing care, and natural waning of the infection.

All well and good—we will contrast bed rest plus medicine to bed rest alone. But the comparison will be valid only if, when our study begins, the patients receiving each treatment are similar: equally ill, equally resilient, and so on.

In some early controlled trials, experimenters alternated assignments, giving every other subject the medicine under test. Practicing doctors could game the system, holding back promising patients, timing their entry so as to afford them the presumed benefit of the active treatment. If research participants on the drug did better, the difference might be due to their having been healthier to start with.

This and other hidden sources of confusion are called *confounds*. Often, confounds result from *bias*, a systematic flaw, such as the pattern of assigning promising patients to receive the drug. This particular problem, the one caused here by meddlesome doctors, is called *susceptibility bias*; participants in one arm are more susceptible to further illness and death than those in the other arm. Bias can lead to spurious findings—in this instance, an inflated estimate of a drug's powers.

In a randomized trial, researchers use something like a coin toss— typically they turn to a table of random numbers—to pair subjects and interventions. In the streptomycin study, once a patient had been accepted, a numbered envelope was randomly selected and then opened to reveal a card with the letter C, assigning that patient to the control condition, or S, for streptomycin.

The streptomycin trial suggests an image of how randomization works: A triage nurse sits at a desk. A line of participants approach her. Without regard to any trait of the person before her, she reaches into a box and hands over a sealed envelope, to be delivered to the trial pharmacist, containing instructions that consign the research subject to the trial's active-treatment arm or control arm.

We need the nurse-and-envelope image because in our exploration of the antidepressant controversy we will encounter experiments that get randomization wrong. They have the nurse do something different, say, handing young patients an envelope with one sort of instructions and old patients an envelope with another. We will need to watch for violations of randomization.

The purpose of randomization is to avoid confounds, especially those arising from susceptibility bias. As the editorialist in the *British Medical Journal* noted in response to the streptomycin trial, "The random allocation has not only removed personal responsibility from the clinician and possible bias in his process of choosing patients, but has on the whole effectively equated the groups—fundamental, of course, to the general comparisons . . ."

The beauty of the randomized trial is that the researcher does not need to understand all the factors that influence outcomes. Say that an undiscovered genetic variation makes certain people unresponsive to a medication. The randomizing process will ensure—or make it highly probable—that the arms of the trial contain equal numbers of subjects with that variation. The result will be a fair test.

A *double-blind* trial includes another safeguard against bias: neither the patients under study nor the observers measuring outcomes know which subject has received which intervention. This uncertainty protects against patients' and doctors' favoring the promising treatment and reporting overly encouraging results in the active arm of the trial.

The streptomycin-versus-bed-rest study had this protection in partial form. Radiologists reading a film were not told whether it came from the file of a patient on medication. But clinicians and patients knew who was getting injections.

Doctors had long believed that morale affected recovery from pulmonary tuberculosis. Group psychotherapy traces its origin to instructive and inspirational meetings for tubercular patients conducted with the support of a church in Boston in the early 1900s. *The Boston Medical and Surgical Journal*, precursor to *The New England Journal of Medicine*, reported that the method outperformed sanatorium treatment. By the 1940s, the understanding of tuberculosis had changed. If getting a shot induced optimism, and if optimism revved up the immune system, no one worried that this potential confound would invalidate the findings.

Assumptions about the nature of an illness affect the design of research. With streptomycin, doctors accepted that antibiotic action, and not hope aroused by injections, would determine outcomes. Different beliefs would make researchers conduct the trial differently.

Scientists favor double-blind, randomized, placebo-controlled trials, but there is no doubt about which element matters most. The British Medical Research Council could do with partial blinding and without a placebo. If a trial is to be run, the essential element, the one that statisticians most hate to forgo, is randomization. Randomization is a great medical advance of the twentieth century, on a par, historians say, with penicillin. Randomization minimizes confounds. The midcentury epidemiologist Archie Cochrane, an advocate of evidence-based medicine *avant la lettre*, has become the movement's hero and icon. Cochrane had little respect for doctors' wishes to spare their patients exposure to placebo and to offer them promising, unproven therapies. Challenged by a colleague who demanded to know how far Cochrane was prepared to push "this randomizing game," he shot back, "You should randomize until it hurts [the clinicians]."

4

As Max Saw It

ROLAND KUHN'S REPORT on imipramine arrived a decade after the Research Council's paper on streptomycin. Scientists at Geigy understood that imipramine would have to be evaluated via the new technology. But what would play the role of the chest X-ray—the basis for measuring the drug's efficacy?

Alan Broadhurst, the chemist who had served as a guinea pig in the early testing of imipramine, contacted Max Hamilton, a German-born British psychiatrist who specialized in statistics. Hamilton had just formulated a depression rating scale. Broadhurst convinced researchers to apply it in clinical trials.

Like Kuhn, Hamilton began with patients. He asked them about the burdens of depression—sadness, disturbed sleep, suicidal thoughts—and attached numbers to represent levels of intensity. He focused on severely afflicted patients in hospitals but also interviewed outpatients. Then he composed a rating scale intended to characterize a discrete syndrome, "affective disorder of the depressive type."

This specificity appealed to Broadhurst. Hamilton's scale made an argument for viewing depression as a conventional medical disorder, characterized by symptoms that could be assessed in a patient interview.

In the 1950s, psychiatry worked differently. Freudians classed patients broadly, as psychotic and in need of a simplified psychotherapy or neurotic and likely to be good candidates for psychoanalysis. Either way, the core disturbance was unconscious emotional conflict, turmoil that might be protean in its expression. Symptoms were mutable—of interest mostly as clues to the origins (in childhood experiences, in sexual repression) of patients' distorted perception and behavior.

Existential psychoanalysis, in Kuhn's version, had more in common with conventional medicine. Kuhn recognized diagnoses. But he remained an analyst in this sense: he did not take patients' initial reports at face value. Kuhn said, "One needs to realize that the symptoms of vital depression are often not spontaneously mentioned . . . They are often concealed by other symptoms which may seem to be more severe. They may not come to the patient's mind even with questioning. Patients admit to these symptoms only as the links of an integral whole in a dialogue that is free and comprehensible."

No one knows precisely how Kuhn arrived at a diagnosis. If less deeply, I, like Kuhn, trained in existential psychotherapy. My mentor, Leston Havens, believed that a doctor should "sit alongside" patients psychologically, looking out at the world with them. If the view was bleak, perhaps they were depressed. Les spoke of the "imprint" of depression. After a group had witnessed a clinical interview, a latecomer might discern the diagnosis in the bodily posture of the observers. Depression was profound hopelessness best apprehended through empathy. The number of symptoms was unimportant. In patients who "put a good face on it" and said chipper things, depression might nonetheless be detected—by psychiatrists, through self-monitoring.

In contrast, Hamilton put stock in the surface manifestations of illness. He built his scale on seventeen rating factors—low mood, work problems, expressions of guilt, and so on—each with points assigned according to severity. Doctors were to act as raters, but in that role they might rely on patients' reports. Under "suicide," the response "feels life is not worth living" merits a score of one point; "wishes he were dead" scores two; "suicidal ideas or gestures" scores three; and a recent history of attempts scores four.

Many Hamilton items correspond to a commonsense take on depression: listlessness, indecision, self-reproach, and the slowing of speech and movement that psychiatrists call psychomotor retardation. But the scale has its oddities. Bodily symptoms such as indigestion, constipation, menstrual disturbances, and backache can contribute ten points. Hypochondria can add four. Somatic complaints were common on the psychiatry wards of the 1950s, where patients might be warehoused in long stays. For Hamilton, sleep disturbance played an outsize role. He gave separate ratings to problems in falling asleep, staying asleep, and waking at a suitable hour. Likewise, anxiety makes repeated appearances. The instrument was one doctor's portrait of depression at a moment in time.

Despite its idiosyncrasies, the Hamilton scale was embraced as a means of documenting the course of a depression. Psychiatrists could run through the checklist and attach numbers to symptoms. The sum was the Hamilton score. Subsequent scores could be contrasted with the baseline to track responses to treatment.

The Hamilton scale tops out at 50, but totals above the low 30s are rare. The field constantly debates definitions of severity, but in simple terms a Hamilton of 30 represents severe depression; 20, moderate; and 10, mild. Most patients in antidepressant trials have scores in the 20s. In typical outpatient practices, Hamiltons average 19 or 20.

As for degrees of change, from early on, the criterion for a *response* was a halving of the initial Hamilton score, improvement that would move most severely depressed patients into the mild category and mildly depressed patients to normality. *Remission*, ending the bout of illness, required driving the total below 8. In the streptomycin study, researchers had used informal categories—"considerable" or "moderate or slight" resolution of the X-ray—and Kuhn had written of full and partial relief from depression. Whether Hamilton's numbers added precision was an open question, but the scale looked scientific.

Between 1959 and 1965, more than a thousand patients were assessed in brief randomized trials testing imipramine as a treatment for depression. About two-thirds of subjects on medication responded, versus close to a third of those in the control arm, a pattern that echoed the outcome for partial chest X-ray clearing in the streptomycin study.

Imipramine, randomized trials, and the Hamilton worked synergistic magic. Its ability to capture the medication's efficacy validated the scale. Meanwhile, the research results validated antidepressants. The new tools served a political role, pushing psychiatry toward mainstream medicine, with its emphasis on diagnosis.

Over time, the scale had extraordinary impact. Increasingly, doctors looked to symptoms, their pattern, number, and severity, to define mental illnesses. As Kuhn had invented the antidepressant, so Hamilton had invented a new understanding of depression.

5

Interlude

The Antithesis of Science

DESPITE THE NEW research tools, antidepressants gained acceptance slowly. To give a sense of the pace of change, I want to share a personal history that a colleague, Robert Liberman, has generously made public.

I have mentioned that by 1965 imipramine had been tested on a thousand patients and shown substantial efficacy. That analysis appeared in a review compiled by two men I came to know later in their careers. Jonathan Cole ran the first major trials of psychotherapeutic drugs in the United States. He was an affable raconteur, at once a top-notch scientist and a low-key ambassador for pharmacology. His younger colleague Gerald Klerman, although by no means humorless, had a sterner brilliance. He would become something like an enforcer for evidence-based psychiatry.

Considering everything from chemical structure to side effects, in their review Cole and Klerman showcased imipramine as a medication that science could characterize in detail, a treatment that had come of age. But they were respectful of objections, among them the argument that "what clinical efficacy these drugs have is mediated by socio-psychological mechanisms, particularly the suggestibility and faith of the patient, the enthusiasm amid zeal of the physician, or both." Cole and Klerman traced the claim for classic placebo effects to a 1961 paper,

"A Criticism of Drug Therapy in Psychiatry," which appeared in a publication of the American Medical Association. Liberman, then a second-year medical student at Dartmouth, was the author.

Regarding imipramine, Liberman wrote that it had been "greeted with much undeserved praise as an antidepressive agent." His approach to the evidence was hardly evenhanded. He highlighted unsuccessful treatments reported by a private practitioner while underplaying a systematic study, summarized in the same journal, that found favorable outcomes. In support of the idea that the drug works via placebo effects, Liberman cited an article that did not discuss depression.

Liberman's paper reflects the scholarship of its time, but it serves now mainly to show how far back the antidepressant-as-placebo argument extends and how little was required to sustain it. In concluding that prescribing amounted to "poor medical practice," Liberman championed mainstream views, widely held by psychotherapists and welcome in leading publications.

When I located the essay, it occurred to me that I knew a Robert Liberman, an advocate for medication use in depression. I telephoned, and he acknowledged the critique as his own, adding that it had a bittersweet follow-on, one that he had discussed in published interviews.

Leaving Dartmouth, Liberman had transferred to Johns Hopkins, where he became depressed. In retrospect, he had suffered episodes since age sixteen. At Hopkins—just after his "criticism" appeared—Liberman was offered an antidepressant. He recovered quickly. He next became depressed while working at the National Institute of Mental Health. When psychotherapy did little for him, he took an antidepressant, to good effect. Still, he was unconvinced.

For another episode, in California in the 1970s, Liberman again chose psychotherapy. It brought no relief. Years later, discussing that course of treatment, he said, "Despite the fact that I did not benefit from their ministrations and even got worse, these psychiatrists never suggested to me that I might improve with antidepressant medication."

Liberman's own doubts persisted. Only after another twenty years of recurrent illness, requiring hospitalizations and finally electroconvulsive therapy, did he embrace antidepressant use. By then, in the mid-1990s, psychiatry had adopted the idea of a midway state between recurrent major depression and bipolar disorder, a variant in which patients never quite become manic but suffer worsening depression over time. Looking at the alternation between Liberman's periods of depression and intervals of productivity, a psychopharmacologist made that diagnosis, although the possibility of straightforward recurrent depression remained in play.

The midway condition can respond poorly to antidepressants—but the consultant had Liberman's favorable past experience to rely on. Ever since, Liberman has been on an antidepressant. Despite his disorder's progressive nature, on medication Liberman has gone fifteen years without a substantial depressive episode. He has been healthier—less burdened by depression—than in his earlier years.

Liberman has integrated his experience into his clinical practice. When he considers openness appropriate, he tells patients that he takes medication daily, a self-revelation that encourages others to adhere to their own drug regimens.

Do we censure those California psychiatrists, the ones who did not prescribe and left their patient on a downhill course? We must be careful not to judge them according to our current awareness of progressive risk to brain and mind. Likely, Liberman's caregivers believed—this position still has its advocates—that without gains in self-understanding, cure does more harm than good.

Still, there is something undoctorly about withholding medication from an ailing patient who has responded to it repeatedly. Not anecdote but ideology is the antithesis of science. Anecdotally, antidepressants worked for Liberman.

Even a skeptic focused on placebo effects might have prescribed for a patient in Liberman's circumstances, but nowhere in medicine do placebos act in the way that antidepressants did for Liberman, consistently interrupting complex manifestations of illness and conferring solid stabilization. Psychiatrists in my generation saw this sequence regularly: psychotherapy failed for patients who believed in it stubbornly, and then antidepressants succeeded. Those cases were convincing.

To return to Cole and Klerman's early review of research on imipramine: The paper was evenhanded in its presentation of the placebo issue that Liberman had raised in 1961. Imipramine has evident side effects. It can make patients so dry-mouthed that they or an interviewer—hearing the tongue cluck as it releases from the roof of the mouth—might guess that they were on medication. The trial would no longer be blind.

Critics argued that antidepressants might appear less effective if tested against "active" placebos—otherwise inert drugs that cause side effects such as dry mouth and constipation and, so, inspire higher expectancy. On this topic, Cole and Klerman found few relevant studies. In one, participants on a symptom-causing placebo fared especially poorly. Had the constipating pill done harm? The jury was out on whether active placebos had a role to play in testing. (To this day, it remains out. There have been few new studies. What you believe depends on how you handle the outlying data—and what you make of the powers of placebo pills in general, a topic we will confront in time.)

Cole and Klerman were likewise frank about the limits to scientific knowledge. In developing antidepressants, drug companies screened compounds that alter the way that nerve cells handle certain chemical messengers in the brain, substances (such as norepinephrine and serotonin) called monoamines. The idea that they matter in depression was the *monoamine hypothesis*. Cole and Klerman cautioned, "The evidence for this view is almost entirely indirect." Even the best-supported parts were "admittedly speculative." Drugs that influenced norepinephrine and the rest often did offer relief, but it was never clear that monoamine abnormalities caused or constituted depression.

I mention Cole and Klerman's circumspection because of the role that the monoamine hypothesis plays in the current antidepressant controversy. Critics complain that faith in medication is sustained by an unsubstantiated belief that drugs reverse depression by boosting transmitters whose deficiency constitutes the disorder. (Marcia Angell writes that the theory has been "broadly accepted . . . by the medical profession.") Particular aspects of the monoamine hypothesis have gained plausibility in recent years—serotonin regulation does have something to do with depression—but for the whole of the time that antidepressants have been available, leading figures in psychiatry, including the pioneering psychopharmacologists, have viewed the theory skeptically. In my training, it was presented as, to use the language I employ in *Listening to Prozac*, "perhaps false and at least incomplete."

The prevailing understanding is not that antidepressants reverse a fundamental deficiency (of serotonin or a related chemical), but rather that the medications restore resilience in the mind and brain, allowing the growth of new nerve cells and the elaboration of new connections between cells. The drugs "permit" depression to diminish by allowing repair and new learning to proceed in brains and persons previously left "stuck" in depression. This theory of recovery has driven research since before Prozac's time.

In the antidepressant controversy, the monoamine hypothesis has become a red herring. In each generation, acceptance of antidepressants has been sustained by complex accounts of the science like Cole and Klerman's.

Another constant, from the early going, has been empirical support from randomized controlled trials. Cole and Klerman entertained a host of caveats, but finally their review attested to imipramine's efficacy: a two-to-one advantage, drug over dummy pills, in the treatment of depression—and the summary numbers were conservative. Some trials had used the drug at low doses. When patients received at least 200 milligrams daily, the results might be stronger.

Discussing randomization, I referred to Archie Cochrane, the guiding spirit for today's curators of evidence-based medicine, the Cochrane Collaboration. Cochrane was a Scottish doctor who practiced in prisoner-of-war camps in World War II, went on to study lung disease, and made his name as an early proponent of randomized trials.

Cochrane, who expressed grave doubts about psychotherapy, was critical of psychiatric research in general. But in 1972, in his influential book on effective health care, when he listed treatments that might improve outcomes for the British National Health Service, Cochrane put antidepressants on a short list with blood-pressure pills, the polio vaccine, cortisone, and antibiotics for tuberculosis.

Cochrane's endorsement and Liberman's troubling history epitomize conflicting attitudes toward depression treatment in the 1970s. Expert researchers considered antidepressants highly effective, but many clinicians refused even to test out medication and remained doubters.

6

Off the Hook

IT MAY APPEAR that with the antidepressant, the rating scale, the randomized trial, and the expert literature review, psychiatry had entered the era of science-based medicine for good and all. Instead, there was resistance, and from unexpected quarters.

By the mid-1960s, Sir Austin Bradford Hill, the principal designer of the British streptomycin study, had become uneasy about the increasing emphasis on the sort of research he had initiated. The pendulum had swung too far. Certain important issues would never be settled through randomized trials. Hill had a special interest in the link between smoking and lung cancer. No one was going to randomly assign people to smoke cigarettes for decades. Judging causes and outcomes, doctors would need to consider other factors, such as biological plausibility and the overall coherence of a body of evidence.

In a lecture that touched on mental health research, Hill went further: "Any belief that the controlled trial is the only way would mean not that the pendulum had swung too far but that it had come right off its hook." Hill doubted that blinding was appropriate in assessing treatments for disorders, like anxiety, with subjective symptoms. To optimize outcomes, doctors would need to adjust doses and observe responses, aware of who was on what—and the clinician's perception might be the most accurate gauge of results. Taking what looks like a swipe at the Hamilton scale, Hill quoted a colleague's comment that it is "ridiculous to scorn subjective assessments in subjective symptoms, and it is unrealistic to make artificially objective assessments." As an example of a task that would require a flexible combination of approaches, experimental and clinical, Hill chose the evaluation of antidepressants.

Roland Kuhn, too, expressed mistrust of rating scales and controlled trials: "In clinical research, most of the statistics are useless . . ." In the 1990s, looking back on psychiatry's failures—no one had found an antidepressant more effective than imipramine—Kuhn said:

> My methods were entirely different from those which are nowadays applied in clinical research. I have never used "controlled double-blind studies" with "placebos," "standardised rating scales" or the statistical treatment of records of large numbers of patients.
>
> Instead I examined each patient individually even every day, often on several occasions, and questioned him or her again and again.

Kuhn had been interested in social functioning as much as symptom relief. What impressed him about imipramine was its capacity to give patients back their lives.

More, Kuhn argued that clinical trials on depressed patients had become impossible because potential research subjects would already have been treated (for instance, with imipramine) by the family physician.

As we have seen, not all doctors or patients believed in antidepressant use. But for those open to drug treatment, imipramine and similar medicines were readily available. Internists likely to diagnose depression generally prescribed for it on their own. Increasingly, the patients who entered trials were those who had already failed on medication. As a result, research was conducted on a population that did not represent the full range of depressed people. Patients who have proved "refractory to treatment" will be less likely to respond to the next remedy tried. The result might be a failure to identify useful drugs. Psychiatric research was a victim of its own past successes.

The situation, Kuhn complained, had been different in the 1950s: "The cases then were much better suited for trials because those today who are suitable for trials don't come anymore to the psychiatrist and even less into clinic. The clinical picture has completely changed because of treatment." I call this difficulty—the inability to recruit representative patients into trials—the curse of Roland Kuhn. We will encounter it repeatedly.

Both Hill and Kuhn wondered whether psychiatry was the right domain for rating scales. This objection may sound antique. For half a century and more, researchers have utilized the Hamilton. Much of what we know about depression—how prevalent it is, what harm it causes, where it registers in the brain, and, yes, which treatments mitigate it—comes thanks to the Hamilton. But it may be that depression is so distinctive and so harmful that its effects emerge even with imperfect measurement.

Because the vast majority of research on antidepressants has used the Hamilton, we will want to know whether the scale is more accurate than Kuhn's method, coming to understand the patient through conversation over long acquaintance. Many researchers complain that the scale has become a lead weight—that it interferes with our ability to evaluate the efficacy of antidepressants. Statisticians' objections to the Hamilton tend to be technical, but we can understand some problems readily enough.

The scale can compact two ailments into one, with confusing results. Consider Max Hamilton's emphasis on physical complaints, such as constipation. If a patient is hypochondriacal and mildly depressed, when a rater adds up the symptom scores, the scale will depict the depression as severe. If a treatment works for that patient, we may conclude that it works for severe depression—when mild depression was at issue. Equally, a medicine that eliminates only the depression (and not the hypochondriasis) will appear half-effective, even though the mood disorder is gone.

Also, the scale equates unequal aspects of the illness. Four points assigned for insistent suicidality are equated to four points attached to four scattered mild symptoms, so that one patient with a middling Hamilton score may be much sicker than another. By 1975, researchers had found that in hospitalized patients, the Hamilton could no longer distinguish between moderate and severe depression, as rated by attending physicians.

The Hamilton is a prisoner of history. The scale captures the depression that Max Hamilton encountered, often an agitated state accompanied by insomnia. Questioned years later, Alan Broadhurst conceded that he had chosen a scale suited to showcasing imipramine, an antidepressant that tends to be calming and sedating. Newer, more energizing antidepressants are disadvantaged. That's another area where the Hamilton scale introduces inaccuracies: comparisons of antidepressants.

These defects are pretty bad. We want a rating scale to contrast treatments accurately. We want it to measure and track patients' level of depression. We don't want patients with mild mood disorders admitted into studies of severe depression.

The scale survived and flourished largely because of its priority. To allow for comparison with old trials, new ones used the scale. The FDA played a role. To prevent pharmaceutical houses from gaming the system, selecting measures matched to a drug being tested, the agency favored the Hamilton. But that the field was paying a price—relying on data that had an ever-more-approximate relationship to the course of patients' illness—was an open secret.

Working in the 1970s, a Danish group headed by the young psychiatrist Per Bech decided to rework the Hamilton so that it would once more serve its original intended role, representing depression as doctors see it. The team asked respected clinicians to rate patients they knew well. Comparing those impressions to Hamilton ratings, Bech and his colleagues found the essence of depression to reside in six factors: depressed mood, guilt, functioning at work and similar tasks, psychomotor retardation (again, a slowing of mind and body), psychic anxiety, and a cluster of negative feelings that included tiredness and pain. The scale did yet better if you expanded "guilt" to include low self-esteem.

Those patients who scored high on the six factors were the ones doctors had called most depressed. When depression became more severe, scores on those items rose. As depression abated, scores fell. The factors clustered, often rising and falling in sync, defining an entity that Bech called core depression. The six items corresponded to depression as doctors see it, and the collection behaved well statistically. This "good behavior" has held up over thirty-five years and more.

The ill-behaved Hamilton factors included suicidality, agitation, weight loss, insomnia, diminished sexual interest, poor insight, and a host of bodily symptoms and concerns. Some items were hard to rate, so that observers disagreed about their severity. Some rose as core items fell. (Notoriously, suicide risk can increase as patients begin to recover from depression.) Some were persistent, seemingly independent of the level of depression.

It's not that the peripheral items bore no relationship to depression. Suicidality can signal mood disorder. But their fluctuations did not do the job that Hamilton had proposed: to represent the changing burden of illness.

Max Hamilton traveled to Copenhagen in 1977 and, in a gracious lecture, largely accepted the Danes' verdict. Of his scale's factors, "Six of them did all the work and the other eleven were, so to speak, passengers which interfered with the work."

Bech called his pared-down scale the HAM-D6, where the original Hamilton became the HAM-D17. The six-factor scale had numerous successes. For tricyclics, it gave a cleaner account of the relationship between dose and response—more medication meant greater efficacy, up to a point—where the full scale did not. The short scale turned out to be sensitive, picking up improvements in mood disorder early in trials, before the full scale registered the change. And the scale eliminated factors, such as insomnia and agitation, that might respond incidentally to imipramine. On the HAM-D6, tricyclics continued to look effective, but arguably (the statistics were inconclusive) at a slightly lower level than the full Hamilton had made them out to be.

I have often wondered why Bech's simplification has not replaced the original Hamilton. Perhaps the problem is that very virtue, simplicity. The Bech is too reflective of the doctor's quick insight: sick or not. If the six items measure the disorder, they do not define it—do not highlight the signal roles of insomnia and suicidality in producing the burden of depression. Hamilton's longer scale seems more mechanical and therefore scientific. Regulators may imagine that, as researchers work their way through seventeen items, in the tedium they lose track of their private judgment and produce something free of opinion, something precise and trustworthy.

All the same, we will need to remember Per Bech's contribution. Developed years before the appearance of serotonin-based antidepressants like Prozac, the short scale would later capture the strengths of the newer medications. They alleviate core symptoms of depression. We're out ahead of ourselves here, but the contemporary antidepressant controversy arises largely from the peculiarities of the Hamilton scale, with its focus on symptoms such as headache that wax and wane spontaneously or stay fixed no matter the treatment. In compiling his instrument, Max Hamilton legitimated the tricyclics and incidentally set in place a mechanism for casting the worth of later antidepressants in doubt.

Despite the preference for complexity, there's much to be said for the gestalt, for doctors' summary impression of their patients' level of depression. When statisticians limit their attention to a symptom collection that tracks the informed gut call, they emerge with coherent data that confirm what doctors see. The result is not happenstance. Bech intended for the revised scale to capture the clinical perspective.

Here's where things stood when I began my training, in the late 1970s. Antidepressants had shown their efficacy in early trials, but the glory days were over. Research would become ever harder to conduct. Outcome data—so long as the full-scale Hamilton remained in place—would prove ever less valid. And as Hill had predicted, rigorous trials would miss truths apparent to practicing doctors free to work flexibly with patients they knew well.

7

Interlude

My Sins

IT WAS IN medical school, on my internal medicine rotation, that I first sat with men and women who suffered depression at the deepest level, the depression documented by Albrecht Dürer in prints, Pablo Picasso in oils, and Max Hamilton in his rating scale. On those wards, these patients were not rare. Thin, immobile suffering souls, prematurely aged, they had the classic depressive habitus, the attitude or physique of the disease.

The rounding doctors found melancholic patients difficult to interview. They spoke slowly and repetitively. We trainees set stethoscopes to their chests, checked the IV lines, and left the room. When a depressed woman—Irma—did not answer his questions, the resident asked me to see what I could elicit.

Other medical students excelled at reading cardiograms. I could sit with silence. With Irma, I ventured the occasional comment: *The pain is too great. There's no point trying.* At psychiatry rounds, where patients were interviewed with us there, I had seen this approach attempted.

Irma responded, if sparingly. A husband had died, and then a daughter, long ago. Life ended then. Now Irma had heart disease. She was content to die.

What was remarkable was Irma's coherence. She was not paranoid.

She was not hallucinating. She was depressed, although that word hardly captures the bleakness. To speak, she had to overcome interference from a brain that transmitted a single message, despair.

Irma lived with a sister who on Irma's good days brought her to group sessions at a mental health center. Irma had never taken medicine.

I was barely off the streets, a student of history and literature. We speak of impressions being seared into memory.

I made my report: resigned, but not suicidal. Irma had consented to treatment for heart failure.

I doubt that the rounding team considered antidepressants. Attention to mental illness was not the routine, and besides, tricyclics affected heart rhythm.

Later, on my psychiatry rotation, I saw depleted depressives in number. I trained on a service of the Massachusetts Mental Health Center, a community hospital in the state system, staffed by eminent psychotherapists. The ward housed many Irmas. In the activity room, they sat still, distinguishable from catatonic patients only by their hand-wringing.

Almost twenty years after Kuhn's discovery of imipramine, Boston doctors treated these patients with psychotherapy alone. Otherwise, depression was allowed to run its course.

Mass Mental was under the sway of an éminence grise, the psychoanalyst Elvin Semrad, a Midwesterner with a knack for coaxing sense out of psychotic patients. In the recollection of a classmate of mine who did a residency at Mass Mental, Semrad saw medications as "chemical straitjackets" and intrusions on patients' autonomy. People needed to inhabit their illness until they felt safe enough to abandon it.

There was irrational confidence in the other direction as well. Leading psychopharmacologists had founded a medical-model service. There, the prevailing belief was that the small collection of available antidepressants and antipsychotics, Largactil's progeny, could cure anything. Often, patients improved and went home. But the medicines could cause movement disorders that mimicked Parkinson's disease. The sight of zombified patients served to justify the skepticism of psychiatrists from the psychotherapy-oriented wards.

Presently, the two cultures would make contact, with trainees from

my generation as a moving force. Having seen successes with pharmacology, they could not let ill patients on psychotherapy services suffer.
Where at the start of my cohort's training, prescribing was scorned,
toward the end, residents went to court to force patients to take medications by injection. Brigadoon vanished.

I left Harvard for a medical internship at the University of Wisconsin, followed by a psychiatry residency at Yale. Both balanced psychotherapy training with biology research. Prescribing was understood as
an art. Nowhere did I see the volume of end-stage depression I had
encountered in Boston—nor have I ever again. And in thirty-plus years
of outpatient practice in Providence, not one of my patients has begun
with or, to my knowledge, moved on to classical, paralyzing melancholy.
Perhaps there is a single exception, an elderly, demented, alcoholic man
who required electroconvulsive therapy.

Where are they, Irma and her fellows?

This chapter stands as further confession. I have said that clinical
understanding must, where possible, find grounding in formal evidence. But if I am honest, there are reasons, beyond the numbers, that
I would find it hard to believe that antidepressants do not work. Among
them is an apparent decrease in the end-of-the-line depression that
was familiar in my medical-school years.

I know of no data on this topic. The Public Health Service conducts
surveys on mental illness, but the prompts are too general to reveal trends
in categories like severe depression. Lacking better evidence, over the
years I have asked medical students, senior colleagues, and mood-disorder
specialists what they see. Their response is uniform: little end-stage
depression, much less (say the oldest doctors) than four or five decades
back.

Asked about their gravest cases, med students say, A patient who
had been doing well in treatment lost his job, could not afford his medicine, resumed drinking, missed his clinic appointments, and after four
months was brought to the emergency room by the police. Paralyzing
melancholy has become an element in a tale of treatment interrupted.

One colleague specializes in neuromodulation, the application of
electricity or magnetic current to the brain. The treatments—ECT,
transcranial magnetic stimulation, and deep-brain stimulation—are reserved for the most seriously depressed. In a series of sixty consecutive

patients referred for assessment, she found only one with the paralyzing condition I asked about. His depression was complicated by multiple
small strokes evident on a brain scan.

I doubt that I would have published this chapter without one final
piece of testimony. In 2014, I attended a talk by Anthony Rothschild, a
researcher at the University of Massachusetts who is arguably our
premier expert on psychotic depression. It is crucial to recognize this
condition—depression accompanied by hallucinations or delusions—
because it tends to respond to antidepressants only when a second
drug, an antipsychotic, is added.

Tony interviews severely depressed patients regularly. I asked about
nonpsychotic depression: Did he still see classic, immobilizing melancholy?

No, he said. There's much less of it. His thought was that primary-
care doctors nip depression in the bud, enough to make a difference.
He spoke of depression as a progressive disease. People used to move
from depression to severe depression to that paralyzing state. Since the
1980s, with the advent of easier-to-use antidepressants, often the down-
ward progress is interrupted.

We still see psychotic depression. Doctors don't diagnose it well, so
it's not treated complexly, and it worsens. The shift is in the prevalence
of end-stage nonpsychotic depression, a worse phase of the straightforward depression that does often respond to simple treatment.

Over long intervals, many things change. We've grown increasingly
aware of dementia, drug abuse, and post-traumatic states; we see them
as separate from mood disorder. We may have made depression a more
limited category, one skewed toward healthier people.

There are no data, and if there were, comparisons over time might
remain unreliable. Still, I'm guessing that the change—fewer like Irma—
is real. With the deinstitutionalization of mentally ill patients, we
should all know people with severe melancholic depression. For the
sweep of human history, they have been with us, sufferers with wast-
ing bodies, tortured eyes, and downturned gazes. They were seen at
the church and in family homes as part of communal life. And now—
rarely.

As I say, I am engaged in confession. Unlike randomized trials, my
observation affords scant protection against confounding factors. Per-

haps my informants tell me what I want to hear. It's only that the shift seems so large, so general.

I know better than to insist on this line of thought. Diseases come and go. Often, doctors cannot explain why. Anorexia has fluctuated in incidence: high in the 1930s, low in the 1950s, with steady increases for decades after.

If treatment plays a role, it's not only antidepressants that have impacted depression. Altogether, we are less willing than we once were to let mood disorders fester. Psychotherapies aim to target depression directly, to interrupt episodes. The adoption of lithium salts to moderate manic depression is the great psychiatric success story of the twentieth century. Surely making inroads against bipolar disorder influences the frequency of end-stage depression.

When severely depressed patients enter a hospital, they are treated vigorously. We are less likely to see them sit in their misery, week after week.

Still, my impression is that end-of-the-line depression is less common in part because—haphazardly, with many a case missed altogether—we treat depression early, generally with antidepressants. Even when it fails at symptom reduction, prescribing may work preventively. Certain studies in psychiatry have conclusions that take this form: A bad outcome, like memory loss, correlates with the length of time a woman is depressed—but the correlation is more robust if you subtract the weeks that she was medicated with antidepressants, without regard to whether the patient responded. Time in treatment confers the benefit.

Do we, now and then, only change the form of the disease, creating mobilized depression? We must, and sometimes to the good. I see patients, still moody, who can raise their children and go to work. As with cancer, with depression we have turned terminal cases into chronic ones. In the worst instance, like the Roman general Fabius the Delayer, prescribing doctors beat a measured retreat, slowing the enemy's advance.

If that delaying effort counts, then the practice that I observed at Harvard, forgoing medicine and letting depression take its course, was, for all its idealism, barbaric. Irma and her fellows were psychiatry's pride then and its shame now.

I was no hero in this narrative. Despite having seen Adele respond to imipramine, I remained intent on my teachers' wisdom, retaining hope that psychotherapy would heal all ills. Recovery on medication seemed second-best. What shifted first was my sense of the required pace of progress. I hated to see patients suffer.

When I say that the attack on antidepressants presents dangers, my perspective begins with patients afflicted by severe classic depression. On occasion, our arguments about efficacy will sound bloodless. We must not find them so. Throughout, we must see people in pain.

Imagine Irma after her first pregnancy, on the death of her husband, on the death of her daughter. Imagine Irma at critical junctures, struggling with progressively more disabling episodes of mood disorder. Might medication have slowed her slide? While her depression was still mild or moderate, should she have been offered a trial of antidepressants?

Surely she should have—unless they do not work.

Because I do not see her like, I believe that they do.

The chain of reasoning that creates that sentence contains a dozen weak links—I have conceded as much. But then, every doctor approaches research evidence from a complexly shaped perspective. I work under this influence, time spent with depression when prescribing was taboo.

8

Permission

OF THE PSYCHOPHARMACOLOGISTS I encountered in medical school, only one made an impression. In my final year, I met Jonathan Cole.

Cole's career spanned the period of modern drug development in psychiatry. In 1953, before imipramine, he helped organize a national conference on psychopharmacology. He went on to head newly established pharmacology divisions at the National Institute of Mental Health. At the NIMH, he supervised the first large-scale trials of antidepressants. Believing in "green thumb" psychiatrists who, like Kuhn, could identify promising drugs through clinical observation, Cole maintained support for informal studies. By the 1970s, Cole was at McLean Hospital, in the Harvard system. I attended his talks. He invited me to his office.

Cole was a congenitally open, happy man. In his later years, residents called him Jolly Old Cole. Cole made no concession to the psychoanalytic convention that gravity and passive listening are the hallmarks of wisdom.

Cole loved to talk about unexpected uses of drugs. For example, he entertained a theory about nicotine. It might act to suppress anger; its ability to take the edge off irritability was part of what made it attractive to smokers.

In his time with me, Cole discussed alternatives to antidepressants. When doctors used amphetamine to energize patients during their hospital stays, some depressives simply recovered. Cole said that when medications such as imipramine failed, he might prescribe amphetamine, especially for patients who seemed apathetic. Stimulants had a bad name. They'd been prescribed for weight loss and abused. If you're referred a depressed patient on amphetamine, Cole said, the doctor is either incompetent or sophisticated.

Cole was interested in the antidepressant effect of drugs such as Valium. They were called anxiolytics—they lysed, or dissolved, anxiety. GPs were criticized for prescribing "mother's little helpers" to bored housewives. Perhaps the doctors were savvy. Cole had seen cases, especially when depression was admixed with anxiety, in which anxiolytics helped altogether, restoring energy instead of depleting it. In one study, Valium seemed more successful in this regard than Librium or Miltown.

Did I know a disturbing fact about Valium? Cole asked. Research had shown that patients prescribed Valium liked the doctor better, a worrisome feedback loop. Maybe they were right to do so.

Prescribing was an art. A patient's requirements might be idiosyncratic because humans are.

Although they were about drugs from other classes, these conversations helped define for me what pharmacologists expected of antidepressants. Many medications could be referred to in terms of a direction, up or down—they induced more or less excitation. On occasion, those same medicines did a more complex and thorough job. They reversed much of a syndrome, many linked symptoms at once. Or they got to the heart of a disorder—in the case of depression, the loss of a future. That job, the one that, when stimulants or anxiolytics pulled it off, occasioned surprise, antidepressants did routinely. I am using Cole's patter to point to how antidepressants act when they work well.

I spoke with Cole in subsequent years, but I remember the early conversations best. I had seen pharmacology as a matter of memorizing the dose ranges for drugs and then avoiding using them. Cole demonstrated that a lively mind could be engaged by the complexities of prescribing.

From early on—since encountering Cole as I left medical school—I have utilized many classes of medication with depressed patients: stimulants, antianxiety medications, antiepileptics, antipsychotics, mood stabilizers, sedatives, and others. Occasionally, patients respond best to a "wrong" drug or the right drug at the wrong dose. Like Cole, I always have a depressed patient or two in my practice who are taking amphetamine or Ritalin by itself and who do well globally.

I mention Cole's approach to depression treatment—that there's more than one way to skin a cat—because of what strikes me as an odd line of argument against traditional antidepressants. Critics have complained that since unrelated sorts of medicine can help in depression, something is suspect about the central group of antidepressants, imipramine and Prozac and the rest. Why are they more "antidepressant" than Valium or Ritalin?

I think that the critics misread the findings. In studies where anxiolytics are tested as depression treatments, they rate well on insomnia, agitation, and anxiety, not the core symptoms. The distinction between Valium and imipramine is real enough.

But if the research results were different, if Valium proved a terrific antidepressant, what of it? Doctors lower blood pressure through varied medications that at the first level act on the brain, kidney, blood vessels, or heart. No one argues that the multiplicity of approaches discredits antihypertensives.

With depression, the expectation of exclusivity seems especially peculiar. If we believe that mood disorders respond to changes in self-awareness, social comfort, and assessment of external circumstances, it follows that, now and again, a medicine that relaxes or focuses the mind might prove useful.

For me, Cole's was a model approach to the work of psychiatry. We try remedies that have been well tested. When those fail, room is left for efforts grounded in less systematic observation. This method resembled the one I used in psychotherapy, trying one line of inquiry and then another, demanding progress. Cole gave me the permission I wanted, for vigor in the treatment of depressed patients—this in an era when infinite patience was the norm.

9

Interlude

What He Came Here For

WHEN I SAY, in a lecture or conversation, that nearly two decades after the discovery of imipramine it was not unusual to meet hospitalized, profoundly depressed patients who had never been offered medication, listeners object that I must be mistaken. But the adoption of antidepressants was far from uniform. If evidence is needed, it abounds in the documents surrounding a famous legal confrontation, *Osheroff v. Chestnut Lodge*. At issue was a treatment that took place in 1979.

Raphael Osheroff was a kidney specialist and an entrepreneur—he owned dialysis centers—who suffered from anxiety and depression. Shortly before he turned forty, Osheroff became depressed and was treated with psychotherapy and tricyclic antidepressants, like imipramine. He improved, but only moderately, so he lowered his own medication dose, then deteriorated, and signed in to Chestnut Lodge, a psychiatric hospital in Rockville, Maryland.

The Lodge had hosted leading midcentury American psychoanalysts, such as Frieda Fromm-Reichman and Harry Stack Sullivan, and Osheroff's treatment proceeded along analytic lines. He slipped further, losing forty pounds or more and becoming so agitated—he paced constantly—that his feet needed medical attention. Despite questioning by a consultant hired by the family, Osheroff's doctors continued to withhold medication.

In 2012, Ray Osheroff sent me a transcript of a treatment planning meeting from early in his stay. It shows the ward staff discussing suicide risk. A psychiatric aide said, "We are very concerned about him because when he looks like he is depressed, he probably is really depressed and the nursing staff feels like we really have to watch him closely!"

In contrast, the ward administrator put Osheroff's problem in psychological terms:

> He asked to be put on medication but I told him that it would interfere with what he came here for! I told him that he needed every neuron to absorb what we are telling him here and that medication would interfere with that. I told him that if his pacing got out of hand we would have to wrap him up in a cold wet sheet pack! The social worker told us that his agitated behavior was reminiscent of the obnoxious conduct that his father had indulged in.

Osheroff explained that he had a contract worth hundreds of thousands of dollars annually that could be voided if he did not return to the office within six months. A doctor at the Lodge scoffed at the deadline: "This business that he created was a giant breast that was going to restore the scenes of adoration that he had with his mother!" The staff anticipated a hospital stay of at least three years, to rework Osheroff's personality.

Osheroff lost control of his business. His marriage ended. After seven months, a friend had Osheroff moved to another hospital, Silver Hill, in Connecticut, where he received antidepressant and antipsychotic medicines. He improved in three weeks, was discharged in three months, and returned to medical practice.

Osheroff's diagnosis was a point of dispute. His psychotherapist claimed to have been treating Osheroff for a personality disorder involving narcissism. A dissenting clinician had emphasized the depression, as had bills sent to the insurer. Osheroff and his expert witnesses later referred to psychotic depression, the condition now generally treated with the antidepressant-antipsychotic pairing.

Osheroff sued Chestnut Lodge for negligence, saying that medication would have spared him lost income.

For psychiatry, *Osheroff v. Chestnut Lodge* was the case of the decade and arguably the half century. It might as well have been *Pharmacotherapy v. Psychotherapy*. Eminent authorities appeared for each side. Witnesses for Osheroff testified that there was no objective evidence that psychotherapy worked for either severe personality disorder or severe depression, while the benefits of medication for mood disorder were amply documented. Gerald Klerman said of *Osheroff* that the issue was "not psychotherapy versus biological therapy but, rather, opinion versus evidence." It might be fairer to say that the suit did double duty, since, in Klerman's view, the facts were all on one side.

They were hard to resist: Osheroff's agony and his financial loss—and then his quick restoration by medicine. In that context, the therapists' justifications for their choices sounded misguided and even cruel. The conclusions that Klerman drew seemed to follow. Depression needed to be treated as illness, and expeditiously. Medicine was effective for that purpose. Where doctors ignored research results, patients suffered needlessly.

A Maryland state medical arbitration panel ruled for the plaintiff, the award was appealed to the courts, and in 1987 the case was settled, largely in Osheroff's favor, before trial. Despite the absence of a court verdict, *Osheroff* was enormously influential. Hospital administrators understood that their institutions would be at legal risk if their staff withheld medications whose worth had been demonstrated in clinical trials.

If not in its content, in its political effect *Osheroff* was like *Roe v. Wade*. A legal process gave a victory to one side in a dispute turning on deeply held, principled views. The result was resentment and a campaign of resistance by believers in the losing cause.

Klerman, who had served as an expert witness for Osheroff, followed up with him. Writing in 1990, Klerman reported that ten years out, supported by psychotherapy and medication, Osheroff had experienced no downturn serious enough to interfere with his work or social functioning.

I contacted Ray Osheroff in February of 2012, when he was seventy-three. He was living in New Jersey with a long-term girlfriend and practicing medicine. He said that he had "gone through bad times" but never again experienced anything like that devastating episode, an experience for which, as he put it, "*depression* was a wimp of a word." He added that his career had never fully recovered and that he had experienced harm in his private life as well.

I don't doubt that Osheroff had a strong personality. On the phone, he sounded irascible—like the kind of person who makes history. (In their discussion, the Chestnut Lodge staff had recognized that the traits they hoped to moderate were ones that had led to their patient's professional success.) Osheroff had a wide range of reference, a sense of humor, a quick mind, and a sharp memory. He could be poignant.

Osheroff described the course of his depression in the late 1970s. It began with crying spells and panic attacks. Then he entered "a deep, dark tunnel." He was beyond sad: "What was worst was the absence of feeling."

Medication restored him. He could cry again. "You are glad to feel sad . . . You appreciate birds, blue skies, the smell of the grass." Elavil, a close cousin of imipramine's, had sustained him for the rest of his life.

Of his time at Chestnut Lodge, Osheroff said, "You were not treated; you were tortured. The literature of torture is most relevant."

Three weeks after our conversation and one week after his last e-mail to me, Ray Osheroff died in his sleep.

In an advocacy piece written in 1990, "The Psychiatric Patient's Right to Effective Treatment: Implications of *Osheroff v. Chestnut Lodge*," Klerman suggested that the case's influence should be extended. Malpractice law had been governed by the "respectable minority doctrine." If a doctor's decisions were ones favored by even a few recognized authorities—and the psychoanalysts who recommended withholding medication were many—then those choices could not legally be considered substandard care. Klerman argued for discarding the respectable minority rule wherever scientific evidence favored a course of action.

In their discussions with patients, Klerman wrote, doctors should review treatment alternatives, highlighting research evidence—this in an era when some analysts practiced in near silence. Under the standard he proposed, statements such as "Drug treatment is only a crutch"—the example is Klerman's—could be used by patients against clinicians in legal actions.

To psychotherapists, Klerman's approach felt like bullying.

Klerman's paper fomented resistance, but from a weakening sector. In 1980, the American Psychiatric Association had adopted a revised "diagnostic and statistical manual," the groundbreaking *DSM-III*. It erased the category "neurosis" and required diagnosis based on checklists of symptoms. Effectively, Hamilton's take on depression had won out over Kuhn's, although perhaps more in the public realm (and on insurance forms) than in the quiet of consulting rooms.

Practitioners continued to believe that mechanical assessments were best understood as quick approximations of what doctors could determine through thoughtful contact with patients. Still, *Osheroff* was a turning point. The settlement's main effect was through financial coercion, via potential lawsuits, but the case exerted moral suasion as well. The facts were so egregious that they pushed opinion in the direction of three practices that seemed linked: attention to diagnosis, reliance on objective experimentation, and the use of psychotherapeutic medication.

As a side note: I have said that psychotic depression most often responds, as Osheroff's did, to combination pharmacotherapy, antidepressant plus antipsychotic. In the era of Osheroff's hospitalization, only clinical lore, and not controlled trials, backed that practice.

I did my residency at Yale in the late 1970s. Two of my teachers, Malcolm Bowers and J. Craig Nelson, were studying psychotic depression. In 1979, just before Osheroff arrived at Chestnut Lodge, they published a case series. In it, the antidepressant-antipsychotic cocktail looked promising. Bowers and Nelson would soon report cases in which antidepressants given singly made psychotically depressed patients' delusions worse.

If Osheroff's psychiatrists had gone with what controlled trials showed—antidepressants help depressed patients—they might have done harm. Silver Hill was staffed by Yale faculty. (My friend Alan worked there then.) That's why Osheroff got effective treatment, because doctors were aware of Bowers and Nelson's experimental work. In general terms, systematic research legitimated antidepressants, but finally it was the grapevine—case reports, anecdote—that saved Ray Osheroff.

10

Anti-Depressed

BECAUSE THE *Osheroff* case records are extreme—tainted by dogma and disdain—they give an unfair impression of psychotherapy's brief against medication. For balance, I want to turn to a graceful document of resistance, one that helped shape views of antidepressants for doctors who favored psychological approaches.

In 1975, the *British Journal of Medical Psychology* published a biting commentary by Doris Y. Mayer, an American-trained, psychoanalytically oriented child psychiatrist practicing in England. Mayer had admirable reach. She wrote an anticapitalist stage play and did anthropology fieldwork in Ghana. As a psychiatrist, Mayer's best-known piece was "Psychotropic Drugs and the 'Anti-Depressed' Personality." The distinctive adjective conveys the argument's considerable appeal.

In her essay, Mayer questioned whether antidepressants worked but then dropped the complaint: "Let us assume that drugs have at least moderate success in alleviating some forms of distress." What did medication offer?

Mayer worried over patients' losing "emotional experience" and the "protective function of unpleasant feelings." Pills might interrupt crises, but patients risked emerging "with lessened rather than enhanced ego strength." Tartly, she countered a narrative that I would later offer: "It is sometimes said that medication makes patients more amenable to psychotherapy. In my experience, it merely makes them more amenable." She recommended drugs only for unbearable mental states.

Her memorable indictment went:

> Not anxious but not at ease; not incapable of working but not capable of working well; not tormented by the children, but not able to enjoy them; willing to be made love to, but not actively loving; neither tense nor relaxed, neither cheerful nor tearful, neither ill nor well, more depressing than depressed, the bland, tranquillized, "anti-depressed" personality of our time.

What a stunning passage! Mayer gave incisive expression to a viewpoint that continues to energize the antidepressant controversy and any number of recent discussions of our culture's valuation of happiness: prescribing represents a failure to appreciate the signal benefits of discomfort.

Despite her essay's compelling title, Mayer's critique was not limited to antidepressants. To support her views, Mayer offered case examples. Only one patient, a grieving widow, took an antidepressant alone, and with her, Mayer described no emotional flattening. (The concern was that medication robbed the woman of the opportunity to mourn.) Another patient was on imipramine along with an anxiolytic, Librium, which would explain the tranquilization. Mayer's remaining vignettes discussed patients on anxiolytics and antipsychotics, along with Ritalin.

Given the prescribing patterns of the time, the state Mayer complained of may have resulted from drugs we would not consider antidepressants. Discussing patients' arriving on medication, Mayer referenced a 1971 drug-use survey. It found that in Britain over 14 percent of adults had taken an antianxiety medication in the prior year.

Use in the States was at that level or above. During 1973, the year prescribing peaked, over a quarter of American adults took a psychotherapeutic medication. Changes in survey methods make comparisons imprecise, but that estimate is higher than the numbers that we worry over today. In the early 1970s, most scrips were for anxiolytics.

Under 2 percent of adults had taken an antidepressant in a given year, and as many as half of those had also taken a "mother's little helper," like Miltown. The odds that Mayer had seen large numbers of patients taking antidepressants alone were slim. The "anti-depressed" label notwithstanding, the bland personality arose from Librium or Valium.

It is interesting to juxtapose Mayer's description with Ray Osheroff's report of his response—glad to feel sad. In my own observation, the early antidepressants could be restorative, making patients more available emotionally and then more engaged as parents and workers. These effects might be apparent even in those who experienced an unpleasant awareness of being on medication, often the price of taking tricyclics.

If Mayer's list of incapacities is evocative, it may be because of its relevance to medications like Prozac. These drugs, the ones that affect serotonin-based brain pathways, interfere with sexual desire. With extended use, they sometimes cause apathy. It seemed that Mayer was looking at Valium, pointing to imipramine, and, with prophetic vision, seeing Prozac.

As for the expression of doubts about efficacy, they arose when antidepressants were among the best-validated treatments in medicine. (In 1974, Jonathan Cole revisited the efficacy literature, now more extensive, with a different young colleague, John Davis, and found much the same level of benefit as appeared in the 1960s data.) Mayer was offering a fallback case. If a reader does not buy the primary argument, that the drugs' mitigation of depression is counterproductive, a weaker, somewhat contradictory complaint stands at the ready. Over time, my impression has been along these lines: often, the claim that antidepressants do not work is in the service of a prior position, mistrust of medication when it does relieve suffering.

11

Interlude

Transitions

IN MEDICAL SCHOOL and then in residency at Yale, I had two interests, psychotherapy and community psychiatry. I worked with wayward youth, parolees, and indigent legal defendants. I ran groups for the gravely mentally ill, made home visits in inner-city neighborhoods, and staffed public clinics.

I might have continued in this vein except that I had begun dating a woman—Alan's friend Rachel, whom I would marry—who lived in Maryland. To join her, I agreed to an increased workload in New Haven in exchange for permission to spend my final six months in the federal government, in Rockville. A Yale professor there ran an office that brought model programs to mental health centers nationally. When that effort fell to budget cuts, I was sent to the agency that oversaw the NIMH and its sister institutes.

My boss was Gerry Klerman.

In the early months, I worked with Charles Krauthammer, then just out of his own psychiatry residency. Followers of Charlie's unsparing conservative political commentary will be amused to learn that he left to become a speechwriter for Walter Mondale in Jimmy Carter's losing reelection campaign. At that point, I ran the Division of Science of the Alcohol, Drug Abuse, and Mental Health Administration, largely because I constituted the whole of its remaining professional staff.

I had an extensive portfolio that included, from my prior life, research on illness and social disadvantage. My main job was to consult with experts and then brief Gerry for presentations to Congress and the White House. He was a large, quick man, and much of our contact was on the move, as in Aaron Sorkin television shows—*The West Wing*, *The Newsroom*—that feature assistants at their masters' heels. Once I'd prepped Gerry, he'd fill his speech with examples I had not provided and arrive at conclusions more sophisticated than those I had proposed.

Under his tutelage, I studied treatment-outcome research. Our focus was proposed legislation, originating in the Senate, that demanded controlled trials in mental health care, with an emphasis on psychotherapy. If therapy failed, federal programs would not pay for it. If therapy passed muster, psychologists would gain new practice privileges under Medicare. Gerry was pressuring psychotherapists: randomize until it hurts.

Gerry had standing because he and his future wife, Myrna Weissman, had conducted the first substantial trial of psychotherapy for depression. The research utilized a simplified version of psychoanalysis called interpersonal psychotherapy, or IPT. The treatment's elements were specified in manuals, used for training via brief instructional courses.

Gerry and Myrna tested IPT's ability, alone and in conjunction with the tricyclic Elavil, to prevent relapse in patients who had recovered from a recent episode of depression. On its own, Elavil outperformed IPT. (In another trial, of depression treatment, the two did equally well.) Surprisingly, combined treatment, psychotherapy plus Elavil, was no more protective than Elavil alone. This result was early evidence that mental health interventions are not always "additive." If each of two treatments gives a benefit, the two together may not give a larger benefit.

The main impact of these trials was to show that psychotherapy could be tested, like any medical intervention. This conclusion encountered resistance. The setup—manuals, quick training—outraged many psychotherapists.

I was one. How many hours had I spent attending seminars and

undergoing supervision in the effort to master particular psychotherapies? That's before mentioning reading, my personal analysis, and
time spent in patient care—followed always by self-criticism. Was I
present, imaginative, spontaneous, kindly, empathetic, and clear? Psychotherapy was an aspiration or destination. And now we were testing its
worth via brief treatments conducted in accordance with mechanical
guidelines.

Consistently, the outcome trials showed efficacy, but each time
they did, I thought, It might have been otherwise.

Gerry dismissed these concerns as naïve. The government and other
payers would demand that treatments prove their worth, and rightly so.

In 1980, with Gerry's encouragement, the NIMH established a
Psychosocial Treatments Research Branch under Morris Parloff, an
expert in outcome trials. (Like my father, he'd been one of the "Ritchie
Boys," German speakers with a scientific bent who served in American
military intelligence in World War II.) Morrie was urbane, with a wry
manner. In group settings, he generally held back. If the discussion
veered in a direction he found unhelpful, when called upon, he would
venture, "I feel like I've said too little already." I worked with him on
research policy.

Morrie estimated that there were 250 schools of psychotherapy.
Each variant might have a dozen targets—schizophrenia, alcoholism,
and so on. You might want to look at those treatments for those targets in, say, a half-dozen patient groups—adolescents, the medically ill,
and more. If so, evaluating each combination of treatment, disease, and
patient type once would require eighteen thousand clinical trials—and
then replication. The government was having trouble finding funding for
a single substantial trial.

But Gerry was set on outcome testing, and in the area he had pio-
neered, depression treatment. The great activity, in the two and a
half years I worked in government, was preparing for a large-scale
psychotherapy trial. Not on his watch, but shortly after, Gerry's vision
carried the day. The research would also set standards for the testing
of medication—and play a role in the antidepressant controversy years
later.

Meanwhile, I was accumulating experience treating depression.
Doctors in federal posts were granted time to teach and practice. I

joined the faculty at George Washington University—but where might patients come from?

An elderly psychoanalyst had been weakened by a chronic and now terminal illness. He was looking for young doctors to take on his remaining patients and try treating them with medication. A professor at GW recommended me. I visited the analyst in his large brick house near Rock Creek Park.

The visit was an assessment: Was I up to the task? There was another agenda. Among the remaining patients was Stephan. In adolescence, he had been delicate, living in an abusive setting. The analyst, call him Dominic, and his wife rescued Stephan, taking him into their home and acting as foster parents. Perhaps because this arrangement demanded secrecy, Stephan had never been referred for consultation.

Stephan was timid and solitary, a career administrator in the federal bureaucracy. Throughout adulthood, he had been pessimistic, scrupulous, cautious, and glum. As Dominic became frail, Stephan had slipped into "double depression," an acute episode superimposed on a chronic state. Double depression was just being discussed in the field, and antidepressants were thought to help. I did not hesitate in prescribing a tricyclic.

The depressive episode resolved quickly, a pattern that was new to Stephan, and he noted that he was less liable to downturns in mood.

Stabilization proved important. Dominic died. Under Ronald Reagan, government workers faced a "reduction in force"—firings. Stephan assumed more varied duties and reported to a different boss. Ordinarily, upheaval at this level caused Stephan to experience mild paranoia, as if organizational restructuring contained threats intentionally directed at him.

The medication sustained more benign views. Stephan understood what he had been told repeatedly, that crises constitute chances to nudge staff forward. He had what he said was a new thought: "I deserve a good life."

For Stephan, so attached to Dominic, I represented entropy: the dissolution of shared memories and assumptions. I was of a cooler temperament than Dominic and likelier, prescribing aside, to throw Stephan on his own resources. The medicine, not I, proved to be Dominic's replacement. It seemed that antidepressants could act that way, as transitional companionship—in this case, at a level that allowed Stephan to begin socializing, if cautiously, with peers from his work-place.

In my clinical practice, the experience of being Roland Kuhn played out over a decade. Repeatedly, I encountered patients who responded to medication as they never had to remedies they trusted more.

With Gerry, I read endlessly about outcome testing based on rating scales. But, as Jonathan Cole had taught, it was clinical care that demonstrated what drugs offered. An antidepressant might free a patient to accept change. I stored that result in my library of potential medication effects.

As for my own development, I had moved from studenthood, with its constant supervision, into private practice. Evenings, I went to an empty office, and people came to me. I was hooked, by the autonomy, the responsibility, and the privilege.

12

Big Splash

BEFORE RONALD REAGAN took office, Gerry Klerman left government, and the Senate bill requiring psychotherapy trials lost momentum. Why had psychologists ever supported the legislation? Payment under government programs was an incentive, but they had another reason to trust in randomized trials—an ace in the hole. In the 1970s, a psychologist had invented a new statistical tool, meta-analysis, and it showed that psychotherapy worked.

As interest in controlled trials grew, psychotherapy had come under attack as mere placebo or worse. Chief among the critics was a German-born British psychologist, Hans Eysenck. Since the 1950s, Eysenck had been writing that research failed to support psychotherapy's central claim, that it lessened neurosis.

In an era when hospitalization was used to treat milder conditions, Eysenck reviewed data on discharges of mentally ill inpatients. Many had never received formal psychotherapy. Eysenck estimated that over 70 percent of neurotics got better with general medical care. Looking at wards where psychotherapy was practiced, Eysenck found that 64 percent of patients responded—and where psychoanalysis was used, only 44 percent.

Psychotherapy seemed to relieve neurosis—until you looked at a control condition. With conventional medical treatment, symptoms faded, and more reliably. Eysenck suggested that therapy might be harmful: "the more psychotherapy, the lower the recovery rate."

The attack was preposterous. When a patient returned to work, his GP might consider him cured even when a psychoanalyst would doubt that the neurosis had budged. As a contemporary commentator put it, Eysenck's finding—less relief among analytic patients—"reflects the probability that the more intensive the therapy, the higher the standard of recovery."

However unreasonable, Eysenck's challenge was a burr under the saddle for psychotherapists. A young psychologist and statistician, Gene Glass, had become frustrated by what he called "Eysenck's frequent and tendentious reviews of the psychotherapy outcome research that proclaimed psychotherapy as worthless." Glass intended, he wrote, "to annihilate Eysenck and prove that psychotherapy really works" by making "a big splash." The occasion was an address that Glass was slated to give to a professional organization in 1976. He later recalled, "I set about to do battle with Dr. Eysenck and prove that psychotherapy— my psychotherapy—was an effective treatment."

The problem was the lack of agreement about how to summarize a body of research literature. Experts did that job all the time, but the review article was a ready forum for the expression of prejudices. Glass complained, "A common method for integrating several studies with inconsistent findings is to carp on the design or analysis deficiencies of all but a few studies—those remaining frequently being one's own work or that of one's students or friends."

Glass believed that Eysenck had ignored inconvenient data.

Intent on doing the opposite, Glass assembled every study he could find that tested a psychotherapy against another intervention or against a placebo condition such as "usual medical treatment." Where Eysenck had located 11 qualifying studies, Glass gathered 475 involving more than twenty-five thousand patients. He then set out to combine the results in clever fashion. Taking a basket of apples and oranges, he would prove that it was possible to study fruit.

But how? One researcher might test psychoanalysis in the treatment of alcoholism. Another might evaluate cognitive therapy for college students made anxious by a hard math problem. To amalgamate diverse studies—to create a class of fruit—Glass turned to a statistical concept, *effect size*.

In his reworking of the Ten Commandments, the poet W. H. Auden admonished, "Thou shalt not sit / With statisticians nor commit / A social science." Because the antidepressant controversy consists largely of arguments about effect sizes, we may need to transgress, if gingerly.

Effect size looks at a group of people and says how far treatment moves those who receive it. The calculation begins with our standard maneuver, subtracting the progress patients make in the control arm from the greater progress their counterparts make in the treatment arm. Then, to make the results of dissimilar studies comparable, the formula brings in a basic measure in statistics, the standard deviation.

We won't get into the math except to say that, for our purposes, a standard deviation is "a lot." To attach a number: If a medical intervention shifts those on it one standard deviation in a good direction, the average treatment user will now be at the 84 percent mark, so that only 16 percent of people in the original group were healthier. A therapy that brings about change at that level is said to have an effect size of one. It shifted the average by one standard deviation—a lot.

Few medical treatments do that well. An intervention may move patients ahead half a standard deviation, a result expressed as an effect size of 0.5. The average treated subject will do better than 69 percent of untreated subjects.

Glass took the concept of effect size from an influential statistician, Jacob Cohen, who, in the 1960s, had developed a field called power analysis. To that point, statistics had been mostly an all-or-none business. When an experiment found a result (for instance, that psychotherapy, more than usual medical care, decreases patients' anxiety), statisticians would say whether the result was "significant"—unlikely to be due to chance alone. By the 1930s, statisticians had adopted a working agreement: only if it achieved certainty at the 95 percent level would an experimental finding be deemed significant, that is, credible. Statistical significance answers the question "Is the result real?" or, more precisely, "Is there only a small probability that it's not real?"

Changes can be real without being noteworthy. A therapy might predictably help people but only by a tiny amount. Cohen's measure looked beyond yes-or-no to say *how much*. Effect size expresses the amount of improvement likely to occur in response to treatment. It's the statistical answer to the Ed Koch question, "How'm I doing?"

Since effect size is not an intuitive concept, Cohen provided a guide. An effect size of 0.2 is small; 0.5 is medium; and 0.8 is large. (He later admonished those who took these labels too seriously that they had been "set forth throughout with much diffidence, qualifications, and invitations not to employ them if possible.") Standard medical treatments tend to show medium effect sizes, just under 0.5.

Gene Glass saw that he could use effect sizes to combine apples and oranges. If psychoanalysis for alcoholism moved treated patients to the 84 percent mark and so did the anxiety therapy (and some others), then Glass would say that therapy in general performed its job at that level, one standard deviation's worth, with an effect size of one.

Glass had collected all kinds of psychotherapy outcome studies. They measured movement toward freedom from delusions in schizophrenic patients and movement toward freedom from snake phobias in healthy college students. In each case, Glass asked how far treatment moved treated research subjects relative to their group as a whole. Combining his 475 studies into one big experiment, Glass found that the effect size for psychotherapy was 0.85—large. Few other interventions in the social or psychological arena work as well. Glass's summary result—high efficacy for psychotherapy—constituted a thorough refutation of Eysenck. Glass had achieved his goal, total victory in the psychotherapy dispute.

13

Alchemy

WE WILL HAVE doubts about that outcome: *total victory.* Dogma-based controversies tend to persist. Besides, each meta-analysis is an experiment, and experiments involve choices.

Glass's approach, including every trial ever reported, sounds uncontroversial. The ideal in research is to respect the contribution of each subject who enters any study. Count everyone.

But even Glass had applied judgment. For example, he found so many trials testing treatments for snake phobia that this specialized therapy threatened to dominate his results. He omitted some of the data sets.

Glass chose not to correct other similar problems. Because psychology departments are housed in colleges, and because college students are curious and in need of petty cash, the easiest studies to perform are of undergraduates made to experience and then recover from unease. When you embrace every experiment, your conclusion, *psychotherapy works,* may mean only that counseling helps venturesome young people with artificially induced problems. What has that finding to do with treatment of depression, anorexia, and the rest? The "count everyone" approach puts meta-analysis at the mercy of what happens to be in the literature. If selecting studies is suspect, using a complete set of trials can be, too.

In 1983, admirers of Hans Eysenck's published their own meta-analysis. Psychologists at Wesleyan University found that in Glass's collection only thirty-two studies contrasted conventional psychotherapy to a placebo condition. Taking results from those trials and using methods slightly different from Glass's, the researchers calculated an effect size of 0.15—small impact—and the benefit came largely from studies involving recruited subjects. With real psychiatric outpatients, the effect size was basically zero.

When they employed methods closer to Glass's, the Wesleyan group found an effect size of 0.42. These results, effect sizes of 0.85, 0.42, and 0.15 (or zero), cover the range. Either psychotherapy is astonishingly effective or as good as many treatments doctors use or a complete bust.

As for Eysenck, meta-analysis left him unimpressed. He wrote, "A good review is based on intimate personal knowledge of the field, the participants, the problems that arise, the reputation of different laboratories, the likely trustworthiness of individual scientists, and other partly subjective but extremely relevant considerations."

Most overviews amounted to an abuse of data.

Glass had conducted one analysis that resembled the Wesleyan group's. He examined trials with three arms, contrasting psychotherapy, medication, and placebo. These studies enroll patients with real disorders—no imipramine for healthy undergrads. Also, research can suffer from "allegiance bias": psychotherapy trials conducted by interested parties show inflated results. (Where experimenters had an allegiance to the therapy under study, Glass found an effect size close to one—a lot.) In three-armed trials, pharmacologists' preferences balance therapists'.

Treating serious patients in more neutral studies, psychotherapy showed an effect size of 0.3, low to medium. Medication yielded an effect size just over 0.5, medium, and Glass argued for cutting that figure to 0.4. For antidepressants such as imipramine, effect sizes ran between 0.4 and 0.5—typical for treatments in clinical medicine. How bad was therapy's 0.3? Glass considered psychotherapy to be *scarcely any less effective than drug therapy in the treatment of serious psycho-*

logical disorders." For Glass, effect sizes between 0.3 and 0.5 in imperfect trials signaled useful treatments.

As we shall see later, that range encompasses most of the recent estimates of antidepressant efficacy, with psychotherapy perhaps running slightly lower. Critics of medical model psychiatry complain that antidepressants were hyped from early on. But Glass's meta-analyses, at the birth of the method, look to be on target.

As for how much faith we should put in meta-analysis, the debate over Glass's work might make us wonder. What does it mean that a collection of studies can give rise to three efficacy estimates: high, medium, and low?

Let's think about what meta-analysis tries to do. The ideal in outcome research is a randomized trial large enough to settle an issue definitively, what's called a gold standard trial. One thousand has come to be accepted as the minimum number of patients for gold standard designation. Many efforts are larger. When researchers worried about the effects of hormone replacement in menopause, they ran controlled trials involving between ten thousand and sixteen thousand women. High-enrollment programs are convincing but expensive. There are no gold standard trials in psychiatry—and not enough in the rest of medicine either. Meta-analysis purports to achieve similar certainty by combining small trials.

By the early 1990s, meta-analysis had moved into the medical mainstream. In one influential effort, from 1992, researchers examined the use of streptokinase, a medicine that dissolves blood clots, in the wake of heart attacks. They found that if statisticians had performed a cumulative meta-analysis each time a new small trial entered the literature, they would have confirmed the effectiveness of the intervention before gold standard trials on the topic were conducted—and saved lives by speeding the acceptance of streptokinase use.

This inquiry was less about levels of efficacy—*How much?*—than statistical significance. The amalgamated data gave an early indication that streptokinase improved survival. The studies under analysis were of two sorts: large trials, involving five hundred or seven hundred patients, and small trials in which the effects of treatment showed up consistently, time after time. Large trials and trials with consistent results give clear signals in meta-analyses—but, of course, even without a special statistical technique doctors might find that accumulation of results convincing.

Is there value in combining results from small trials with conflicting findings? And can meta-analysis answer *How much?*

In 1997, doctors from the University of Montreal, writing in *The New England Journal of Medicine,* contrasted meta-analysis and the gold standard. The team identified a dozen large, randomized trials, each testing at least a thousand patients, where the same question—Should the treatment be used?—had been answered in prior meta-analyses, forty in all. The topics were diverse: streptokinase, but also magnesium in the treatment of heart attacks, chemotherapies for breast cancer, and so on. The outcomes measured were straightforward. The commonest was death.

The news from Montreal was discouraging. When a gold standard trial showed that a treatment worked, a third of the time the prior meta-analyses had failed to find efficacy. When the gold standard trial found insufficient or negative evidence, a third of the time "the meta-analysis would have led to the adoption of an ineffective treatment."

Meta-analyses lead doctors in the right direction four times in six. Coin flips would lead them in the right direction three times in six. But then, doctors can do better than fifty-fifty, as when they make note of areas where many small studies and a large one point in the same direction, areas where meta-analyses only confirm the obvious.

In the Montreal study, what meta-analysis proved worst at was what it was designed for, measuring the magnitude of effects. The Canadian researchers came down where Hans Eysenck had. They looked favorably on the suggestion that doctors read trials individually and exercise judgment.

Why can't meta-analysis perform alchemy, turning a heterogeneous mixture (of data) into gold? There are many reasons, some highly technical, but one that is easy to understand concerns what is effectively a loss of randomization.

Meta-analyses are studies of controlled trials. Each trial arrives at the triage desk and is accepted or rejected. And most meta-analyses are performed after the fact. Experts who know the research literature propose entry criteria, admitting this sort of study and not that one, and then run the numbers. Like psychotherapy trials, meta-analyses display allegiance bias. The outcomes favor views held by authors who have a professional or financial stake in the result. Researchers found this pattern in competing meta-analyses on straightforward questions such as whether formaldehyde exposure causes leukemia.

Even where everyone's hands are on the table, meta-analysis can prove tricky. A recent example involves surgical safety checklists. Reformers had hoped that if before, during, and after an operation, nurses catechized the surgical team on issues such as whether the incision site was properly marked, then patients would fare better. A celebrated meta-analysis of twenty-two small trials—it led to widespread adoption of the operating-room discipline—found that checklists reduced complications and deaths dramatically, by 40 percent. But a subsequent study of 200,000 surgical operations in Ontario, half performed before and half after the implementation of checklists, found no benefit: no fewer deaths, no fewer return emergency-room visits, and no fewer surgical complications.

Here, probably the problem was what gets published. Hospitals whose innovations fail bury the result. Successful efforts get written up. Meta-analysis is at the mercy of what makes its way into the literature.

Public health advocates had celebrated the early meta-analysis, and the disappointing large-scale research tested their devotion to *evidence*. Their tendency was to defend checklists, based on a detailed examination of the virtues of this or that program—again, the close reading of small studies. In truth, medicine relies on judgment: doctors have a good sense of what works, they find confirmation in well-performed research, and they feel justified in discounting even large-scale studies, based on possible flaws. In Ontario, was the training adequate? Public health experts still support checklists, although with acknowledgment that they are unlikely to offer the impressive benefits first reported. On the *How much?* question, the meta-analysis had been misleading.

Few discussions of the antidepressant controversy acknowledge this truth: In psychiatry, we lack large trials, and meta-analyses are imperfect substitutes. The particular shortcomings are significant. The antidepressant controversy is about *How much?* On the simple question of whether antidepressants outperform placebos, the meta-analyses are in agreement: Medications work. The debate is over the magnitude of the effect size.

This dispute has a fantastical aspect. Meta-analysis does not constitute sublime guidance. Even in neutral hands, it provides only suggestive findings. Often, it amounts to argumentation.

Since meta-analyses are what we have, in this book I will refer to them repeatedly. But often I will try to supplement their findings through attention to the constituent trials. That's where the fun is, and the promise of wisdom as well, in the quirks of carefully conducted small-scale research.

Still, whatever the limitations of Glass's invention, its influence would be hard to overstate. In mental health care, when experts argue over the worth of treatments, almost always it is meta-analysis that drives the debate.

14

Interlude
Providence

RONALD REAGAN CAME to office. His budget director, David Stockman, announced a ban on social research. The ukase covered much of my portfolio, including the effects of poverty on health. I left the government.

Baby in tow, my wife and I landed in Providence, Rhode Island, where I had been invited to head the outpatient psychiatry departments for three hospitals, including the principal general hospital. Here, too, Reagan played a role. My mandate was to create services for the flow of patients expected to burden clinics as, with budget cuts, community mental health centers lost funding. I would be doing public psychiatry in the private, not-for-profit sector.

With few resources for independent outpatient work, I tasked my staff with supporting the medical and surgical departments. The doctors were fine with our offering psychotherapy, but what they wanted most was for me to prescribe for their patients. The psychotherapeutic medications were considered effective but hard to use.

My strongest connection was with the gastroenterologists. I lectured on ulcers and helped with research on the acceptance of hepatitis vaccines. As a result, I was referred a cluster of patients like those Kuhn had treated, with hard-to-diagnose GI complaints. These men and women, employed in unrewarding service-industry or line-manufacturing jobs, came with stories of disrupted childhoods, conflict-ridden marriages, workplace abuse, and money troubles. They experienced their problems as physical, and they mistrusted talk.

My patients had failed to respond to a series of drugs targeting bowel motility, and sometimes anxiety as well. I am writing of what were considered tough cases, "somatizers" with mood disorder. Although the tricyclics caused stomach and intestinal side effects, the GI patients did well on them. Antidepressants allowed patients to face adversity without being thrown into despair. Not every case was successful, but the successes could be dramatic. They reinforced the lessons I had learned with Adele and Stephan. Antidepressants helped patients who had failed to respond to treatments they believed in, and the benefits were broad.

I described the experiences of those years in a monthly column for a psychiatric trade paper and in my first book, *Moments of Engagement*. Psychotherapy remained my main interest, but there was no avoiding this related issue, how prescribing colored that effort. I described a woman with psychosomatic complaints who blamed her troubles on her family. On medication, she shocked me by saying of an impasse, "It wasn't just my husband, it was me." How many therapy sessions—and what delicacy—would it have taken to earn that insight?

I made note of a tendency in the social workers I brought on staff. They arrived mistrusting medications and the young doctors who managed their use. Then, not long into their tenure, they would begin to demand that I prescribe. Because drugs sometimes accomplished within weeks what psychotherapy did (or failed at) over years, social workers had become a tribe in danger of losing faith in its own customs.

What I wrote at the time (really) was "The issue is not efficacy nor evidence." The improvement that caught the social workers' and my attention might have little to do with items on the Hamilton scale. A patient would be relieved of a hard-to-define impediment and go on to create a new social environment and then flourish.

I have nostalgia for those days. I retained values from medical school—favoring psychotherapy, urging my staff and my patients to give it more of a chance. And then there was something pleasant about prescribing *malgré soi*. I am a fan of Rex Stout's mysteries. The setup is

that his detective, Nero Wolfe, never leaves the house on assignment—
except in the novel you are reading, the unique case that requires extraordinary means. My use of antidepressants was that way, always in
despite of misgivings. And then there would be uplift, if the remedy
turned out to be a right one after all.

If I dismissed questions of evidence and efficacy, the profession did
not. Starting in 1982, clinics at the University of Pittsburgh, George
Washington University, and the University of Oklahoma began enrolling patients—250 in all—for the depression-treatment study that
Gerry Klerman had championed. It had four arms, testing interpersonal
psychotherapy, cognitive behavioral therapy, imipramine, and placebo
pills.

In 1986, a researcher presented preliminary data. *The New York
Times* relayed the conclusions in a story headlined "Psychotherapy Is as
Good as Drug in Curing Depression, Study Finds." The article's key
paragraph read:

> The study found that two relatively new forms of psychotherapy, cog-
> nitive behavior therapy and interpersonal psychotherapy, achieved
> results comparable to a standard antidepressant drug, imipramine, in
> reducing the symptoms of depression and improving the functioning
> of patients. All three therapies completely eliminated serious symp-
> toms in 50 to 60 percent of the patients treated for 16 weeks.

The explanation continued, "While 50 to 60 percent of the patients
who received either the psychotherapeutic treatments or the drug
reached 'full recovery' with no serious symptoms, fewer than 30 percent
of those given the placebo reached full recovery."

The field's largest experiment—the Treatment of Depression Collaborative Research Program, or TDCRP—had validated every method.
Think of it: *full recovery in most patients*. On reading the account, I
experienced relief. As always, my thought was, It might have been
otherwise.

15

Best Reference

ACTUALLY, IT WAS otherwise. With the newspaper article's appearance, all hell broke loose. Scientists who served as advisers to the trial complained that the preliminary report misrepresented the research findings. Because of disputes over statistical methods, it would be 1989 before the study's results appeared in a professional journal.

The Treatment of Depression Collaborative Research Program had one purpose, planners had written: "to advance the scientific study of the effectiveness of different forms of psychotherapy." The organizers looked for therapies standardized for use as brief treatments. Two were available: interpersonal psychotherapy, or IPT, and cognitive behavioral psychotherapy, or CBT.

IPT represented the Freudian strain in psychology, therapies aimed at emotional self-understanding. CBT, with roots back to Pavlov, relied on educational approaches to help patients correct maladaptive thoughts. This one trial, of CBT and IPT for depression, would stand in for Morris Parloff's eighteen thousand experiments. The overarching question was, Does psychotherapy work?

The planners argued over the selection of a control condition. Ideally, IPT and CBT would have been compared to fifty-minute conversations with experts who had been trained *not* to bolster patients' interpersonal functioning or reasoning processes, but no one had designed a placebo psychotherapy. Also, having pressed psychotherapists to test their practices, pharmacologists now worried that the NIMH trial would be a put-up job, enlisting a healthy population, not real patients. The pharmacologists asked for what would later be called a *comparator* arm.

A comparator—you can stress either the first or second syllable—is an established treatment that serves to "validate the sample." In a trial with properly diagnosed patients, the comparator will produce an expected level of change. If the group is unrepresentative, the comparator will fail, and the trial results can be dismissed.

The obvious comparator was imipramine—in the organizers' words, "The best reference drug to use would be the drug with the longest history of use and for which a large amount of efficacy data exists with this patient population." The control condition would be a placebo pill. But in the 1980s, "brief psychotherapy" lasted at least sixteen weeks, an eternity for depressed patients. To minimize suffering and prevent suicides, the researchers decided to supplement placebo administration with emotional support. The patients on pills (placebo or imipramine) would attend sixteen or more twenty-to-thirty-minute "advice and encouragement" sessions with experienced psychiatrists.

The NIMH researchers wrote that this clinical management was "*not* a no-treatment condition or an 'inactive' placebo condition." They considered it "minimal supportive therapy." The question under study was whether IPT and CBT could outperform modest nonspecific counseling.

The answer was, yes and no. When the experiment had been run and the numbers crunched, the NIMH researchers reported that the data showed a "consistent ordering of treatments at termination, with imipramine plus clinical management generally doing best, placebo plus clinical management worst, and the two psychotherapies in between but generally closer to imipramine plus clinical management." The details told a more particular story. Interpersonal psychotherapy had performed better than placebo and almost as well as imipramine. Cognitive behavioral therapy had failed. CBT had been contrasted to placebo-plus-support through twenty or thirty statistical analyses. On none did the psychotherapy demonstrate superiority at a level that achieved statistical significance.

One of the trial's advisers was Donald Klein, a pharmacology pioneer I had met while working for Gerry Klerman and whose theories I would rely on in *Listening to Prozac*. Klein summarized the NIMH results in provocative fashion: "It is not simply that imipramine is better, faster, and cheaper than CBT, but that the whole basis for the belief that cognitive psychotherapy is doing anything specific has been placed in jeopardy."

The TDCRP had been designed as the finest outcome trial that research technology would allow. Do we imagine that, in response, cognitive behavioral therapists began (à la Gerry Klerman) to warn patients that CBT might work no better than supportive conversations? We do not.

Psychologists argued that the trial did not contrast psychotherapy to "treatment as usual" but rather to a supportive therapy that was not, in the end, all that minimal. Some of what CBT provided (expert attention, reassurance, direction) was duplicated in the placebo arm, and when the benefits of that care were subtracted away, CBT proved to offer little extra.

Then there was the matter of enrollment. Interviews conducted during the sign-on found that what volunteers wanted was free psychotherapy. They needed a Hamilton score of 14 to enter the trial. Perhaps people who were not depressed had listed false symptoms and then given the impression that they were "responding" to placebo (or any offering) by giving honest answers once the trial began. Consultants who had seen the raw data found evidence of "baseline score inflation," as this problem is called, with high Hamilton scores plummeting within days. The resulting puffed-up response rate in the placebo arm was hard to compete with.

Defenders of CBT also questioned the study's implementation. At two sites, CBT appeared to have been performed in rote fashion. Perhaps early critics of the trial had been right: manualized therapies could not duplicate the real thing, therapy built around creative or spontaneous efforts with patients.

But finally, cognitive therapists set the results in context and went about their business. Although the enrollment, sixty patients per arm, was large for the time, TDCRP was hardly of gold standard dimensions, and prior small studies had been favorable. Adherents of CBT might be advocates of controlled trials, but in defense of a treatment they found useful in practice, they listed endless reasons to keep the faith, and likely they were right. Subsequent research has suggested that CBT performs as well as other psychotherapies.

The NIMH trial had paradoxical results. It was designed to test psychotherapies, and CBT bombed. But previously, cognitive behaviorism had been a bit player, a curiosity dear to hyperrational types for whom psychoanalysis represented mysticism. Now, because a team of experts had taken CBT seriously, the field did. CBT failed to outperform placebo—and gained legitimacy.

Imipramine's fate was equally paradoxical. The drug did its job, validating the patient sample, but in time the results of the collaborative study would be used to foster doubt about antidepressants.

16

Better, Faster, Cheaper

IMIPRAMINE ENDED EPISODES of depression. The NIMH researchers defined "recovery" as a Hamilton score below 6. By this standard—it suggests solid mental health—over 40 percent of those who entered the imipramine arm recovered. Half as many subjects recovered with placebo. Whatever distortions the recruitment process produced—and it does seem that some participants had exaggerated their symptoms—overall, the recovery numbers suggested that it had attracted patients with substantial mood disorders.

But what if, instead of using imipramine to test the trial, we want to use the trial to test imipramine?

The NIMH study was designed to evaluate psychotherapy. Since imipramine was meant as a comparator, it was prescribed according to methods used in prior research where antidepressants succeeded. Clinicians were to push the dose up to a good level and hold it there. But the trials that served as models lasted six or eight weeks. To accommodate psychotherapy, the TDCRP lasted sixteen.

Jan Fawcett, the psychiatrist who wrote the manual for drug administration, later said that he had always entertained misgivings about the medication protocol. With the rigid plan, a research subject might be dosed heavily, show no response, suffer agitation and indigestion, and persist with those symptoms for months. Patients would be exposed to risk and discomfort, and imipramine's score sheet would be blemished by bad outcomes rarely seen in settings where doctors can adjust regimens. As the trial proceeded, Fawcett recalled, participating pharmacologists became demoralized.

There are, so far as I know, no published accounts of how much medication patients in the TDCRP took, but worrisome indicators came to Fawcett's attention.

Doctors were beginning to regulate patients' imipramine doses according to blood levels, a practice that later became common. The intention was to keep the concentrations in a "therapeutic window," a range in which medicine is most effective. A classic study found that patients with proper drug levels were 70 percent likelier to respond than those with readings below or above the window. Once the NIMH trial had ended, Fawcett learned that ten participants had reached toxic drug levels—enough imipramine to cause disturbances of electrical conduction in the heart. It was lucky that no one died. The blood levels ran almost triple what they should have. Given the level of overdosing in these ten patients, many more of the volunteers must have been at less alarming levels that were nonetheless outside—above—the window.

Donald Klein developed concerns that the trial's design had caused problems at the other extreme—below the therapeutic window. Knowing that patients would be stuck at whatever dose the imipramine had been increased to, prudent clinicians might have been cautious in prescribing for relatively healthy patients. Klein wrote, "It is quite possible the milder patients received ineffective, small doses."

The trial's method—drawing blood only late in the trial, withholding laboratory results from prescribers, and forbidding dose decreases—had the virtue of simplicity. If you provided blood levels to prescribers, would you offer them pretend data for the placebo group? The TDCRP avoided complexity and still got the wished-for confirmation: real patients. But if half the TDCRP participants had blood levels outside the therapeutic window, then the study results might understate imipramine's benefits by a third. That's a lot of efficacy left on the table—a lot of difference between what the trial reported and what imipramine does in doctors' offices.

Sir Austin Bradford Hill had anticipated this dilemma, the need to choose between simplicity and full efficacy. He said, "It may well be asked, therefore, in the planning of a trial, which is the more important—for the doctor to be ignorant of the treatment and unbiased in his judgment or for him to know what he is doing and to be able to adjust what he is doing so as to observe closely the results and then make unbiased judgments to the best of his ability . . ."

The NIMH trial was blinded, but that precaution, meant to minimize bias, almost certainly skewed the results anyway, against medication.

If the study underestimated the value of imipramine, it may also have overstated the effects of placebo pills. I have mentioned problems that can occur at the start of a trial, when patients may exaggerate symptoms. Later, we will consider ways in which baseline score inflation has clouded our understanding of antidepressants. For now, let's consider distortions that can occur as participants leave a study.

What drives people away? When researchers ask, patients give consistent answers. In the group on placebo, almost all who leave do so because the treatment isn't working. On the drug side, dropouts for side effects predominate.

Placebo arms lose sick patients and retain healthier ones: people who get better spontaneously, people who were not depressed to begin with, and people who respond to minimal supportive psychotherapy. Describing what happens in the drug arm is more difficult. If participants know from experience that their depression tends to remit with, say, psychotherapy, even a mild drug side effect may cause them to seek help elsewhere. These dropouts may include the most naturally responsive patients in the sample. For some patients, drugs will work partial magic, relieving half their symptoms, say, and instilling hope of more improvement to follow—so that quite fragile and vulnerable patients are carried along.

When participants exit different arms of a trial for different reasons, the study is said to suffer from *differential dropout*. Differential dropout ruins randomization. The placebo arm will have retained patients who were resilient to start with. The medication arm will have retained a sicker group. The experiment is back where it would have been if the triage nurse had assigned healthy people to take placebo and gravely burdened ones to take medication. This distortion—*dropout bias*—can produce results that understate antidepressants' worth.

The NIMH researchers worried in advance about differential dropout. A third of patients did quit early—but fully 45 percent of those given placebo. In the placebo group, patients who left the study tended to be those who had been severely depressed to start with.

Dropout bias tends to be greatest when researchers base their calculations on patients who stick with a trial, what is called a *completer analysis*. If only healthy patients persist in the placebo arm of a trial, a completer analysis will reverse reality, giving placebo credit for having driven off people who are still suffering.

In an alternative approach, an *intention-to-treat analysis*, researchers include results from all patients who enter a trial. Any who drop out are assigned the last Hamilton score recorded before they left. If a patient quits toward the start of a trial, her final Hamilton score will be the initial one—no improvement. The intention-to-treat analysis does not reward treatments for their failures.

In the completer analysis, looking at severely depressed patients who stuck with the program, the NIMH trial found that, contrasted with placebo, imipramine was four times as likely to induce a recovery—good efficacy. In the intention-to-treat analysis, counting all severely depressed patients who started the trial, it found that imipramine was six or seven times as likely to induce a recovery—fantastic efficacy. Arguably, imipramine was much more helpful than the completer analysis had shown it to be.

Okay. Researchers decide whose results (everyone, or those who stick it out) to include in an analysis—but which results?

We can count Hamilton points. On average, did patients on imipramine shed more symptoms than patients on placebo?

Another choice is to count people or instances of improvement. How many people responded—that is, shed half their symptoms? How many recovered—that is, exited depression? Response and recovery are categories. When they count people, researchers are doing a *categorical analysis*.

Because they help some patients a lot while leaving others unchanged or worse off, antidepressants look most effective in categorical analyses. Because in the course of a study many people will shed a few symptoms, placebos do well in analyses that look at averages.

The NIMH trial had that pattern. In terms of average outcome, imipramine always outperformed placebo, but only in a few calculations were the differences statistically significant. It was when they looked at categories—How many people did well?—that researchers found the most decisive evidence of imipramine's superiority.

Interpreters of outcome studies have choices: Completer sample or intention-to-treat? Categorical analysis or attention to averages? But what measure should we be talking about? Having met Per Bech, we may be wondering about the clinical gestalt.

The NIMH study employed an instrument called the Global Assessment Scale. Raters summarized each subject's well-being in a single number, considering social, psychological, and occupational competency. On the global scale, imipramine's efficacy was apparent even in average scores. This result is common. If an experiment includes a scale based on global impressions, where observers say how each research participant is doing overall, that measure will best capture antidepressants' advantage over placebo.

Can we use the NIMH trial data to develop a portrait of imipramine? We know that the medication was administered poorly to reluctant patients, people hoping for free psychotherapy. Even the strongest of the trial's results do not capture imipramine's inherent efficacy. But the data give an impressionistic picture. Imipramine will rarely shine "on average." Its strength is in bringing about substantial change in the large subset of patients it works for. The benefits are not limited to the syndrome the Hamilton recognizes. They extend to overall well-being.

Later, when we think about meta-analyses, we will be able to put our tools to work. Does a collection include the NIMH study, using the results as if they represented a fair assessment of imipramine's potential? If so, do the researchers rely on a completer analysis? The answers will give us a sense of what genre we're encountering—what sort of narrator is telling the tale.

Regarding the NIMH-led collaboration, if the news was not as good as reporters had claimed, it was not all bad either. A representative of the psychodynamic school, interpersonal psychotherapy, had shown its worth, and the field's old friend imipramine had done yeoman's work. These successes covered most of what mental health professionals relied on in the treatment of depression.

One more irony emerged. This scrupulous effort, designed by top-flight academics, had led to controversy and calls for reinterpretation. The contentious aftermath suggested that it was hard to conduct outcome research in a way that produced definitive or even convincing results. But the general understanding about the TDCRP was the reverse: it had demonstrated that randomized trials of depression treatment were feasible. As Gerry Klerman had hoped, they became the standard of evidence for psychotherapy.

17

Interlude

Tolerably Good

WE ARRIVE AT the modern antidepressant era. In late 1987, while the NIMH trial data were being analyzed, Prozac was approved for use. Knowing that it took the world by storm, we may imagine that Prozac arrived to fanfare. In truth, journals reported a range of outcomes, including modest and discouraging ones. A typical overview concluded, "Although [Prozac] should be added to formularies, its use should be reserved for treatment of those who do not respond to or do not tolerate tricyclic agents."

The new drug's promise was in the domain of side effects. Prozac was part of a class of medications that, because of the way they influence the brain's handling of neurotransmitters, were called selective serotonin reuptake inhibitors, or SSRIs. The SSRIs did not typically cause constipation, dry mouth, and the rest, although some patients complained of nausea.

In the column I wrote for psychiatrists and later in *Listening to Prozac*, I reported on my patients' response to the new medication. As they recovered from the condition we had targeted, depression or obsessionality, some noticed gains in self-confidence and social ease. I was interested in the intersection of technology, culture, and ethics: If an intervention could influence personality reliably, would doctors embrace that potential? Would we all?

About Prozac as a treatment for mood disorder, I had less to say. My summary verdict mirrored the profession's consensus: "a reasonable main effect, diminished side effects." My guess was that Prozac's special territory would be mild and chronic depression. SSRIs might influence depression indirectly, through creating a biological and psychological context that allowed recovery to proceed. The medicine's best use, I thought, was in conjunction with psychotherapy.

Later, as more results emerged, the efficacy research was encouraging. Early in 1993, while *Listening* was in press, the *British Medical Journal* reviewed sixty-three studies that compared SSRIs to tricyclics directly. The drugs worked equally well, an impressive result, since most studies used the Hamilton scale, which favors sedating antidepressants. Because they had thirty years of experience with imipramine, clinicians had a fair read on Prozac.

When Prozac arrived, I was caring for a number of depressed patients whose symptoms had lingered despite trials of psychotherapy and tricyclics. Often, Prozac helped—as it should have. A study of treatment performed in the 1990s found that when chronically depressed patients who had failed to improve on imipramine were switched to Zoloft, another early SSRI, 60 percent responded and 32 percent remitted. (As awareness of the chronicity of depression increased, *remission* replaced *recovery* as the term for the near disappearance of symptoms.)

Imagine that you are a psychiatrist practicing in the early 1990s. Among your patients are ten heartbreakers with obdurate mood disorder. Tricyclics have not budged it or them. You prescribe Zoloft. Now, you have only four nonresponders. That benefit alone might have made the SSRIs the most valuable new treatment to emerge in your career.

In time, I switched many patients from a tricyclic to an SSRI, not least because they demanded the change. I did see some new recoveries, but I recall being more impressed with another outcome, improved tolerability. I fear that I have not conveyed how hard the tricyclics were to live with—how unpleasant chronic constipation and grogginess can be. In a study where patients who failed on imipramine were offered Zoloft and vice versa, the switch only worked in one direction. Patients who had done poorly on tricyclics gave SSRIs time to do their job. Moved from Zoloft to imipramine, subjects quit the drug trial.

Tolerability turned out to be a more important determinant of drug use than anyone had anticipated. Like Valium in its time, Prozac was doctor- and patient-friendly. Compared to the tricyclics, the SSRIs were simpler to manage and safer in overdose.

In my book, I had foreseen and feared that Prozac might become the pill for the age, allowing people to endure or ignore the stresses of postmodernity. What I had not signaled was that Prozac would remake the treatment of major depression.

When a drug is well tolerated, doctors prescribe it early, before an episode of depression settles in to stay, and they prescribe it for lengths of time, to create an interval of calm in which patients can consolidate change. Prozac altered the skilled use of medication and, more generally, doctors' approach to depression.

From my own practice, let one example stand for many. Caroline came to me out of concern for her marriage. Anxious and intense, she was embarrassed to find herself in a psychiatrist's office. Caroline had made her mark as a copywriter in an advertising agency. Her ideas had dried up, which made her feel useless and desperate. Simultaneously, the demands of parenting had come to seem overwhelming. Caroline retired to devote herself to her two young daughters.

Time at home did not solve Caroline's problem. When the girls were in school, she found herself paralyzed by dread. She took to napping by day. At night, the apprehensions were worse. When her husband expressed concerns, Caroline amplified them. She feared that he had married the wrong woman.

Caroline was in an unrecognized, full-blown bout of depression—in retrospect, probably her third or fourth. Facing the same problem a decade earlier, I might, if months of talk therapy failed, have proposed a trial of imipramine. We would have struggled with doses and side effects, all the while wondering whether we were on the right track. The new antidepressants were preferable not because the odds were more in their favor, but because they were easy to use and, by then, socially acceptable. As Prozac gained popularity, it was understood that antidepressants might stabilize you while you "worked on your marriage."

With Caroline, I was not looking for incidental effects, like bolstering confidence. I was out to interrupt a depressive episode. After a week on Zoloft, Caroline felt less desperate. After a month, she had the will and the energy to tend to her daughters. The recovery had a cognitive aspect: Caroline's sharpness of thought returned.

Caroline was not a thorough "good responder" of the sort I had written about in *Listening to Prozac*. She remained cautious and prone to self-doubt. Whenever anything went wrong—in the marriage, in parenting—it was her fault.

Her husband, Greg, had joined us for occasional sessions. He was affable but evasive. He did not share his wife's worries about child care. Caroline never achieved enough assertiveness to enforce her standards. Greg budged, but only slightly.

Because Caroline was less prone to catastrophizing, that small movement on Greg's part sufficed. With her husband barely on board, Caroline returned to work. She had missed the office, with its deadlines, intrigue, and camaraderie. She was gifted with words and adept at epitomizing human needs and foibles in compact dramas. A great harm of depression was that it had blocked her from exercising her talents.

For years, Caroline visited me intermittently, for conversations that included psychotherapy, medical attention, and some guidance. Leston Havens used to say, "We need our doctors." People with depression, he meant, as much as those with diabetes.

By the 1990s, the standard of care in psychiatry called for long-term use of antidepressants in chronic cases. If a patient had suffered three serious episodes of depression, the thought was that when an antidepressant worked, she should be left on it "indefinitely," at full dose. The recommendation was grounded in the observation that after a third episode further bouts are all but inevitable, and they are likely to be progressively more disabling and closely spaced.

Studies suggested that antidepressant maintenance prevents recurrence. Interruptions might expose patients to deterioration. Since I had few depressed patients from whom I could not elicit accounts of two prior intervals of depression, almost all my patients were in a third or later episode. Despite the research result, often I tried tapering the medications. Once they were restabilized, patients might enjoy long intervals off antidepressants and free of mood disorder.

Following an intermittent strategy with imipramine was dicey. Even the second time around, the dose had to be eased up slowly, so that weeks would pass before the patient saw a full effect. The SSRIs made practice easy. You could restart the medication at a full dose, from day one. Often, patients noted an immediate slight uplift. Zoloft was nimble.

Caroline had runs of nine or ten months when she was on Zoloft and longer stretches when she was off medication. When she began to slip, the antidepressant offered enough prompt relief to allow her to continue doing what she valued.

What helps people like Caroline? Psychotherapy? Work? Family? Medicine acts as a catalyst, allowing for thriving under the ordinary constraints of the culture. Kuhn had said that he was less focused on patients' symptoms than their lives. I, too, cared about overall well-being. It seemed to me that Prozac and Zoloft and the rest helped my depressed patients achieve it.

In time, objective evidence emerged that bore on this topic, the effect of medication on life as it's lived. To assess general medical care, researchers developed scales that measure health-related well-being. The instruments ask about vitality, happiness, job attendance, task completion, social engagement, and more. Taking everything into account—the mental, social, and physical—how do ill people fare? Two antihypertensive drugs may lower blood pressure to the same degree, but because it has milder side effects, one may allow for a better life.

Although not created with depression in mind, well-being measures are relevant since mood disorders are so burdensome. Tracked through quality-of-life interviews, the progress of patients on SSRIs is remarkable. Drugs outperform placebo in the early going. By the three-month mark, patients who began depressed—gravely burdened—score within national norms in well-being. Even though some patients retain residual symptoms, on medicine depressed patients do as well as their never-depressed neighbors, and the effect persists.

In one study, researchers took chronically depressed patients who had responded to Zoloft, kept some on the drug, switched others to placebo, and followed the patients out to eighteen months. If their emotional functioning slid, their social functioning did not. For those maintained on medication, whenever measurements were taken, these patients—who began with multiyear histories of mood disorder and poor ratings of well-being—reported functioning better than average, healthy people in the community.

One fine point bears mention. In cases where the placebo matched medication in terms of symptom relief, it fell behind on social functioning. The quality-of-life scales captured antidepressant benefits that depression-symptom scales miss.

The quality-of-life research, mostly academic and from good centers, reflects the clinical picture. Antidepressants exert a broad influence. If an SSRI allows a patient to resume fulfilling work, her well-being will improve, never mind that some depressive symptoms linger. Even partial relief can lead in good directions.

What does this constellation look like, well-being in the face of lingering depression?

One patient, Luke, shared a poignant moment with me. After years of work paralysis when off medicines and then years of effort on them, he published a series of papers and finally earned academic tenure. Luke brought champagne to the next therapy session and invited me to join him in celebration. What a miracle—except for this detail: Luke said he could not feel deep pleasure in the event. That capacity had not been restored.

If depression remained a daunting adversary, still, Luke's life was transformed. Tenure gave him permanent membership in an academic community, along with the chance to teach and explore what he loved. It is not only medicine that maintains well-being. Once we function competently, the world may pitch in.

18

Better than Well

WRITING ABOUT PROZAC and personality, I coined two phrases, *better than well* and *cosmetic psychopharmacology*.

The first theme came from a patient who had prided himself on his cynicism and irascibility. He had said that on Prozac he was "better than baseline," more comfortable and less prickly than he had been even before his episode of depression had begun. He was ambivalent about his newfound equanimity, but in conventional terms (and his wife's) it represented change to the good. When other patients offered similar reports, their focus was assertiveness. Relief from depression aside, on medication they were more confident and outgoing.

The second idea came from an ethical and practical challenge I had faced. A patient would respond to Prozac in this fashion—better than well—and then come off medication. Months later, still mostly free of depression, she might return to my office. She had functioned more effectively while on Prozac. Would I offer it again?

This sequence made me wonder: Might a doctor prescribe for a person who had never been ill, to provide a boost in social ease? I called this potential use of medication cosmetic psychopharmacology, on the model of cosmetic surgery. Both efforts employed medical technology to move a person from a normal state to another normal state that is better rewarded in the culture. The discussion in *Listening to Prozac* energized the study of what ethicists call *enhancement*, medical interventions used for purposes other than the cure or prevention of disease.

Better than well referred to enhancement in psychiatric patients. *Cosmetic psychopharmacology* referred to enhancement in people with no mental disorder.

I first outlined these concepts in essays ("Metamorphosis" and "The New You") addressed to colleagues, saying that they must have seen what I had.

Later, in an interview, Jonathan Cole recalled that, treating patients with Prozac before the drug came to market, he had noticed some who "were clearly better than they had ever been before in their lives," adding that "there were just enough of them to make a difference." Cole called me "the *Listening to Prozac* man." Later, he retrieved my name: "Peter Kramer can be somewhat foggy but he makes valid points." Oh, dear. All the same, Cole confirmed the better-than-well phenomenon.

Coles's conversation was with David Healy, a noted critic of drug companies and arguably our most important historian of psychopharmacology. Healy asked the Swedish neuroscientist Arvid Carlsson—he would later win the Nobel Prize in Physiology or Medicine—about cosmetic psychopharmacology. Carlsson ventured, "I think that is true now with [Prozac] and all these drugs. There are people who feel so much better, who didn't have any diagnosis really."

This expert testimony spoke to the concepts' plausibility.

So did prior research. One motivation for developing serotonin-specific antidepressants had been the hope that they would influence phenomena beyond mainstream depression. These included obsessive-compulsive disorder, impulsive aggression, and atypical depression, where patients eat and sleep too much—and often suffer from social anxiety and low self-worth. In different ways, serotonin regulation had been implicated in all these problems. When I noticed personality effects in response to Prozac, I had reason to suspect that I might be onto something.

Was I? After *Listening to Prozac* appeared, researchers began to address cosmetic psychopharmacology and the better-than-well phenomenon.

The earliest studies asked whether healthy people experience personality change on medication. To mention one trial from a handful: David Healy looked at twenty normal subjects, including members of his research team at the University of Wales. They took either Zoloft or reboxetine, a medicine (not marketed in the States) that alters the way the brain handles norepinephrine. Later, participants who had been on one medicine were given the other.

Some volunteers did well on Zoloft, others on reboxetine. Unfavorable reactions to each drug also occurred. People who were suited to Zoloft reported feeling less prone to emotional upset when on it. In contrast, those who responded to reboxetine might experience unpleasant agitation on Zoloft.

When participants responded favorably to Zoloft, they became more sociable. Overall, the authors reported, "On their preferred drug, subjects scored lower on aggression, agitation, hostility, psychasthenia [low-level obsessions] and somatic anxiety, while scoring higher on social desirability."

Healy stressed a point that we considered when discussing how attention to average outcomes understates antidepressants' worth: on a given drug, some patients fare well and some especially poorly.

More recently, neuroscientists interested in ethics tested whether the SSRI Celexa could make thirty normal volunteers "prosocial." The subjects were paired off and put in a game where, with money at stake, they could make choices that would spare others harm, but at a cost of unfairness to themselves. On the SSRI, more than when on placebo or an antidepressant that affects norepinephrine, the participants behaved collaboratively, avoiding choices that would injure other people.

Because the issue is not clinical—few if any doctors are medicating "squeaky-clean" people, with no hint of depression—cosmetic psychopharmacology has been of interest mainly to philosophers. No one can say with certainty whether SSRIs induce self-assurance in healthy people. But what research there is suggests that personality effects are common and that on SSRIs people gain social comfort.

Funding is more readily available for studies of illness. Some trials of fair size have looked at the better-than-well phenomenon, personality change in depressed patients.

In 1999, Lisa Ekselius and other Swedish researchers examined more than three hundred moderately depressed patients drawn from primary-care clinics. In the trial, participants were given an SSRI (Celexa or Zoloft—with no risk of getting placebo), in treatment overseen by their general practitioners. This design has advantages. Depressed people will volunteer since all participants receive effective treatment. The doctors know the patients well. We are in Roland Kuhn territory, avoiding distortions that arise in trials that use placebos.

In Ekselius's hands, Celexa and Zoloft were outstanding treatments. In six months, 75 to 80 percent of patients who entered the trial and over 90 percent of those who completed it improved substantially on measures of depression. These figures resemble the ones Kuhn had reported four decades before.

(We should bookmark this result so that we can return to it when we discuss placebo effects: Do we believe that virtually all depression seen in general medical practice would respond to dummy pills?)

The better-than-well question is, When depressed people improve on an SSRI, do they experience personality change as well? On medication, the Swedish patients became less anxious and less aggressive. They scored higher on measures of socialization and social desirability. The study tracked many traits—detachment, suspicion, obsessiveness, and others. The authors observed, "After treatment, significant changes in the direction of normalisation were seen in all scales." Personality shifts occurred even in the few patients who did not get less depressed. Statistically the gains in sociability had almost no correlation with change in mood.

These results—reliable relief from depression and, independently, normalization of maladaptive personality traits—go a long way toward explaining the enthusiasm for these medications.

Others replicated the Ekselius experiment. UCLA researchers found decreased "harm avoidance" (that is, increased boldness) in patients with obsessive-compulsive disorder who improved on Paxil. Evidently, you did not need to start out depressed to experience personality effects from medication. Controlled trials told a similar story. In 2000, a team at Beth Israel Hospital in New York studied more than four hundred patients with dysthymia—chronic low-level depression. Those who recovered on Zoloft showed the greatest lessening of harm avoidance, with patients on imipramine and placebo trailing.

What causes what? Do people naturally become less timid and more sociable as they emerge from depression? A Finnish study suggested as much, but it was not a controlled trial, and its design might have led it to miss medication effects. Conversely, do antidepressants bring about personality change that facilitates recovery from mood disorder? Considering this question, researchers have focused on a trait called neuroticism. The coinage, from Hans Eysenck, encapsulates negative thinking, uncomfortable self-consciousness, and emotional vulnerability and instability. A 2008 Canadian study found that SSRIs work via their ability to mute neuroticism. When it drops, then depressive symptoms do, too.

Fortunately, the field has a painstaking randomized trial on this topic. It comes from a prolific group at the University of Pennsylvania and Vanderbilt University, largely psychologists interested in psychotherapy. In 2009, the Penn-Vanderbilt team reported on 240 depressed patients treated with Paxil, cognitive therapy, or a placebo pill.

For depression, both psychotherapy and Paxil outperformed placebo. But with medication especially, the greater change was in muting neuroticism. On Paxil, "patients reported changes in neuroticism and extraversion that were 4 to 8 times as large as the changes reported by placebo patients." On medication, patients gained confidence, social ease, and emotional stability.

Placebo did not diminish neuroticism. Paxil did, and the effect was consequential. After an initial four-month trial, the team followed the patients for another year. Patients whose neuroticism scores had dropped suffered fewer depressive episodes. Even patients who stopped treatment retained protection—so long as they had first improved on Paxil. Patients whose neuroticism fell during cognitive therapy remained liable to recurrent depression. In the researchers' words, "Perhaps the most surprising pattern we observed was the relation between neuroticism reduction during acute SSRI treatment and subsequent resistance to relapse."

What Paxil did *best* was to make people less fragile, the effect that my patients had discussed with me. This change proved more stabilizing than anything that psychotherapy or placebo use did.

Paxil, the Penn-Vanderbilt team wrote, "appears to have a specific pharmacological effect on personality that is distinct from its effect on depression." The results, they said, "support the notion that SSRIs' effects on personality go beyond and perhaps contribute to their anti-depressant effects."

The studies on SSRIs suggest that my main error was in caution—in my having written that "on occasion" medication caused personality change. On antidepressants, patients feel and become more emotion-ally secure much of the time. In the Penn-Vanderbilt study, when Paxil (contrasted to placebo) was considered a treatment for neuroti-cism, the effect size was 0.6, in the high-medium range. Today, SSRIs' better-than-well effect is less controversial—less contradicted in the literature—than the notion that SSRIs constitute a reliable treatment for depression. That is also to say that the antidepressant debate is possible only because conventional rating scales miss the drugs' influ-ence on quality of life and traits such as neuroticism.

Because of these findings and, more, because of doctors' own observations in the course of patient care, medical practice has changed. Twenty years ago, if an episode of depression ended, everyone was satis-fied. But having seen the shift in temperament that can accompany antidepressant use, doctors began to worry over patients who, although technically free of depression, remained diffident, socially withdrawn, emotionally brittle, and insecure. Whether to prescribe in these cases is a difficult question.

In *Listening to Prozac*, I warned about "diagnostic bracket creep," the tendency of disease categories to expand to embrace what medication does. The Penn-Vanderbilt findings blur that issue. Perhaps attention to personality traits constitutes basic care—prevention of recurrence—and without any change in our definition of illness. For depressive patients, neurotic traits no longer seem benign. In the minds of some doctors, the state I called better than well is a facet of ordinary health.

Often, in discussions of the antidepressant controversy, I am chal-lenged about the *better than well* coinage: *How's that working for ya?* The idea is that when there is doubt about medications' ability to perform their main job, treating depression, it is ludicrous to think that they might do more. But the issues, interrupting depressive epi-sodes and reshaping personality, are distinct. While the clamor against antidepressants has been in crescendo, the better-than-well hypothesis has received increasing confirmation and proved increasingly relevant to clinical care.

If this attention to my thought has been gratifying (it has), it also represents a common sequence in medical practice. Work with patients inspires certain ideas, a doctor floats them, colleagues confirm the observations, patient care shifts, and along the way research offers further support. Today, we are so focused on error that we may imagine that folly is the rule in medical practice. My impression is different. Clinical wisdom tends to pan out, if in general terms. Often, systematic trials suggest refinements, experience adds further pointers, and so on. The back-and-forth takes place in the context of current scientific knowledge—the context of biological plausibility. This process, progress through a virtuous dialectic between less and more formal observation, is the norm. Grand revelations of error, although important when they occur, are the exception.

19

Interlude
Old Dream

WITH *LISTENING TO PROZAC* on the bestseller lists, I received inquiries from men and women who believed that they resembled characters in the book's vignettes. I referred most callers to psychiatrists in their hometown, but some of these readers found their way into my practice.

Moira was one. I tell her story to illustrate a transition that Prozac brought about.

Moira was a special-needs counselor at a liberal arts college. Although skilled, she was not well regarded at her job. She was too deliberative, too tentative, not upbeat enough with students. She had chosen her career for altruistic reasons—her brothers were learning disabled, and she had seen how much support they needed—but now she considered her work pointless. Often, she phoned in sick.

I suspected that Moira had dysthymia, chronic low-level depression. She saw herself as having a negative personality. Cynical and gloomy, she discounted much and expected little. The case histories in my book had made her wonder whether there was another way to be.

Moira's passivity and pessimism had worn her husband down. The marriage turned rocky, and Moira had nowhere to turn. She had long preferred isolation to socializing.

Moira had undergone psychotherapy in the past and did not want more. She lived north of Boston, so frequent visits to Providence would be inconvenient. Besides, Moira said, her problems were biological. All her family members had the same affliction. On her father's side, she said, they were black Irish—which surprised me. Moira was a strawberry blonde with pale skin and freckles. She corrected herself: black-mood Irish. The men drank and got surly. The women were like her, sour and solitary.

Moira wanted me to prescribe for her. I can't say why I considered the request. Only rarely do I monitor medication without doing psychotherapy. The exceptions are patients treated by a handful of Providence-based psychologists and social workers whom I have known for years and whose work I trust. Partly it was that Moira did remind me of past patients who had done well on SSRIs. Partly it was that she struck me as especially self-aware.

Perhaps I was influenced by an image from an old sociology text about a rural Irish community. A normally sociable woman spends the winter sitting listlessly in front of the turf fire, emerging haggard in springtime. In the village, the behavior—the level of depression—is considered unremarkable.

I compromised: a few sessions, and then Moira would need to find a doctor closer to home.

On an antidepressant, Moira had more zest and energy. She thought clearly. Some of what had held her back had, indeed, been chronic low-level depression.

The drug response was partial. Any month would include bad days. Still, most things came more easily.

We discussed whether to pursue the remaining symptoms. Moira said that she was getting what she had expected from medication. She saw more possibility. She was decisive.

Moira made use of the good intervals, mending fences at work and at home. I did not know how to assess the degree of benefit, but Moira's husband was pleased. Members of the extended family noticed the change. Moira was frank about its basis. She had gotten help. Others should, too.

Moira never did switch to another doctor. She saw me four or six times a year. Every meeting, she would report on a relation—a sister, later an aunt, then cousins—who had modified some depressive condition with medication. The accounts were detailed, full of implications for children, marriages, and careers.

Drugs failed often enough. Some relatives expressed contempt toward others who resorted to antidepressants. Mostly though, the family was pulling itself out of a long slump. Moira saw me for years, and for the whole of that time she brought news of progress in the lives of a network of relatives.

Moira changed jobs, leaving academia for banking and human resources work, a transition she was able to make, she said, because she could bear stress and, more, foresee continuity in her efforts, a precondition for ambition. She entered an executive-training track and received mentorship from senior staff. The outcome was welcome, my sentimental preference for higher education over the financial sector notwithstanding.

Perhaps what was at issue in Moira's family was *folie à plusieurs* or, more properly, its reverse, health by contagion. There are examples: various crazes for hypnosis. But the reason that, in contrast to mass hysteria, health contagion is not a commonplace is that while symptoms are easy to catch, resilience is not. My impression was that I was hearing about a sea change in response to a new technology.

In a medication-naïve group, as Moira's family seems to have been, antidepressants' broad-spectrum reach can prove transformative. For years, day after day for most days, people are debilitated by corrosive melancholy—and then, not. I have said that muting emotional vulnerability may be what antidepressants do best. I should have offered a longer list: lessening neuroticism, keeping patients stable once they recover, and mitigating chronic mild depression. Those capacities are among the drugs' strongest.

We worry about misuse of antidepressants, and with equal justice we express frustration about the drugs' limitations. But before Prozac, even groups with health insurance and access to doctors might harbor a large reservoir of untreated depression. The personality of the new medications—ease in prescribing, relative safety in overdose, social acceptability, and favorable impact on social functioning—allowed for the spread of mental health care at a level with little precedent.

In my own work in the 1990s, I was impressed with the SSRIs' adjunctive role in psychotherapy. The antidepressants might allow a patient to see the world as less hostile. I could then encourage him to undertake new efforts, in therapy and in his daily life—to elaborate the early medication-based change, in expectation that we might soon cut back on the pharmacotherapy.

Outside my practice, many patients wanted only to be prescribed for. Even for them, something like psychotherapy might occur. If you want to withdraw from destructive relationships, it helps to be able to tolerate separation and loss. Similarly in the workplace: emotional security sets the context for negotiation and perhaps also for insight—for owning up to your tendency to, say, rub people the wrong way.

On medication, even when symptoms lingered, patients might, in time, show themselves better able to manage practical challenges. Standard outcome measures might miss this benefit. Practicing doctors saw it continually. Not ideally, not without gaps and risks, but on a scale that had never occurred before, Prozac became a partial fulfillment of an old dream, psychotherapy for the masses.

20

Spotting Trout

WE COME NOW to the opening salvo of the current antidepressant controversy. In June of 1998, Irving Kirsch, a psychologist then at the University of Connecticut, and his former graduate student Guy Sapirstein published a paper that seemed quixotic. It was meant to cast doubt on the usefulness of all antidepressants, including tricyclics. Because of the paper's title, "Listening to Prozac but Hearing Placebo: A Meta-analysis of Antidepressant Medication," word of its publication reached me immediately.

I admired the essay for its chutzpah. To my reading, "Hearing Placebo" was to the 1990s what Doris Mayer's "'Anti-Depressed' Personality" had been to the 1970s, a cri de coeur against the encroachment of medication into the domain of psychotherapy. The lead author, Kirsch, a pioneering theorist in the science of placebo effects, seemed to be out to twit authority. His paper was larded with calculations bound to leave pharmacologists sputtering.

"Hearing Placebo" was presented as unconventional. It appeared in an online journal before those were mainstream, and the editors preceded the text with an introduction that cited the study's "clearly arguable statistical methods." Their preface began:

The article that follows is a controversial one. It reaches a controversial conclusion—that much of the therapeutic benefit of antidepressant medications actually derives from placebo responding. The article reaches this conclusion by utilizing a controversial statistical approach—meta-analysis. And it employs meta-analysis controversially—by meta-analyzing studies that are very heterogeneous in subject selection criteria, treatments employed, and statistical methods used.

As remedy for the research's shortcomings, the editors took another extraordinary step. Simultaneously, they published expert commentary, including dismissive responses.

Two critics, Donald Klein, the Columbia University researcher, and the late Robyn Dawes, a psychologist expert in statistics, offered thorough refutations. But the essay would not go away.

As its subtitle indicates, the paper is built around a meta-analysis. Searching the literature for randomized trials of medication treatment for depression, Kirsch had identified nineteen whose data he considered adequate. The trials involved sixteen drugs, not all of them antidepressants.

Kirsch found effect sizes on the order of 0.4, with SSRIs coming in a bit higher—scores that Kirsch conceded were "remarkably similar" to the 0.5 effect size appearing in other overviews. Klein's essay argued that Kirsch's statistical approach was disadvantaging to medication—and any correction would have pushed the results far into the acceptable range. Nothing in the numbers was shocking.

Klein also found Kirsch's choice of material for the meta-analysis prejudicial. Certainly, it was selective. A recent Cochrane report on Elavil located thirty-seven studies published before 1998 that had efficacy data suitable for analysis. Looking at not one drug but sixteen, Kirsch found only nineteen trials with data he could work with.

Kirsch's process seemed to cull studies in which antidepressants underperformed. In a set of Wellbutrin trials, he embraced one with weak results and dismissed similarly designed studies, reported in the same paper, that showed higher drug efficacy. Kirsch included the NIMH collaborative trial (the TDCRP), which we know was not designed to show imipramine to best advantage; incorporating that study,

Kirsch used average Hamilton scores and completer analyses. He was not telling a tale in which medication would play the hero's role.

When a critic assembles an unfavorable collection of trials and finds that SSRIs have medium effect sizes, shouldn't the psychopharmacology community celebrate?

But Kirsch suggested other ways to view the results. He said that three-fourths of what antidepressants did could be accomplished by dummy pills. Then he questioned that last bit of change, the 25 percent. His idea was that standard placebo pills did not generate *enough* hopeful expectancy since, unlike antidepressants, they did not cause side effects. We are back to the "active placebo" argument, the one that Cole and Klerman had left hanging.

Kirsch believed that his meta-analysis contained pertinent evidence. We will recall that he had analyzed sixteen drugs used in depression-outcome research. Four of those were not classed as antidepressants, and they performed as well as the twelve that were.

Simplified, Kirsch's argument ran: Since the "non-antidepressant drugs" ought not to work, we can think of them as active placebos, dummy pills with side effects that signal to patients, "You're on medication." But in the trials analyzed, the non-antidepressant drugs worked as well as antidepressants. If ineffective pills with side effects work as well as the "real" drugs, perhaps *all* the apparent efficacy of antidepressants, including the tenacious final quarter, arises from imagining.

I have said that in reading a meta-analysis, often it is only when we look at the studies it gathers, the individual research papers, that we understand what is at issue. Let's examine the reports on what Kirsch called "non-antidepressant drugs."

The four were a thyroid hormone (liothyronine); a Xanax-like medicine (adinazolam); a barbiturate (amylobarbitone); and lithium. Kirsch considered these medicines active placebos—drugs with no inherent efficacy for depression, ones that treated mood disorders only through causing stray bodily effects and so arousing intense expectations of cure.

The most outrageous element in the mix was the study of thyroid hormone and lithium. Russell Joffe, a Toronto-based researcher, had been interested in what to do next when antidepressants fail. In practice, often psychiatrists would continue the treatment but add a small daily supplement of lithium or thyroid hormone, not because low-dose lithium or thyroid is effective on its own, but because either can help the antidepressant to work. This approach is called *augmentation*.

To test augmentation, Joffe began with fifty patients who had been prescribed full doses of a tricyclic—imipramine or a related drug, desipramine—and had not responded. For some (in a two-week trial, conducted in the early 1990s) he merely continued the antidepressant along with a second tablet, a dummy pill. The rest also stayed on the antidepressant but with low-dose lithium or thyroid added as an augmenter.

Only a few patients in the antidepressant-continuation (imipramine-plus-placebo) arm improved.

The antidepressant-plus-lithium group and the antidepressant-plus-thyroid group did better, with triple the response rate.

Augmentation looked like a promising strategy.

Good news, then: Many patients improve on antidepressants. Of those who don't, most will respond when the antidepressant is supplemented by a modest dose of thyroid or lithium. So, yes, low-dose thyroid and lithium combat depression *if you give them along with a full dose of an antidepressant.*

And thyroid and lithium are psychoactive substances. Joffe's study hardly showed that just anything works for depression. Instead, it confirmed what practicing psychiatrists believed, that certain substances with marked influences in the brain can help catalyze the action of antidepressants.

Imagine that you're testing a new formulation of gasoline. It does well in some cars but poorly in others. Thinking that the balky cars may have water in the gas line, you pour in an additive—a "water remover"—and now the engines run fine. A friend says to you, Looks like that additive is a terrific fuel! No. Gasoline is a terrific fuel. Sometimes it needs an augmenter.

Kirsch's inclusion of the Joffe study brought out a glimmer of humor in Donald Klein. In his refutation, "Listening to Meta-analysis but Hearing Bias," Klein said that coming across the Joffe data in the Kirsch essay was "like finding a trout in the milk."

The reference is to a diary entry by Henry David Thoreau in 1850.

During a dairy strike the prior year, deliverymen had been accused of diluting milk with stream water. Countering the notion that circumstantial evidence cannot be conclusive, Thoreau wrote, "Some circumstantial evidence is very strong, as when you find a trout in the milk." "Hearing Placebo," Klein was implying, contained internal evidence that Kirsch had not set out to conduct a dispassionate inquiry into the virtues of antidepressants.

The two other "non-antidepressant drugs" hardly qualify as active placebos either. Xanax had been commercially successful as an anti-anxiety drug. During its development, some scientists had hoped that because of its structure, it might show antidepressant effects as well. The pharmaceutical house Upjohn set out to develop a Xanax variant—adinazolam—that would have stronger antidepressant properties, through acting on brain pathways that involve serotonin.

In trials, adinazolam did sometimes relieve depression in the early going, but its antidepressant powers were unimpressive, and it showed hints of a problem called rebound—a sharp uptick in symptoms after initial improvement—so it never came to market. Still, the drug had been designed to treat depression through conventional means. By citing a trial where, for some weeks, adinazolam succeeded, Kirsch was hardly demonstrating that any random pill could duplicate the effects of antidepressants.

Kirsch's "non-antidepressant drug" category had one final candidate, amylobarbitone, a barbiturate. Medications of this class—Seconal was a leading brand name—were used to treat anxiety and insomnia.

The study caught in Kirsch's sieve was designed to address a practical problem. Wary of drug side effects, primary-care doctors tended not to prescribe the older antidepressants at full doses. Might low doses work? Since generalists were comfortable prescribing barbiturates, might they be substituted? In the trial, patients were given any of four pills: placebo, the barbiturate, 75 milligrams of Elavil (a low dose), or 150 milligrams of Elavil (a standard dose, also on the low side).

By the study's end, four weeks out, the more realistic dose of Elavil had significantly outperformed placebo on three scales, including the Hamilton. The barbiturate and the lower dose of Elavil were indistinguishable from placebo. On two scales, the full dose of Elavil outperformed the barbiturate.

Not much to go on. The authors' main conclusion, as regards efficacy, was "After 28 days, [Elavil] 150 mg/day was significantly better than the other treatments." The authors suggested that any barbiturate benefit may have been due to scale items rating sedation. If primary-care doctors wanted to treat depression, they would need to leave their comfort zone and prescribe a full dose of antidepressant.

In his analysis, Kirsch merged the results from the two doses of Elavil, a choice that made the antidepressant look less distinctive. But to be clear, the study authors found that barbiturate did not treat depression as well as an adequate, if modest, dose of Elavil.

After scouring the literature, Kirsch had managed to present—this was my impression—not a single example of what he had expected to find, a medication that ought not to have possessed antidepressant effects but that (through the impact of pill taking enhanced by drug side effects) alleviated depression anyway. This part of Kirsch's paper stood as testimony against the active-placebo hypothesis.

I don't mean to claim that antidepressants are the only medicines that can help depressed people. As Jonathan Cole taught, often patients will flourish on the "wrong drug." I do mean that, in my view, Kirsch had failed to demonstrate that the final chunk of benefit, the advantage of antidepressants over placebo, was due to anything other than the drugs' action on relevant pathways in the brain, their "pharmacologic potency."

Even after Donald Klein pointed out problems along these lines, Kirsch continued to claim that his 1998 paper demonstrated that non-antidepressant drugs work as well as antidepressants. In 2000, he wrote, "Some active drugs that are not considered antidepressants (amylobarbitone, lithium, liothyronine, and adinazolam) show the same effect on depression as that shown by antidepressants." He made similar claims in papers published in 2005 and 2009, still referencing "Hearing Placebo."

In 2012, when interviewed by Lesley Stahl for *60 Minutes*, Kirsch said, "We even looked at drugs that are not considered antidepressants: tranquilizers, barbiturates. And do you know what? They had the same effect as the antidepressants." Was he still referring to adinazolam and amylobarbitone, based on the same two trials?

"Hearing Placebo" had been intended as a debunking report, and yet it had found adequate effect sizes and (despite assiduous efforts) no grounds for diminishing them. I imagined that the paper would carry little weight in evidence-based medicine. I was wrong, and wrong more generally about the historical role that "Hearing Placebo" would play. I had seen it as a rearguard action. It was in the vanguard, the start of a resurgence of doubt about antidepressants.

21

Hypothetical Counterfactual

WITH HIS TROUT-IN-THE-MILK remark, Donald Klein questioned the evenhandedness of Irving Kirsch's analysis. Robyn Dawes raised a more fundamental concern. He objected to Kirsch's account of what placebo is and does.

In essence, Dawes's complaint was that Kirsch saw placebo as something solid—a treatment. When doctors prescribe an antidepressant, it helps people directly, through its pharmacologic potency. Kirsch thought of placebo the same way: when researchers offer a dummy pill, patients improve because of it.

The back-and-forth between Kirsch and Dawes centered on technical questions about effect sizes. That discussion is beyond our pay grade, but we can approach it by addressing a topic we need to think about anyway: What else, beyond the inherent efficacy of medication, helps people improve (or seem to) in drug trials?

Kirsch considered the placebo arm to encompass two healing elements, the passage of time, which he called "natural history," and a more powerful factor, the core placebo effect. Although Kirsch did not define this core, the implication was that it had largely to do with placebo as we ordinarily imagine it, a pill that induces hopeful expectancy.

To Dawes, in contrast, the placebo arm had a single function: to capture the "hypothetical counterfactual," what would have happened to patients in a trial's active treatment arm had they not gotten the effective ingredient in the pill. In this view, controlled trials can tell us only about the treatment under test—here, antidepressants. The studies tell us nothing about the comparison intervention, placebos. (The parallel is not exact, but, when you time yourself as you jog, the result tells you nothing about the watch.) Placebo tracks what happens without antidepressants, progress that will differ from trial to trial.

Dawes did not break them out, but all sorts of influences play a role. Springtime arrives and daylight hours increase. The economy turns a corner. To the extent that depression is responsive to these external factors, a study conducted in favorable conditions will show better-than-usual outcomes in the placebo arm. Because of circumstance, the influence of "natural history"—time—will vary from study to study.

The design and implementation of the research will matter, too. Think of a trial where patients visit the test site frequently and meet at length with supportive, directive clinicians. We will expect enhanced placebo responses, due to the more intensive "minimal supportive psychotherapy."

Other factors come into play. Patients may distort their symptom reports in hopes of pleasing the caregiver. The term of art for this tendency is *demand characteristics*. Often, patients provide what they think doctors demand. The propensity for looking sick early in a medical encounter, in hopes of engaging the caregiver, is the *hello effect*. Toward the end of treatment, courteous participants may tell a rater that they are better when they are not—the *goodbye effect*. The personalities of staff and patients (and, again, the intensity of contact) will determine the strength of demand characteristics.

We have already encountered baseline score inflation. It is not only would-be participants who exaggerate. Raters under time pressure to recruit participants may puff up patients' symptom counts at the start of a trial so that they appear to satisfy the minimum requirements for entry. Subsequently, scores will fall, whether or not the patients get better.

By this account, what Kirsch calls the placebo effect (all influences other than natural history) contains diverse elements, such as demand characteristics and baseline score inflation. And then, yes, there is the classic placebo response, hopeful expectancy. To the extent that it alters the course of depressive episodes, it, too, will differ from study to study, depending on the shape and color of the pill and the stiffness of the starch in doctors' white coats.

To express the jumble of influences in the control arm, Gerald Klerman wrote of a "package of placebo effects." I will go further and call the package a *grab bag*. In different trials, the contents of the sack—their amounts and proportions—will differ.

Because the control arm packages distractions that we want to see beyond, because it absorbs happenstance influences, placebo administration will produce levels of improvement that vary from trial to trial. If not, we would have no need to run placebo arms. We could compare medication results to a universal number, the placebo effect. Dawes argued that Kirsch was making more or less that mistake, assuming that placebo, like imipramine, had a discoverable "efficacy."

Dawes thought that it rarely made sense to refer to a proportion of treatment effect as being accounted for by "placebo." In early drug trials, when untreated patients were plentiful and the NIMH had yet to demand that study participants be offered encouragement, placebo arm results ran low—showing, say, half of the change seen in imipramine arms. Later, with score inflation and supportive psychotherapy, the proportion rose to three-quarters. But imipramine was still the same chemical, with the same inherent efficacy.

When Kirsch compared drugs to placebo, often he expressed outcomes as percentages: "75% of the response to the medications examined in these studies was a placebo response, and at most, 25% might be a true drug effect." Marcia Angell would echo this claim, writing that Kirsch's early research had demonstrated that "as judged by scales used to measure depression, placebos were 75 percent as effective as antidepressants."

But this formulation may tempt us into all sorts of error. For instance, we might be tempted to say that dummy pills *do* a great deal— that they *do* three-fourths of what antidepressants do. But when it comes to increased sunshine, rising salaries, demand characteristics, and score inflation, the placebo pill contributes nothing. The influence of classic placebo effects—hopeful expectancy—may be minimal.

In contrast, Gene Glass's measure, the effect size, gets these matters right, using placebo only for purposes of comparison. When, as in
the trials Kirsch assembled, we discover an effect size of 0.4 or 0.5, we
know that antidepressants will move a typical patient to the lesser level
of depression of someone at the 65 to 70 percent mark in the control
group—never mind whether days are long or short and skies blue or
gray.

We may recall that in calculating effect sizes, a key step is the one
we encountered when we first discussed randomized trials, subtracting
the progress patients make in the control arm from the greater progress their counterparts make in the treatment arm. That operation—
subtraction—treats placebo not as a valued remedy but as a collection
of nuisance variables to be tossed out.

The important point is conceptual: The placebo is a pale doppel-
gänger, taking the form of the active intervention but lacking the en-
livening element. Its insubstantiality—its ability to shape-shift and
capture circumstance—is the placebo's glory. But we must not become
too enamored of placebo. It is there to be thrown away.

22

Two Plus Two

TO SEE CLEARLY, to determine how well antidepressants work, we want to subtract placebo outcomes from treatment outcomes. But what if we can't do that either? Surprisingly, Robyn Dawes and Irving Kirsch were in agreement on this point: Subtraction can give a wrong result, causing us to underestimate how much antidepressants offer. The drugs may be doing more than our indicators, such as effect size, suggest.

Here we come to a detail in statistics that is unfamiliar even to most doctors. For subtraction to give an accurate account of how well a treatment works, the research results need to have a property called *additivity*. Additivity is so automatic an assumption that it emerges—becomes easy to grasp conceptually—only when it fails. The standard way to illustrate additivity problems is through thinking about experiments with alcohol. Vodka is the active medication. Tonic water is the placebo.

Say that we want to measure vodka's ability to impair dexterity. The problem is, we don't have vodka, only premixed vodka tonics. We also have tonic water. We will give participants tonic water without alcohol and measure their motor performance. Then, we will serve vodka tonics and remeasure. When we subtract the deterioration on tonic from the deterioration on vodka tonic, the difference will represent the inherent capacity of vodka to cause impairment.

We begin our test by warning participants that they may become drunk. Then we administer our placebo, tonic water.

Tonic is useful because quinine, the soda's bitter ingredient, masks the taste of alcohol. Our introductory remarks suggest to participants that they may be getting tonic laced with vodka. The tonic induces expectancy—of intoxication. Despite the absence of alcohol, our research subjects feel and act tipsy, and their performance—quickly placing pegs in holes—is three points below normal on a scale that measures dexterity.

For the second arm of our experiment, we again imply that we may be supplying a strong cocktail, and we do serve a heavy vodka tonic. Our participants' dexterity falls four points.

Okay: Alcohol plus expectancy produces four points of harm. Expectancy alone causes three points.

We take the result from the vodka-plus-expectancy arm and subtract the result from the expectancy-alone arm. Seeing the remainder, one point, we will conclude that alcohol has little inherent efficacy—little ability to impair motor skills.

Although the arithmetic is right, we will suspect that we have failed to capture vodka's potential. We seem to have subtracted too much.

Luckily, in our imagined experimenting, we are missing something else besides straight vodka: We have no medical ethicists. We are free to engage in deception.

Now, we tell people that they are in a tonic-water taste test. In one arm of our trial, we do give tonic. We ask our participants to complete a survey displayed on a computer screen and sneakily measure their motor performance. People remain dexterous—unimpaired.

In our second arm, we serve heavy vodka tonics, as strong as those we poured in our first experiment. We discover that alcohol alone is highly impairing. Even with no expectancy—no belief that they are drinking alcohol—our research subjects fumble, because they are drunk. The scores fall not one point but almost the full four.

So, vodka plus heightened expectancy causes four points of impairment. Vodka alone causes almost four points of impairment.

Our first conclusion, that drinking vodka is harmless, was wrong. We had subtracted too much.

The problem is with additivity. The two causes of impairment, tonic-driven expectancy and alcohol's direct brain effects, are not additive. Expectancy caused three points of change, and vodka alone caused (almost) four, but vodka-plus-expectancy did not cause seven. It caused four—and almost all of the clumsiness could be duplicated by vodka-drinking alone. We can't subtract three points of expectancy effect from the four points of vodka-plus-expectancy because, whatever it might do on its own, the expectancy added little impairing power to the combination.

In the first experiment, tonic worked via expectancy. In both experiments, vodka worked via direct brain effects. Where interventions operate through different means—and especially where one intervention is powerful on its own—additivity may not apply.

Give enough vodka, and we can cause any degree of impairment, right up through blackouts. With high doses of alcohol, any subtraction will give a misimpression of liquor's potential for harm.

Percentages are equally misleading. Considering an experiment parallel to the one I have suggested, Dawes wrote, "At the extreme, the claim that as someone passes out, a certain proportion of his or her problem is due to placebo effects would be met with ridicule. And it should be." Of our first experiment, it remains true that you could get three-quarters of the alcohol effect through tonic-and-suggestion-induced expectancy. What is not true is that three-fourths of a vodka tonic's effect is *due* to the tonic (or expectancy). Alcohol is preemptive. On its own, it does the work of expectancy and more.

Turning to depression treatment, say that for a given depressive syndrome, psychotherapy reduces Hamilton scores by five points. For the same condition, an antidepressant also gives five points of benefit. What do we imagine the combination, drug plus talk therapy, will do?

It would be unusual—unheard of—for the treatments to be fully additive. We will not see ten points of benefit.

When Gerry Klerman first tested interpersonal psychotherapy, he found that giving it along with Elavil did not confer protection more substantial than that observed with Elavil alone. Recently, an all-star team—it included researchers from the Penn-Vanderbilt group that had studied Paxil and neuroticism—looked at psychotherapy and vigorous prescribing as remedies for hard-to-treat depression. The result was similar. Although each intervention is known to be effective individually, for most patients the combination conferred little benefit beyond what they gained from medication alone. For some subgroups, medication on its own was more helpful than medication and cognitive therapy.

We can find examples to the contrary. But the common outcome in psychiatric research is, two and two do not equal four.

Like alcohol and tonic water, antidepressants and the placebo grab bag appear to act through different mechanisms. Studies of electrical activity in the brain suggest as much. According to outcome research from UCLA, in the prefrontal cortex, a brain region thought to be important in depression, patients who eventually respond to antidepressants show decreased activity in the early going. Eventual responders to the control condition—dummy pills plus low-level counseling—show increased activity. (Patients who experience no early brain-wave change tend to remain depressed.)

If these measurements are relevant—if they reflect the course of recovery from depression—then it's not that placebo-plus-counseling moves the brain a certain distance and then the medication induces further progress. Both interventions cause change, but in opposite directions. The characteristic placebo-arm action (increased energy use in the prefrontal cortex) never appears in medicated patients and cannot account for the favorable response that they enjoy. When medicine works, it does so in its own way, via its inherent efficacy.

Similarly, contrasting patterns of brain activity have been found to predict responsiveness to antidepressants and psychotherapy.

Perhaps, as various experts have suggested, depression is a "stuck switch" problem. Strong direct intervention—counseling or medication—perturbs parts of the brain, freeing them to respond to circumstance. But the forms—the direction—of perturbation may differ.

Our understanding of local brain activity and what it means in depression is limited. Finally, no one knows what the contrasting response patterns mean. But in a suggestive way, the brain studies support the conclusion that medication-and-psychotherapy trials introduced: Placebo and antidepressant effects are unlikely to be additive. Much of what medication accomplishes, it achieves on its own.

In an outcome study, effectively we are testing a highly heterogeneous mixture, antidepressant-plus-grab-bag, to obtain a measure of
change. The placebo arm, too, gives us a measure of change, some due
to psychotherapy effects and some to expectancy, good weather, and
patients' farewell gifts.

How much shall we subtract?

Not the whole. The boost from minimal supportive psychotherapy?
The medication covered much of that territory on its own.

In antidepressant trials, almost certainly, full additivity does not
apply—and yet our calculations, including ones for effect sizes, assume
it. Virtually every formal estimate of antidepressant efficacy arises from
a premise, the right to subtract, that is unproven and likely wrong. Our
estimates of drug efficacy run too low.

In much of medicine, additivity is not at issue. The control
condition—bed rest, in the streptomycin trial—merely tracks the fluc-
tuation of illness with time. Because mood disorders respond to both
psychological and chemical influences, the testing of antidepressants
is different. To his credit, Kirsch said as much. The conclusion in
"Hearing Placebo"—that antidepressants have low efficacy—was, he
wrote, "based on the assumption that drug and placebo effects are additive. The additive assumption is that the effect of the drug is limited
to the difference between the drug response and the placebo response.
Alternatively, these effects might not be additive. It is possible that the
drug would produce the same effect, even if there were no placebo effect." Kirsch was open to the possibility that antidepressants are like
vodka in our vodka-tonic example. Drug-based change might preempt
placebo effects, and not just those arising from emotional support.
Even expectancy effects—classic placebo effects—might not be additive; medicine might work even if you did not know you were on it.

Elsewhere, Kirsch wrote:

> It is also possible that antidepressant drug and placebo effects are not
> additive and that the true drug effect is greater than the drug/placebo
> difference . . . Alcohol and stimulant drugs, for example, produce at
> least some drug and placebo effects that are not additive . . .
>
> If antidepressant drug effects and antidepressant placebo effects
> are not additive, the ameliorating effects of antidepressants might be

obtained even if patients did not know the drug was being administered. If that is the case, then antidepressant drugs have substantial pharmacologic effects that are duplicated or masked by placebo.

Here again, Kirsch is saying that even if dummy pills elicit classic placebo effects, subtracting the resulting change from change that drugs produce may lead to error.

Kirsch presented reasons to believe that additivity might apply after all, but they were, to my reading, unconvincing or undercut by results in his own later research. And Kirsch had always seemed open to the other possibility—non-additivity. "Hearing Placebo" contained a challenge to the psychopharmacology community: Either its drugs did not work or, if additivity did not apply, its methods gave imprecise results.

Because standard psychiatric drug trials have psychotherapeutic components and because antidepressants sometimes preempt the effects of psychotherapy, we cannot count on additivity. This uncertainty presents a challenge for evidence-based psychiatry: Our controlled trials, conventionally analyzed, may not reflect reality. Despite our use of randomization, they are likely subject to a consistent confound, arising from a technical bias against antidepressants. We know that antidepressants work. We cannot say how well.

23

In Plain Sight

WHEN PEOPLE HEAR the word *depression,* they tend to think of two different conditions. The first is acute and intense, a variant of Irma's profound and paralyzing melancholy. The second is milder but persistent, a bleak state composed of sadness, lethargy, apathy, emotional vulnerability, and a poor sense of self. In my medical-school years, this lesser disorder was understood as a form of neurosis; for most of my time in practice, it has gone by the name *dysthymia.*

The current American diagnostic manual has eliminated dysthymia as an independent entity, integrating it into a group of chronic depressions. But the World Health Organization still recognizes dysthymia as a diagnosis, and the major research on low-level depression—thirty years' worth—concerns dysthymia. I will stick with the term here.

Dysthymia entails sadness or emotional depletion, with a scattering of other symptoms, on most days, for years. Dysthymia is grave enough. Sitting with a dysthymic person, you feel yourself very much in the territory of depression.

Dysthymic patients are walled off from pleasure and vulnerable to disappointment. They feel defeated by minor humiliation. Dysthymia may wax and wane, but its worst phases are never far from consciousness. For many, the symptoms seem to extend to the core of personality. Dysthymia is debilitating. Studies show that in the long run, endless minor symptoms are as disabling as severe episodes spaced out in time.

Often, my dysthymic patients are plagued by writer's block or the equivalent condition for artists, mathematicians, scientists, planners, and homemakers. The patients complain of loneliness, although I might have difficulty understanding why. They can be insightful and incisive, empathetic and wise—regarding others, anyway.

In psychotherapy, dysthymic patients can be especially engaging. Because their struggles are chronic, they dig deep. Although, as we shall see, the objective evidence is thin, I have always considered psychotherapy to be especially helpful in dysthymia.

That said, the psychoanalytic literature makes note of a frequent problem: neurotic patients who gain insights may have trouble translating them into action, trouble with "working through." On this front, antidepressants can be especially useful—so I found increasingly as I began to prescribe. By the late 1990s, if a patient showed improved self-understanding but still could not set brush to canvas, and if depressive symptoms persisted, I might recommend a trial of medication. Often, an antidepressant supplied the final element—hope, drive, calm—that set recovery in motion.

For some patients, medication did the whole job: They gained energy and direction. They felt fine. For others, the initial uplift was subtle, a diminution in the fixed sense of inadequacy. Small changes allowed for big ones. To mount an exhibition, to risk moving toward marriage, to stay afloat and then succeed in the office workplace—these achievements create new and supportive contexts, ones that enhance mood and bring life meaning. I came to think of SSRIs as catalysts for working through.

In a general sense, research results confirmed these observations. In the early years of evidence-based medicine, in psychiatry, dysthymia research was at the forefront.

I have referred to evidence-based medicine without saying much about it. The movement announced its presence through a manifesto in the *Journal of the American Medical Association* in 1992. The goal of EBM, as doctors called it, was to get practitioners to rely less on clinical experience and more on findings from formal outcome trials.

Standard definitions of evidence-based practice are innocuous. One in wide use refers to "the integration of best research evidence with clinical expertise and patient values." The devil is in the application. Notwithstanding the lip service given expertise and values, from the start devotees emphasized randomized trial results to the exclusion of all else. Too often, EBM entailed an uncritical embrace of meta-analyses. The practical effect was to disqualify most evidence, from biological plausibility to less formal experiments to clinical experience and observation.

As a result, clinicians had mixed feelings—I did—about evidence-based medicine. To the extent that it implied the existence of an opposite—superstition-based medicine?—the term was insulting. The more compact expression for *evidence-based medicine* is *medicine.*

That said, evidence-based medicine has had its victories, instances in which the application of meta-analysis in underexplored areas proved illuminating. The first major EBM-based study in psychiatry—it appeared in 1999—was of this sort. It concerned persistent low-level depression. The authors—the lead was a psychiatrist-epidemiologist, Mauricio Silva de Lima—would go on to substantial research careers in evidence-based medicine. In this pioneering paper, reviewing controlled trials, they found that commonly used antidepressants work for dysthymia and more vaguely defined chronic minor depressive disorders.

De Lima introduced readers to a measure favored in evidence-based medicine, the number needed to treat. Effect size looks at average symptom change—how much help treatment gives a typical patient. In contrast, the number needed to treat counts people—how many enjoy a substantial benefit; that is, how many enter a category like remission or response. De Lima wrote, "The NNT [number needed to treat] is an estimate of the number of patients a clinician would have to treat in order to observe one outcome due to that treatment"—one response or remission more than the doctor would see with the placebo grab bag. As with golf scores, lower means better.

In the treatment of dysthymia with antidepressants, where the measure of success was cutting symptoms by half, de Lima found a number needed to treat of just below 4. The findings in actual studies are more favorable to medication than those in the following example, but a simple way to think about the dysthymia results is this:

If you treat a typical group of four patients, two will do well on medication—but one would also have done well on placebo. You need to treat four patients to get one additional favorable response.

Having encountered additivity, we may mistrust this operation, subtraction. It is true that number needed to treat can be tricky. When our two patients respond to medication, we cannot conclude that only one is being helped by the drug. It may be that in both cases the anti-depressant is supplying remoralization directly, biologically. It's just that one of the patients would have been equally buoyed by attention from doctors and the passage of time.

It may be best to think of number needed to treat as a means of comparison—a tool used so widely that it allows efficacy levels to be contrasted across disciplines. In that case, how good is a number needed to treat of 4?

Matching his results against those found in a standard textbook (*Evidence-Based Medicine: How to Practice and Teach EBM*, by David L. Sackett), de Lima concluded that a number needed to treat of 4 was favorable.

This conclusion is counterintuitive. How terrific can a one-in-four hit rate be? But the number needed to treat is always humbling. We're used to taking Excedrin and having our headache go away. Ideally, the number needed to treat is one, and before we give the matter thought, we may expect success to occur at that level.

The figures Sackett provided showed that doctors make a differ-ence with a small proportion of the patients with whom they intervene: Give 250 people a cholesterol-blocking drug for a year and you prevent one bad cardiac outcome, like a heart attack or sudden death. (Today, the number-needed-to-treat estimates for statins run between 25 and 100.) Roto-Rooter ten blocked carotids, the arteries that supply blood to the brain, and you prevent one bad outcome—stroke or death—in the subsequent two years.

In the textbook's reference chart, the only intervention with a low number needed to treat was medicating patients with very high blood pressure. If the risk was severe enough, you could see a number needed to treat of 3, where what you were forestalling was heart attack, stroke, or death. But treat patients with slightly lower and still abnormal blood pressures, and the figure leaped to 128, for five or six years of daily treatment.

Until the late 1990s, the number-needed-to-treat measure had largely been applied to preventive interventions. Since then, researchers have developed data on treatment of existing illness. Standard medications for heart failure, stroke, and chronic obstructive pulmonary disease have numbers needed to treat of 20 or higher. Only with antibiotics for specific indications, such as bladder infections, do you get numbers needed to treat as low as 3. Oh, and Excedrin in the treatment of headache? If your criterion is reduction of pain by half, the number needed to treat is north of 5. The decision, whether to recommend the treatment, is vastly more complex, but looking at response rates alone, SSRIs for dysthymia work as reliably as Excedrin for headache.

For medications expected to give near-term benefit, a number needed to treat in the mid-single digits signals high efficacy, and numbers needed to treat of up to 10 can identify useful drugs. For grave diseases with few alternative approaches—relentless cancers—doctors may resort to treatments that benefit only one in hundreds of patients.

Dysthymia's number needed to treat of 4 has an extra advantage. For blocked arteries, you give the full surgical treatment—widening the passage—without knowing who will be helped. Antidepressants are different: dysthymic patients whose symptoms don't budge can come off the medication and pursue a different remedy. If we think about our hypothetical four patients, in short order two of them, the nonresponders, may no longer be taking the antidepressant.

Effectiveness for dysthymia goes a long way toward explaining Prozac's rise to popularity. Imipramine might have done the job equally well, but was so hard to live with that it was reserved for highly symptomatic patients.

This property of SSRIs, their efficacy for dysthymia, is the great open secret of the antidepressant debate. I know that I've given Marcia Angell a hard time, but I take her opinion as a touchstone, an indicator of where sophisticated nonpsychiatrists stand. Evidently, the critiques that Angell reviewed did not mention research on dysthymia. Speaking to the *Boston Globe* columnist about my Sunday Review piece, she had complained, "In his article, Kramer says it's well established that antidepressants work for chronic and recurrent mild depression, but where is the evidence for that? That screams out for a reference. Should we believe it just because he says that?"

The paper I had discussed was easily accessed. I had cited the recovery rates, and they matched those in the first reference to pop up if you plug *dysthymia* and *meta-analysis* into Google. The study, from 2011, was an updating of de Lima's, and the new version found much the same level of benefit. And long before, in 2002, the Cochrane Collaboration had invited de Lima to contribute a version of his overview of the literature. He had worked with Joanna Moncrieff, of University College London, who would go on to write papers with Irving Kirsch and become an outspoken skeptic about the use of antidepressants in the treatment of depression. De Lima and Moncrieff's summary, posted on the Cochrane website, was straightforward: "Drugs are effective in the treatment of dysthymia." This indication for drug treatment was at once officially recognized and absent from public discussion.

The dysthymia research is not extensive. De Lima's 1999 study covered fewer than two thousand patients, and the 2011 follow-up, which excluded older studies, fewer than fifteen hundred. That said, the evidence is compelling. Drug companies have not sought FDA approval for antidepressants in the treatment of dysthymia, so the field has been spared the distortions that commercial trials entail. The research has been university-based, conducted by academics following their own standards. Often, the trials were conducted in clinics where patients received their usual care.

Gathering material for review, statisticians worry about "file-drawer bias"—the tendency for disappointing research to remain unpublished—and they have ways of analyzing data to see whether unfavorable small studies remain hidden. The methods are based on the premise that, because many careers depend on them and because the results tend to be convincing, large trials will find their way into print. Small trials will have a tougher road to publication, and preferences on all sides—editors', sponsors'—may lead to unfavorable research's being deep-sixed. Where there's no publication bias, we expect that the average of many small trials will match the average of the few large trials. The dysthymia lit-erature has that pattern, the one that suggests that publication bias has not been a factor.

Moreover, the studies show strong, consistent results. One research group tried to estimate the number of unpublished, less favorable trials that would need to be unearthed for the dysthymia findings to come into question. The answer was: many more than there are published trials altogether. That same calculation applies as readily to future re-search. The conclusion, substantial antidepressant efficacy, is likely to hold up indefinitely, an unsurprising prospect since in practice the medicines work with great reliability.

It makes sense that virtually all the dysthymia research should have found its way into print. Throughout the twentieth century, psycho-therapists had claimed neurosis as their domain. When antidepressants became available, pharmacologists doubted that they would work for depression that looked like a component of personality. Trials that showed drugs falling short would have been welcome.

The field had been exactly wrong. In 2008, Bruce Wampold and other psychologists at the University of Wisconsin reviewed outcome studies. (I am a great admirer of Wampold's work on psychotherapy out-come. He finds that factors common to therapies, such as the doctor-patient relationship, account for much of the efficacy and that the specific benefits of cognitive behavioral therapy in particular have been oversold.) Wampold reported that "medication was significantly more ef-ficacious than psychotherapy in the treatment of dysthymia." His caveat was that trials of the usual duration, often only four months, are brief; psychotherapy's benefits may appear later. By the same token, medica-tion, if patients stayed on it, continued to work for dysthymia for a year or more.

Later, we will consider the "severity hypothesis," which holds that antidepressants work best (or only) for highly symptomatic, grave de-pression. But even exponents of that view make an exception: when they dismiss medication as a treatment for mild and moderate mood disorder, they note that antidepressants work for dysthymia. That is to say, medication works for the sort of mild depression that doctors are most likely to prescribe for, mild depression that persists.

It is hard to know why the dysthymia research has not gotten more play, but inattention to it has clouded the antidepressant debate. Far from being placebos, antidepressants have repeatedly been shown effective for a debilitating mental illness.

As late as the 1990s, doubt remained over antidepressants' usefulness in the treatment of chronic, low-level depression. Against expectations, meta-analysis based on consistent trials demonstrated that medication can be effective, and with a highly acceptable number needed to treat. Shortly, psychiatrists became adept at combining interventions, medication and psychotherapy. The application of antidepressants in the care of dysthymic patients is a key development in mental health care in the last half century, and EBM was the motive force.

24

Trajectories

DESPITE THIS PROGRESS in understanding and using antidepressants, the turn-of-the-millennium years proved difficult for psychiatry as a profession.

The field had entered into an increased, and increasingly questionable, involvement with the pharmaceutical industry, and yet drug development had stalled. In 2002, *The Lancet* published an editorial titled "Just How Tainted Has Medicine Become?" Spending on prescription drugs had doubled between 1997 and 2001. As Pharma thrived, it seemed that the medical disciplines had been absorbed as subsidiaries. In the essay's illustrative case, an editor of *The British Journal of Psychiatry* had been paid for his association with an "educational organisation" sponsored by the manufacturer of an antidepressant, Effexor—and he had just published a paper favorable to the drug.

Prozac's popularity had come to be seen as a mixed blessing.

On the upside, for years public health advocates had pushed for primary-care doctors to recognize depression, and now they were treating it regularly. With well-tolerated medications available, patients were more likely to identify themselves as suffering from mood disorder and more willing to seek care. Memoirs multiplied. Surely stigma had been lessened.

But a survey initiated in the early 1990s found that antidepressant use quadrupled in the next ten years. That medication was being over-prescribed became a commonplace. Drug companies played their part, with the airing of cartoonish direct-to-consumer ads and the hiring of svelte young women to serve as drug reps to aging male physicians.

Soon antidepressant prescriptions topped 100 million annually, with sales on the order of $10 billion. The boom altered the pharmaceutical industry's relationship to psychiatry. Long disfavored, mental health researchers briefly became royalty. Budgets of university departments doubled and doubled again, via drug company funding. With cash came influence. Outcome research long left to academics now was managed by Pharma overseers, who put their stamp on the resulting journal articles as well. Pharmaceutical houses were accused of hiding data about unsuccessful outcome trials and negative drug effects—withdrawal syndromes and suicide attempts.

Concern grew about doctors' receiving payments from industry. Academics were found to have skirted their universities' rules for reporting income. Ordinary practitioners who prescribed in volume were invited to conferences at resorts.

I had felt relatively insulated from drug company influence. I gave no sponsored talks. When—rarely—I attended one, I viewed the graphs skeptically. Everyone knew which researchers were tight with Pharma. In 2008, the *BMJ*—the new incarnation of the *British Medical Journal*—would put me in exclusive company. The publication named one hundred or so "independent medical experts," authorities it considered unbiased commentators, not under Pharma's influence. I was one of six psychiatrists on the roster.

Still, there was no escaping shame and frustration. My profession had sullied itself—and to what end, beyond personal gain? Chemicals previously set aside had been brought off the shelf and tested, and some—Remeron, Pristiq, Viibryd, and other antidepressants—had passed muster. But they were largely "me, too" drugs, similar in their effects and mechanisms of action to antidepressants already in use. Since Prozac's early days, there had been no breakthroughs.

Meanwhile, the depressed patients who responded easily had already been treated, and psychiatrists increasingly saw the remnant for whom there was no ready remedy. Daily, the field faced the limitations of its methods.

In this troubled atmosphere, Irving Kirsch's next salvo landed. Through a Freedom of Information Act request, he had obtained files of trials on new antidepressants that pharmaceutical houses had performed for the Food and Drug Administration. Now, he could answer the leading complaint about "Hearing Placebo," that it was based on an arbitrary collection of research. He had a complete sample, 100 percent of the FDA studies.

In 2002, Kirsch published his conclusions, under the title "The Emperor's New Drugs." He found the effects of antidepressants to be lower and the power of dummy pills higher than he had previously estimated them to be.

Kirsch had analyzed data on three antidepressants, Prozac, Effexor, and Serzone. Medication outperformed placebo by only two points on the Hamilton scale, the equivalent of losing one symptom. Placebo, to use Kirsch's formulation, did 80 percent of what drugs did. A reanalysis in 2008 included trials of Paxil as well and found an effect size for the four antidepressants of 0.32, a small effect. To his credit, Kirsch included a reminder: if additivity did not apply, the medications might work better than the calculations suggested.

But Kirsch thought that the drugs' reach was limited. A British health authority, the National Institute for Clinical Excellence, or NICE, had decided that Hamilton score differences of less than three and effect sizes of less than 0.5 were not clinically meaningful. In Kirsch's analysis, antidepressants met the NICE minimum only for very severe depression. Other psychiatrists, including Jamie Horder of Oxford and Nassir Ghaemi of Tufts, later criticized Kirsch's handling of the data. Their calculations showed efficacy for moderate levels of depression, too.

Still, the outcomes were weak, and Kirsch's conclusions proved influential. It became commonplace for popular writing to suggest that antidepressants do not work at all—the conclusion I find dangerous. By and large, leaders in psychiatry embraced the Kirsch summary. They had to, if they had associated themselves with drug company research.

If the "Emperor" critique displayed any of the transgressive wit I had been inclined to credit Kirsch with, it was along these lines, challenging pharmacologists to accept that their pills are glorified placebos or acknowledge that much of their research was shoddy. I had no trouble embracing the second option. Many Pharma-sponsored studies are terrible—certainly for answering our *How much?* question. Because of the way that the FDA structures the approval process, the incentive is for drug companies to demonstrate that a new medication is minimally useful but very safe. One response to Kirsch's analysis—the data show limited efficacy—is to say that the industry accomplished what it had set out to do.

Otherwise, I wasn't sure that antidepressants had failed at the level that Kirsch suggested.

We'll remember, from our discussion of Gene Glass's work, that in meta-analysis full samples have a downside. Glass had risked letting phobia treatments dominate his results. In Kirsch's analyses, a particular antidepressant, Serzone, played the role of exposure to snakes.

Serzone had been developed and tested because its influence on the brain's handling of serotonin was distinctive. Its special chemistry might make Serzone less likely than SSRIs to cause diminished sex drive and other adverse effects. But the drug had floundered in outcome trials.

That pairing—repeated failed efforts, followed by drug approval—follows from the FDA's ground rules. The FDA has long required companies to produce two favorable randomized trials. The manufacturer can initiate any number of studies in which the medication does poorly so long as, in time, two sets of good results emerge. Behind the policy is the assumption that outcome research is hard to conduct well. If a drug is shown to work and that efficacy is confirmed in a second trial, the agency will be inclined to offer physicians access to the treatment.

The FDA has other requirements. It mistrusts high dropout rates and would be reluctant to approve antidepressants associated with suicides or suicide attempts. To retain and protect research subjects, the industry builds social support into trials, making participation especially pleasant—never mind that placebo response rates skyrocket. The goal is to ensure high patient "adherence"—sticking with the project—and to cut the risk of bad events, until finally two trials arrive in which a drug's effects are discernible over the background noise.

Drugs are patented in the early going, so companies are always racing the patent-expiration clock. Make your mistakes fast, is the attitude. Pharma has come to emphasize patient flow, which has meant abandoning universities for drug-testing mills. These for-profit sites run multiple experiments simultaneously, attracting steady streams of research subjects through nonstop marketing enhanced by inducements for participation. The patients are atypical, even untrustworthy, but numerous enough so that trials can be completed expeditiously.

The research submitted to the FDA, in other words, is not designed to demonstrate new drugs' optimum efficacy. It is designed to produce two successful trials quickly in settings that retain patients and avert disastrous outcomes.

Perhaps wanting to feature Serzone as having few side effects, the manufacturer began its testing with inadequate doses. Even prescribed properly, Serzone looked like a weak antidepressant.

In this instance, because the FDA wanted to give doctors an extra option, access to a medicine that acted through distinctive means, uncharacteristically it looked past full-scale Hamilton scores to subscores (like Per Bech's) and took account of factors such as differential dropout.

Although it gained FDA approval, Serzone did not hold up in the marketplace.

After an initial period of vigorous adoption, it slipped down the list of popular antidepressants. In 2003, a watchdog group, Public Citizen, petitioned the FDA to ban Serzone, claiming that it caused liver disease. Serzone's manufacturer, Bristol-Myers Squibb, declined to defend its drug, although it remains available as a generic.

Kirsch's summary calculations had more patients from Serzone trials than from trials of any other drug. As Serzone kept flunking the Hamilton, the pharmaceutical house had kept running studies. When you "analyze everything," the medication that needed the most trials will dominate.

Looking at Kirsch's second paper, if we drop the Serzone data and consider outcomes for the remaining antidepressants, then calculations like Horder's would show about three Hamilton points' worth of benefit overall, with Effexor and Paxil meeting the NICE standard easily and Prozac lagging.

This distinction—two points or three—may seem trivial, but in experts' discussions it received plenty of ink. A report showing that the SSRIs satisfied one clinical-excellence criterion (but failed another) would hardly have made headlines.

As for the second benchmark, requiring effect sizes at the 0.5 level, NICE seemed to abandon it shortly after it was issued. A more usual target is 0.4, roughly equivalent to a number needed to treat between 4 and 5. In demanding more, NICE had been requiring antidepressants to test out better than do many drugs commonly used in medicine.

The three-Hamilton-point criterion is worth thinking about. A depressed patient can shed three Hamilton points by sleeping better or by improving marginally on scattered items, say, constipation, agitation, and depressed mood. Those advantages (of drug over placebo) might be welcome, but why would a health-standards group consider them sufficient?

The answer is that the averages obscure substantial benefits to the patients for whom drugs work. Three Hamilton points' worth of difference, drug over placebo, corresponds to many additional responses in patients on antidepressants.

In the wake of Kirsch's "Emperor" challenge, researchers studied how symptom improvement distributes itself in drug trials. One team included John Davis—I have mentioned his early work with Jonathan Cole—a senior psychiatrist who made *BMJ*'s list of unbiased medical experts.

In 2012, Davis and colleagues (the lead author was Robert Gibbons, of the University of Chicago) published a summary of the complete set of Eli Lilly–sponsored trials of Prozac. The group found an advantage of Prozac over placebo of only 2.6 Hamilton points. But looking beyond averages to people, the results were reassuring. Doctors needed to treat between four and five patients to get one additional response. Data on Effexor were along similar lines.

Not every result in the Gibbons analysis was this favorable, but the overall lesson was consistent: You don't know what antidepressants do until you examine files from individual patients. A small average difference in Hamilton points can correspond to a favorable number needed to treat.

Overall, even in these halfhearted trials, patients on antidepressants tend to find relief. Further insight into the pattern of response came from research led by John Krystal, the Psychiatry Department chair at Yale. He had access to the entire collection of Eli Lilly's full-dose tests on Cymbalta, a newer imipramine-like antidepressant that influences the brain's use of both serotonin and norepinephrine. The Cymbalta trials had comparators—Prozac, Paxil, or Lexapro—so Krystal got to assess commonly prescribed SSRIs, too. He asked, Given a pill, either drug or placebo, what are the odds of a depressed person's following one or another trajectory, toward health or toward continued dysfunction?

For participants on medication—whether Cymbalta or SSRIs—Krystal found two curves, response and nonresponse.

A quarter of patients were nonresponders. They did not get even the boost enjoyed by a typical patient in a placebo arm. Their Hamilton scores stayed flat, as if the medicine had interfered with their enjoying the contents of the grab bag, such as emotional support. Apparently, these patients had adverse reactions. Like members of David Healy's research team, they felt crummy on a given antidepressant. Adverse responders do better on dummy pills and likely would do better on no medicine than on the antidepressant being tested.

These profound nonresponses—no change—weigh down average results in the drug arms of the outcome trials. Many nonresponders are dropouts.

Three-quarters of the participants on medication fit a "trajectory responder" curve. They got steadily better.

Most people on a response trajectory were responders in the conventional sense as well: their Hamilton score dropped by half. The rest traveled along a similar but flatter curve, losing symptoms at a lesser pace. The authors suggested that with longer follow-up, patients with less dramatic trajectory responses might improve more and reach the conventional response mark.

To review: participants on medication had two trajectories, nonresponse and response—and most people on the response path got substantially better.

The placebo group had a single trajectory. Patients on placebo improved slowly, falling ever farther behind patients on the favorable medication paths. That is not to say that no one recovered on placebo. Some people lost many symptoms, and some deteriorated. But the placebo results clustered, following a single curve, as if a single sort of thing was happening to people in the trials' control arms.

Krystal's method revealed the pattern we have encountered repeatedly. Typically, the placebo grab bag results in a loss of scattered symptoms. Medication gives different results. On antidepressants, a quarter of participants feel so uncomfortable that they don't notice the support that participation in a trial can bring. Three-quarters progress steadily, with most making marked progress.

Importantly, Krystal sees what doctors see. On antidepressants, some patients improve steadily. Others do poorly and need to come off medication. Doctors don't see averages; they see patients. In patients, the drugs work.

In retrospect, Krystal's results add a dimension to the Dawes-Kirsch discussion of percentages. Kirsch had written that his results meant that "for a typical patient, 75% of the benefit obtained from the active drug would also have obtained from an inactive placebo." We can see now that the percentage formulation risks seducing us into another sort of wrong thinking. If antidepressants put some patients on a highly favorable trajectory while placebos mostly lead to scattered symptom losses, then when someone recovers on medication—when a given person's Hamilton scores drop decisively—we would not want to say that 75 percent of that change is *due* to placebo effects. First, since a quarter of patients on medication see no change, placebo duplicates only 60 percent of the improvement in those (many) remaining patients who do well on medication. And second, it simply doesn't look as if placebos (which bring about small change often) have much to do with marked responses.

The trajectory model—like the reports on energy use in the brain—argues against additivity. Medication acts on its own. Presumably, patients who improve on it are not getting a placebo response plus extra help—they're experiencing a reaction set in motion by the drug's pharmacologic potency.

If so, clinicians are not being fooled. Failures announce themselves clearly; patients will say that they feel no better. As for successes, since practitioners give real antidepressants, their patients will not be on a placebo trajectory. When they improve, they will be on a (medication) response trajectory, at one or another slope of progress.

Irving Kirsch's "Emperor" paper stimulated inquiries that the field should have undertaken long before, asking how average outcomes relate to individuals' progress in drug trials. The results suggest that effect size, which Gene Glass had made a standard in mental health research, hides more than it reveals. But Glass had been right when he wrote that effect sizes in the 0.3 to 0.5 range might be reasonably equivalent and fair indicators of efficacy. Sometimes, antidepressants with effect sizes just above 0.3 help three-quarters of those who take them. In office practice, antidepressant responses might be closer than we imagine to what-you-see-is-what-you-get, with only occasional obfuscation by placebo effects.

Those results were not ones that Kirsch had championed, but the new clarity stood as a tribute to his ability to capture the field's attention.

25

No Myth

DISCUSSING THE INSPIRATION for this book, I mentioned Nora, whose life was restored when she began taking antidepressants and who entertained doubts about their worth. In my practice, encounters of this sort became common in the wake of Kirsch's "Emperor" article. But the other trend that concerned me, doctors' dismissal of antidepressants, gained momentum only later. I date that change to 2008, when a justly influential study appeared in *The New England Journal of Medicine*.

Efficacy was not the main topic. The lead author, Erick Turner, from Oregon Health and Science University, would later express concern that his contribution had been misinterpreted as a blanket rejection of antidepressants. But Turner had analyzed the FDA data, and like Kirsch, he had found modest drug effects.

Turner was reviewing publication practices. Considering research submitted to the FDA, he found that medical journals had given space only to reports of studies that validated antidepressants. Results from unfavorable trials either did not find their way into print or were presented in combination with other research, in ways that might obscure the disappointing outcomes. The exceptions involved Prozac and a form of Paxil, for which full data had long been available because of prior protests about the manufacturers, Eli Lilly and GlaxoSmithKline.

Some trials, Turner understood, might have been so flawed that they did not merit publication. Also unclear was how journal editors ought to have proceeded; preliminary results showing modest efficacy for an experimental drug, one that might never make it to market, had little news value. Still, no one doubted that the pharmaceutical industry was inclined to conceal unfavorable information. Surely, for every drug that did gain approval, doctors and the public should have had access to all the data.

New research rules were promulgated in 2007, before the Turner exposé. Drug companies were required to register trials in advance and post results to a public database. But Turner's paper reinforced the movement for transparency.

For our purposes, the important figure in Turner's paper was an overall effect size, 0.31 (signaling a modest impact), that matched Kirsch's calculation. Turner took pains to avoid misinterpretation: each antidepressant remained demonstrably superior to placebo. Discussing whether antidepressants were worth taking, Turner cited the quality-of-life research—patients whose depressive symptoms linger still enjoy improved well-being. And he rejected the NICE standard, saying that it was "doubtful that [Jacob Cohen] would have endorsed NICE's use of an effect size of 0.5 as a litmus test for drug efficacy."

Disclaimers notwithstanding, because of that 0.31 figure, Turner's paper lent support to the view that antidepressants have little to offer. But his analysis, too, had been dominated by drugs that had accumulated disappointing trials, and the FDA's standards guaranteed that there would be many.

I have never considered the FDA data to be a good source of information about drug efficacy. In "candidate-drug trials," as the research on proposed new medicines is called, contact with raters is extensive and supportive, so placebo response rates run high. The patients who sign on rarely resemble the depressed patients I have seen, now or in my training. In some cases, drug doses are held low. The research simply does not address the question that interests us: to what extent medication, thoughtfully administered, is likely to help a typical depressed person.

That said, when the Turner report appeared, I wondered whether the sample he had assembled—of trials never meant to show full drug efficacy—might nonetheless contain *some* usable information on the way antidepressants might work in clinical practice.

Because the FDA believes that it is difficult to recruit representative patient samples—here, groups with typical cases of depression—the agency favors trials with comparators. If in a candidate-drug trial, an antidepressant with known reliability (such as imipramine) does not outperform placebo, the trial is said to have "failed." The presumption is that the experiment was poorly executed or involved an unrepresentative group of patients. In that case, if the new antidepressant stumbles, too, the FDA will be especially forgiving.

Kuhn's opinion was that what trials need most is suitable patients. The FDA was in accord. I wondered what would happen if we adopted the agency's view that the most informative tests are those where a reliable antidepressant such as imipramine succeeds and "validates the sample."

Comparator-validated trials might be interesting for a second reason. Psychologists who consider the classic placebo effect important in depression treatment have been proposing a new sort of evidence. They say that trials with three arms—two antidepressants plus dummy pills—produce elevated placebo response rates. The thought is that when participants know that they have a two-in-three chance of being on an antidepressant, they will have heightened expectations and do especially well—better than in trials where the odds are fifty-fifty. In the more complex trials, drug response rates rise, too, although to a lesser degree. Because of the high placebo response rates, trials with comparators should pose an especially tough challenge for medication.

Knowing that two colleagues, Michael Thase, of the University of Pennsylvania, and Arif Khan, of Duke University, had the FDA material banked in their computer systems, I asked them to do a run of trials with comparators. The results have not been published, which means that they have not gone through editorial and peer review. Still, the statistical procedure is straightforward, based on files available to many research teams.

The FDA collection contained thirty-four candidate-drug trials (with 8,134 patients) that had three arms: placebo, comparator, and a new drug that was eventually approved. Imipramine and Elavil played the benchmarking role most often, but, as patients began to avoid studies with older drugs, new antidepressants, often Paxil, filled in.

In nineteen trials, the comparator failed. In them, the effect size for the new drug over placebo was 0.29, about what Kirsch and Turner found in their analyses. In aggregate, then, the FDA studies—most conducted without a comparator—resemble failed three-arm trials.

In fifteen trials, the comparator succeeded. Its benefit over placebo reached statistical significance. There, where the patient sample proved valid, the effect size for the candidate drug was 0.45.

That figure is familiar. It parallels the effect size for imipramine in Gene Glass's research. It corresponds to a number needed to treat of 4.

In this complete collection of studies, response rates were effectively identical in three- and two-armed trials of the same antidepressants. If patients do calculate the odds of receiving medication, then drug trials don't show much in the way of classic placebo effects. The rise in placebo responses over the years is more likely due to the supportive factors in drug trials—we will get a glimpse of them shortly— and increasing problems with enrollment. Typical depressed patients do not sign on as subjects in candidate-drug trials. In that context, comparator-validated trials, ones in which imipramine performs as expected, become all the more important.

When I mentioned the comparator-validated results to John Davis, he shared analyses from his own wide-ranging review, also as yet unpublished. They told the same story. Davis had examined an extensive collection of trials, some conducted in academic settings, some unpublished, in which imipramine had been used as a comparator for Prozac, Zoloft, or Celexa. In studies involving thousands of patients, the new drugs matched the old consistently, and both outperformed placebo, with effect sizes overall in the 0.5 range, typical for medical treatments in general. (Because Davis's collection included some high-quality trials, the effect sizes ran higher than those calculated from the FDA collection.) As Kuhn's curse would predict, decade by decade the measured efficacy has fallen for all drugs, but in each time period, the new antidepressants kept pace with imipramine.

Davis's analysis should prove important. In its graphs, each of the new drugs tracks imipramine, equaling it in efficacy, but with a steady falloff over time, a sign that it is the trials, not the drugs, that are failing. The FDA's methods, whatever their flaws, have provided doctors with a set of medications that perform as well as imipramine.

Unpublished studies can be only so convincing, so we are lucky to have published analyses to bring to bear. Per Bech and his colleagues have used a different approach to finding valid information in the FDA files, by using their compact Hamilton scale. That choice might mitigate a flaw in the data. If raters game the system, admitting patients whose main claims for entry are headache and constipation, the Bech scale will ignore widely prevalent irrelevancies.

Bech examined a collection of studies similar to Turner's, including the unpublished research. Wherever Bech could break down the data—wherever he could run the numbers on core depression factors—antidepressants worked, so long as they were used in full doses. Bech found effect sizes ranging from about 0.4 for Prozac to 0.6 for Lexapro.

Even looking at failed and unsuccessful trials, sweeping in all the data, if you limit your attention to core symptoms, you find that antidepressants perform at acceptable levels. (The strength of the numbers may reflect medications' ability to ameliorate what Bech calls the dimension of depression, the cluster of core depressive symptoms as they appear even in sloppily diagnosed patients.) Our doubts about efficacy reflect artifacts of measurement—confounds in trials that evidence-based medicine tends to embrace. Pare down Max Hamilton's scale to the essentials, and, to quote Bech's charming conclusion about Prozac and its fellows, you see that "no such myth of mere placebo activity is in operation for second-generation antidepressants."

In his *New England Journal* paper, for each antidepressant Turner had contrasted the high apparent effect sizes that a reader might have arrived at if he had access only to the published studies and a lower effect size that emerged from the complete data set, including unpublished studies. Applying the shortened scale, Bech found effect sizes for Prozac, Celexa, Lexapro, and Cymbalta *higher* than those that Turner had derived from the published, favorable studies. (One antidepressant, Remeron, fell just shy of matching the published FDA number.) The result held for full drug doses and most often for lesser doses as well. The apparently inflated estimates of antidepressant efficacy, the ones calculated based on uniformly positive published studies, were arguably too low.

Bech's results suggest that while psychiatry had corporate, professional, academic, publishing, and oversight scandals, as far as treatment efficacy was concerned, there was no clinical scandal. Arguably, the most relevant effect sizes for antidepressants were *higher* than the published ones. Doctors don't go through life mentally integrating trial results; but any automaton who had regulated his practice that way would have been in danger of *underprescribing*.

There's no excuse for drug companies' and the FDA's failing to inform doctors and the public fully. At the same time, I don't think that it's coincidence when a scale representing the clinical viewpoint documents levels of efficacy that correspond to doctors' impressions of how well antidepressants work.

These approaches—looking at core symptoms, comparator-validated trials, trajectories, and response rates—all find ordinary efficacy for antidepressants, even in the candidate-drug trials.

Advocates of evidence-based medicine complain about doctors' tendency to stick with what has worked for their patients; the profession should be more responsive to research results. But clinical experience acts as ballast, often usefully. Kirsch's "Emperor" paper and Turner's critique of publication practices arrived in the early years of the new millennium. The reports, with their calculations of modest effect sizes, may have led some doctors to stop prescribing antidepressant medication or to cut back on its use. I feared (and observed) that result. But subsequent analyses have been reassuring. Antidepressants work as well as they ever have. Doctors' steady judgment may have been more accurate, more useful in the service of good patient care, than the fluctuating research results.

Finally, here's my take on the FDA studies: They performed their job, allowing the agency to identify useful medicines, ones that patients can live with, ones that have transformed the face of depression. Beyond that, the trials are a lousy source of information about antidepressant efficacy, and it's shocking that an important medical question, about the proper treatment of mood disorder, has been debated using them as a reflection of reality.

As for how flawed the testing process is, we'll see in a moment—next—when we take a trip to a clinical center to observe commercially sponsored drug trials. They're disturbing. Reading outcome studies, we may envisage patients coming to see their doctors and getting either medication or identical-looking placebo pills. Industry drug testing is no longer like that. Industry drug testing is an industry in itself, one that produces results ever less reflective of typical clinical encounters.

26

Interlude
Pitch-Perfect

THE CENTER SITS in a prosperous community just outside one of America's second-tier cities. Across the city boundary, the usual urban tensions are on display. Middle-class migration to the suburbs and the loss of union jobs—we are in October of 2012—have left behind an underclass short on resources. Spotty gentrification downtown has not rescued the poor, but the exurbs are flourishing.

The center building is a glassed cube with views in one direction to prosperous businesses and in another to gracious homes. Decorated sparely—art photos, leather couches—its second-floor waiting room is a reassuring setting. The ambience strikes a balance between implications of comfort and competence, warmth and expertise.

The personnel are part of the picture. They have the thin, up-scale multicultural look of students at a selective university, which is where most were a few years back. Like the decor, they radiate competence and caring—but caring within limits. Professionalism prevails.

In contrast, the clientele on the couches are overweight and modestly dressed. Most are unemployed or underemployed, which is why they can visit the center during the day. They live far from here, some in subsidized housing or homeless shelters.

These men and women are, for all that, valuable. Research subjects are hard to come by. The staff is intent on retaining them.

The for-profit clinical research center is a recent phenomenon. Both pharmaceutical houses and the Food and Drug Administration have turned demanding. Outcome trials are expensive. A comparison of drug and placebo in a hundred subjects will cost $10 million, and companies sometimes spend much more—approaching $100 million. No one leaves drug testing to amateurs.

The clinic I am visiting is influential. Most major trials today are multisite. If you are on an antidepressant approved by the FDA in recent decades, chances are that some of the testing for it was done here. The center enrolls more than a thousand new research subjects a year, two-thirds of them in studies of depression. More mental health visits take place here than at the local university or veterans' hospital, in part because research entails more frequent attendance than does treatment under today's austere standards of care.

The center serves as an auxiliary to the health-care system. Strapped financially, state facilities focus on grave impairment, so uninsured men and women who are slightly less ill will get their mental health care here. Perhaps this pattern will change under Obamacare; more likely, not.

Screening is thorough. Often, it is at the center that subjects will learn that they are pregnant. First diagnoses of cancer, heart disease, hepatitis, and HIV infection are common. Pickups of drug abuse may lead to treatment elsewhere. Sometimes it pays to clean up a subject, getting him off street drugs and into a Pharma protocol.

Since a dozen trials run simultaneously, there are economies of scale. When the clinic recruits for an anxiety study, the intake team may diagnose mania and refer the patient to a different trial, for bipolar disorder.

Overlap matters because subjects are precious. Between advertising (on daytime television), leafleting (at drop-in centers for the mentally ill), and event sponsorship (including meals at soup kitchens, via a local ministry), the clinic may spend a million dollars a year on recruitment, one thousand per new participant. This budget would be higher but for the clinic's good reputation. It depends on professional contacts and word of mouth—on its history in the community.

Support begins with transportation to the center. Most research subjects arrive by van. The routes extend to poor rural areas, journeys of many miles. More trips are from the inner city. The van drivers, selected and trained to be personable, know the regulars—men and women who participate in multiple trials, one after the other. The drivers are raconteurs, listeners, and facilitators, coaxing their passengers to interact companionably. In rating sessions, when interviewers ask subjects what in the past week has given them pleasure, they may reply, *The ride in.*

The van is a social hub. Riding along, I hear a somnolent woman—unemployed, living in the projects—speak of her girl gang, regulars who have been through many studies of bipolar disorder. Some are in the van. The posse has seen Sheila quick and witty, so they tolerate her as she is now, slowed by the depressive phase of the illness. The ride structures Sheila's day. It brings her from the shelter to the center and later to a welfare-to-work program.

Talk of misfortune is common. Center participants are exposed to theft, violence, and petty humiliation. The passengers function as a support group.

Much of the conversation is upbeat. One research subject reminisces about a sister who was raised at an orphanage and has just returned from a reunion with a foster parent. The driver offers parallel examples from the lives of people he knows. The discussion turns to sports. Music is a popular topic, and, perhaps oddly, high fashion.

I ask the passengers how they decided to join a study. Money was a factor. Although considered volunteers, subjects are paid between $40 and $75 for attending a rating session. Most trials begin with weekly visits, later cutting back to twice a month. Public support—welfare—in the center's region runs to about $300 a month, so study participation may increase patients' income by 50 percent or even double it. The extra money may represent the whole of a subject's discretionary income.

Research review boards put caps on incentives, so as not to implicitly coerce people into undertaking a risk not in their interest. It is true that $50 would hardly compensate a middle-class worker for chunks of time taken out of the day. Intake visits can last six hours. A follow-up of ninety minutes would count as a brief rating session.

For the poor and depressed, the attraction is apparent. Here is money you can earn without confronting personal limitations that make holding a job difficult. The clinic's drivers will come into the house and get you moving. No employer will do as much.

For the duration of a trial, participants enjoy higher income, richer social contacts, attention from doctors and nurses, access to transportation, time in an attractive setting, structured days, and a sense of purpose. In the bus, talk turns to cash gifts given to adult children. That's a luxury the extra income affords, the ability to be generous. Even on placebo, these patients ought to get better.

Incentives are only part of the story. The van passengers are proud to do their part to advance medical science. They also say that they are getting good psychiatric care, that it's built into the research.

For all that, the psychological careers of these participants are choppy. Once a study is over, they will not be able to afford the medicine that helped them, or it may be unavailable. These patients will relapse and then be candidates for future trials. If they haven't relapsed, it might be in their interest to make out that they have. The weeks in drug studies may compose the best intervals in the year.

The same is true for participants who have been on dummy pills and responded to the benefits that center attendance provides, not least the opportunity to discuss pain, adversity, and private history.

Its strengths leave the research center vulnerable. It will retain subjects who benefit from social support. If they talk up the program and attract others with a similar bent, word of mouth will amplify this problem. A focus on recruitment and retention guarantees high rates of placebo response.

Twice in two days, I heard deeply depressed patients, men who spoke with excruciating deliberateness, say that they had not encountered anyone socially outside the center. The only pleasurable part of their week was the ratings interview.

Many riders struck me as capable and personable. Depression had made them downwardly mobile. Part of what the center offered was time in a prosperous setting that should have been their due.

Not all participants arrived by van, and not all were unemployed. Some middle-class patients intended to make a contribution to science. Some came because all prior treatments had failed.

Still, most participants had incentives to exaggerate depression ratings at the start of trials. Reading about demand characteristics, I had imagined that they were subtle, grounded as much in the urge to please authority figures as in the wish to be accepted for a study. In practice, the influence of the test setting on depression-scale answers was pronounced and self-evident. During interviews, I heard obvious distortions: fairly healthy people "endorsing" symptoms (saying they had them) in order to join a trial, and in the later going, seriously impaired people attesting to improvement, pretty clearly in hopes of pleasing the rater. Likely, some inaccuracy occurred in the other direction, too: some subjects clung to the sick role. Any drug response coexisted with ratings movement related to a trial's place in the subject's life.

And then there was adversity. Bad things happen to people with scant resources: muggings, evictions. Dispiriting events insert a random flux into research subjects' progress. It is hard to measure treatment effects in a maelstrom.

For patients with disrupted lives, the clinical center is a point of stability. It inspires loyalty because it aspires to excellence. Mornings, while the vans are on the road, the doctors, nurses, pharmacists, technicians, and raters gather in a state-of-the-art meeting room. An administrator projects a spreadsheet on a screen. The array displays every patient's interview and lab test results, with abnormal findings and missed appointments highlighted in red.

Where is Mr. Smith? Attending a funeral. His rater has sent condolences. She'll phone again Wednesday. The protocol's reevaluation deadline is Friday. We're on it. He'll make it in.

Mr. Doe's liver enzyme levels are just above the study's norm. Does another trial tolerate them? The primary-care doctor has been notified.

Miss Roe's lab results show marijuana use. She is entering counseling and has vowed to stay clean. She's out of the current study but will be retested and considered for one starting next month.

Years ago, I attended rounds at a justly celebrated "assertive community treatment program" that followed the chronically mentally ill via contact with their employers and landlords. I had not seen follow-through at this level. Nor had the mental health and general hospital clinics where I'd worked enjoyed the efficiency of the research center. This quality comes through to study participants—reliable attention.

Of course, the center's work product is not health. It is successful trials, ones that detect daylight between a test drug and placebo if any is to be found.

Drug companies demand high patient retention; even 10 percent "attrition" may be unacceptable. Losing subjects means risking differential dropout, which destroys the ability to confirm the superiority of drug to placebo. Business and science require that the clinic atmosphere be congenial. The center honors that imperative, erring in the direction of support, but with awareness that too much coziness will send placebo responses through the roof.

The raters embody this delicate strategy. The best possess a capacity for empathy modulation that verges on the eerie. The young women (all raters are young women) offer warmth up to a point. Everyone is attractive, and no one is seductive. The community maintains itself. If a new hire does not fit in, the group will extrude her.

Once you've seen rating sessions, you no longer wonder where placebo responses come from. Drug studies can be tedious. One patient begins a visit by having his blood pressure taken. There is a discrepancy between two readings. The trial requires successive measurements in a narrow range. The protocol specifies a long interval before retesting. The rater fills the time with talk of the patient's past work achievements. The patient, agitated at first, begins to assume the rater's calm demeanor.

I see some stiff, mechanical encounters, focused on rating forms. But most interviews look like psychotherapy. That effect is especially evident with Allison, the center's most admired rater. She is known for combining high retention rates with accurate ratings.

Allison never works her way down a checklist. She lets study participants reveal themselves. She starts by catching up, as with an old friend. What has become of the child who had trouble with the law?

To me, the ideal diagnostic interview resembles an assessment by a neonatologist in the delivery suite. She admires the newborn, fiddling with its fingers and toes—all while answering the mother's anxious questions. Within minutes the doctor knows whether all is well. If not, she will have a diagnosis in mind or a plan for arriving at one.

Allison's rating sessions are like that. She understands how it is to raise teenagers on a budget or care for ailing parents. Her manner suggests experience and tolerance.

One interviewee, Verna, struggles at work and blames others for her misfortunes. Because of a grievance with a superior, Verna has applied to change assignments. Unlike the disrespectful boss, Allison listens quietly, accepting Verna's premises. Laying out complaints, Verna begins advising herself not to act impulsively, so as not to endanger her prospects. She sees justifications for staying put—clearer responsibilities, less chance of failure. She becomes better able to weigh the relative merits of the different postings.

Elements of the Hamilton emerge. Verna's sleep has improved. She is eating better. Still, Verna's willingness to socialize has not returned. Hearing the conversation, you might not know that depression ratings are at issue.

I congratulate Allison on a masterful performance. I believe that I know just how much Verna's remaining impediments are due to depression and how much to stable character traits.

Allison sighs, "We're stuck with her." In the initial interview, Verna endorsed every Hamilton item and at high levels. Having entered the study with an impossibly elevated depression rating, she is bound to show improvement, whether on medication or placebo. If time spent with Allison helps, that change may further weaken the study's ability to discern medication effects. Although welcome, Verna's recovery will burden the trial.

When the designers of the NIMH collaborative trial referred to "minimal supportive psychotherapy," clearly they had not seen Allison in action. Nothing about her influence was minimal. I've supervised colleagues and trainees, in psychiatry and social work, who had nothing like Allison's knack for sizing up situations or setting people at ease. Many patients come from families where neglect or misunderstanding is the norm. Being listened to thoughtfully makes patients feel acknowledged, never mind that Allison's motivations—accurate ratings, subject retention—are off to the side. Unless their depression is unbudgeable, research subjects interviewed by Allison will show improvement.

Through the van ride, contact with other enrollees, conversation with Allison, and the general structure of the center, the assessment process offers purpose, meaning, structure, companionship, attention, reassurance, respect, trust, insight, health care, financial support, and a safe and attractive physical environment. The interview takes what feels like generalized disaster and redefines it as discrete symptoms of illness. In antidepressant trials as they are run today, the contrast is not between dummy pills and active pills. It is between psychotherapy plus dummy pills and psychotherapy plus medication.

From our discussion of additivity we know that with this setup—where much of the placebo effect is a psychotherapy effect—conventional calculations fail. Because medication preempts some of what psychotherapy does, when we subtract placebo-arm results from drug-arm results, we will subtract too much.

In my residency, the group-therapy instructor had a mantra: *No one's the worse for a good experience.* He meant that psychoanalytic interpretations were not all we offered. The research center provides a good experience with no need for the classic placebo effect, hopeful expectancy attached to a pill, to make a showing. When you see the center in action, you do not wonder why responses are high in control arms of trials or why drug efficacy is hard to demonstrate, even for antidepressants that test out as well as imipramine.

Implicit therapy has its insidious side. If a drug carried grave risk and if the van travelers were well informed about it, would they feel free to decline enrollment? Or is the center's role in their lives so critical that they are, in effect, obliged to consent and, so, unable to protect themselves? It is easy to imagine disaster, medical and ethical.

The competence and skill that center workers bring to their tasks also raise questions. Why does this excellence attach to a commercial enterprise beholden to drug companies and not to our public health system? Why is affordable, competent care not widely available for this most treatable of mental illnesses, depression? The organization I had envisaged when I ran outpatient clinics at not-for-profit hospitals finds its incarnation here, in a center serving Pharma.

Set aside medication and psychotherapy: The depressed might benefit from emotional support given in the drop-in center or subsidized housing block. They might benefit from encouragement to get up in the morning, from rides to appointments, from a chance to socialize, from contact with service people who treat them with respect. If modest monetary incentives are compelling, why not use them to reward successful participation in job training? The candidate-drug-testing enterprise is built on failures in our social architecture.

Although it enrolled homeless people, the center I visited did not focus on attracting them. The risk of dropouts was considered too high. But for other "contract research organizations," often small centers involved in addiction research or the early safety testing of antipsychotic drugs for schizophrenia, homeless shelters are a primary site for recruitment. I was seeing the less sleazy end of the commercial-drug-test spectrum, and it was queasy-making enough.

Carl Elliott, a colleague since *Listening* days, has written extensively and critically about for-profit drug testing and the selection of participants, saying, "It seems inevitable that the job will fall to people who have no better options." In cancer care, in dementia care, the same is not true—a wide array of patients sign on to test unproven remedies. The research benefits from a different source of misfortune: for some conditions, there are no good treatments. With depression, the efficacy of our current medications insures that the poor will act as guinea pigs for new ones.

The center staff expressed awareness of the ethical quandaries attaching to their work. More often, they praised the clinic as a corrective to a flawed health-care system. Raters believe that drug development and testing are critical to progress in medicine, that the marketplace is the right context for that effort, and that it is fair to deliver the impression of caring, skilled treatment because assessment amounts to just that.

Without wanting to dismiss that argument entirely—I had seen the important role that the center played in subjects' lives—I felt unease every moment I was there. I was witnessing a process that was disconcerting on both moral and scientific grounds.

My visit made me think that we had come to a dead end as regards the testing of new antidepressants. The curse of Roland Kuhn is in full effect. Cases of uncomplicated depression are hard to find. Because research subjects are rare, the very poor fill the gaps. Raters must be especially supportive. And so on. These difficulties increased my sympathy for the FDA's position about what signals efficacy. If two favorable trials emerge in this context, you're dealing with a highly useful treatment.

27

Trials

MY VISIT TO the center also made me despair of rating scales, the basis for almost all discussions of antidepressant efficacy. In my earliest writings, I'd criticized the mechanical assessment of patients. Like Roland Kuhn, I believe that the depth of a person's despondency may become apparent only gradually. In the here and now, grave depression can manifest itself in three symptoms, and mild depression in a dozen.

What I had failed to appreciate were the difficulties attending a seemingly simple task, checking off boxes on a ratings list. The center produces assessments of illness severity. They are hard to deliver. If we misread the whole person, we will misread the detail.

Take this moment from an interview I witnessed. Middle-aged, high-strung, beaten-down, Albert is four weeks into a drug trial, on antidepressant or placebo. The rater asks, "When you are in a stressful situation, does your voice quake?"

"Under stress?" Albert's voice goes up a pitch, cracks, and wavers. "I would say no," Albert croaks.

The young woman fills in a bubble on her tablet: Is it yes or no?

The answer may seem obvious. The Hamilton scale is an observer rating. It's the interviewer who assesses the level of anxiety.

But times have changed. In the interest of uniformity, drug companies have broken down each Hamilton factor into clusters of questions. The interviewer poses them, the patient answers, the response gets sent off to Zurich or New York, where statisticians integrate the data to arrive at a Hamilton score. In theory, the rater may make the judgment, but in practice, patients' responses often determine the result.

Behind the response is a reality. Perhaps Albert is less self-conscious, so the tightness in his vocal cords bothers him less than it once did. Perhaps, on the contrary, he is suffering insidious worsening of his anxiety. If we care about providing a useful drug for patients or sparing them exposure to a useless one, we will want to know how Albert is faring.

A later question goes, "Facing stressful events, do you notice your heart racing?"

Sometimes, Albert says, but he does not experience the sensation as anxiety. Feeling better, he has begun leaving his comfort zone. Also, he wonders whether the rapid heartbeat is a side effect of the pills.

Yes or no?

I have mentioned Allison and her reputation for accurate assessment. Her mantra was *Rate what you see.*

Flouting drug-company requirements, Allison filled out forms only at the end of loosely structured interviews. She had an inner register of levels of depression. If she knew that on a given day a patient was a 24, he was going to come out a 24, or nearly—not, she said, because she forced the numbers, but because she rated factors in light of the overall picture.

Max Hamilton had intended for his scale to be applied by doctors who knew patients well, and Allison was true to that spirit. Still, her method verged on treating the Hamilton as if it were a global impression scale. She used the factor ratings to convey the subject's well-being.

The center leaned toward Allison's approach—toward *Rate what you see* more than *Record what patients say.* Still, I saw staff dutifully filling in bubbles in real time.

That's what drug companies want. The single suicidality rating on the Hamilton will emerge from a dozen probes about self-destructive impulses. But structured interviews can inhibit self-revelation. You have high reliability (numbers everyone agrees on) with low validity (numbers that misjudge patients' true states).

Precision without validity is noise. If patients are reluctant to endorse symptoms once a study is under way, placebo response rates will float upward, with lots of subjects scoring as better while they never appear well. Our true drug effect will be ever less visible.

At the clinical center, this problem is readily apparent. One older man, Eddie, who looks gravely depressed, gives upbeat answers to probes from the Hamilton. Here's my guess: Because his depression makes conversation intolerable, he is hoping to speed the session along. The interviewer looks to be a novice; I pull her aside to share my concern. Might Eddie, now scoring as much improved, be at risk for suicide?

Other patients are hard to pin down. Doug seems unfamiliar with what is expected—or else he is not playing the game.

How long does it take you to go to sleep?

"I pay that no mind."

If you wake up, does it take you a long time to get back to sleep?

"I watch TV."

Do you have trouble concentrating when you talk to people?

"I don't talk to people."

Voluble patients can be equally inscrutable. Francine, a methodical rater, is interviewing Lois, a recently laid-off legal secretary who is every bit her match.

How is Lois's appetite?

Lois offers a long explanation: Apathetic, as she is now, she's disinclined to cook. When she doesn't cook, she eats less. But then, with effort, most afternoons, she prepares dinner for her husband. When the food is in front of her, she eats—and makes up for what she misses early in the day.

Clearly, Lois is still depressed. Clearly, too, Francine is trying to answer a questionnaire item derived from a factor on the Hamilton scale—*Somatic symptoms: gastrointestinal: loss of appetite*. Unintentionally, she has nailed down a different item, about work and activities. The lack of motivation to cook fits there, I would say.

Eating may have a diurnal rhythm. Classically, depressed people feel bad early in the day and better later on, so perhaps Lois's hunger has, in fact, been affected. Still, she seems to be denying a change in appetite.

I have a fair impression of the level of Lois's depression—toward the severe end of moderate—and I imagine that Francine does, too. But what of this Hamilton factor?

Appetite is the simplest item on the list. Ten minutes into Francine's inquiry, I still cannot decide whether the capacity is intact. Francine taps a tablet-style computer, sending a rating through the ether. Will it clarify a drug's efficacy or muddy the waters?

Even forthcoming responses can add randomness. Carlotta, an over-burdened single mother, has largely recovered from a nasty depression. Because she has no child care, her young sons are in the interview room, bickering ceaselessly. When the rater asks about irritability, Carlotta says she has it in spades. My guess is that context plays the determining role. In a calm setting, Carlotta might deny that she is on edge.

We have spoken of noise in the data, and here it is, in the form of hard-to-code rating questions. Whether Albert's voice quavers, Doug suffers insomnia, Lois retains appetite, or Carlotta feels testy—interviewers' notations will determine the averages for drug and placebo. The Hamilton figures are as likely to subtract as to add information.

Time at the center made me appreciate Per Bech's approach all the more. The Hamilton scale's core—low mood, low energy—is surrounded by factors that are hard to rate. If telltale items are drowned in a sea of nonsense, good drugs and placebo will look similar.

Perhaps *Rate what you see* offers the least misleading approach to factors that resist assessment—but it leads to worries. Will interviewers make unwise use of the freedom to add fudge factors? Believing that a patient is on medication, a rater may write off symptoms as side effects. Believing that a patient is on placebo, a rater may dismiss improvements as passing fluctuations of mood.

The center's director exhorts his staff to ignore their impressions about who is on what. When trials end, surprises emerge. Patients with characteristic side-effect profiles turn out to have taken dummy pills. Hunches cause failed trials. *Rate what you see* must reflect earnest efforts to gauge patients' level of illness.

For what it's worth: I had no clue about which study participants were on medication—I mean, none based on side effects. It's kosher to imagine that people who get better are on medication—that way, you treat placebo effects, if they occur, as real. When a research subject reported a typical Prozac response, fewer symptoms and greater social ease, I guessed that an antidepressant was responsible. Likewise, dramatic worsening early in a trial made me suspect an adverse response to medication. But mostly these patients and their lives were so complicated that there were no obvious indicators.

What was reasonably clear was patients' overall mental health. More than once in my visit, I heard the center's director venture a guess about a Hamilton score. "What's Wes today, a 21?" Unsurprised, Wes's rater would confirm the number. It is a perverse truth that patients are well-known here, as they might be in a clinic dedicated to treatment. Something is perverse, too, about the need to convert gut impressions into Hamilton scores. If the FDA ignores global impression ratings out of fear that drug companies will game them, why not have trials run by dedicated nonprofits?

The Hamilton scale is a dead letter. Hearing Lois describe her eating and Doug his sleep, I was impressed with how attention to symptom factors obscured what seemed knowable, patients' levels of depression. Researchers see through a glass darkly; clinicians, face-to-face.

Throughout, the patient population was eye-opening. Candidate-drug trials ask whether small indicators of medication effect emerge in unresponsive, partly treated, or immensely disadvantaged patients who have an investment in the process. We are left to speculate about how well the antidepressant will, through its inherent efficacy, help in uncomplicated depression.

As I say, we're at a dead end, and all comers are welcome to put their spin on the murky findings. My impression is that the modest effect sizes Kirsch and Turner derive from the FDA files, 0.3 counting even failed trials, should be read as encouraging. It is no surprise that those numbers identify drugs that in doctors'—in Lisa Ekselius's—offices, with more typical depressed patients, still yield 80 or 90 percent response rates.

Imagine handing Lexapro or Effexor to doctors a half century back and having them run a trial—with no elegant setting, no pert raters, no van transport, no payment, no fetish for Hamilton factors, and no anxiety about participant retention. Imagine that their patients have depression within coherent lives. In the absence of time machines, I won't pay or collect, but my bet is that the clinic staff would say (as Roland Kuhn's staff did) that they were working with a miracle drug. When it emerges from the clinical center—or some lesser facility doing similar work—that's what a small effect size signals.

28

Sham

MIGHT PLACEBO PILLS prove equally miraculous? In outcome trials, in ordinary experience, antidepressants work. If we entertain doubts about them, it's because of the claim that inert tablets would do as well. The consequences of that possibility go beyond the thought that patients might be spared cost and harm. If sham treatment cures depression, it is an especially tractable disorder. If apparent antidepressant responses result from classic placebo effects, then doctors and patients are easily misled.

Think of how a primary-care doctor, call her Viola, gains familiarity with antidepressants. For depressed patients, she may routinely recommend any number of remedies: exercise, bright lights, marriage counseling, and "tincture of time." When those fail or work halfway, she will prescribe. Then, based on her experience, she will make an informal calculation, about how much the medicine (as opposed to more time, more exercise, and the rest—factors whose influence she can subtract out) aids in her patients' recoveries.

What Viola can never see is the change due to the mere facts of prescribing and pill taking. They are inherent in every instance of medicating depression.

True, Viola may have inklings. Working with patients like Adele, the schoolteacher who got more, not less, despondent in the face of dramatic treatments for her thyroid disease, I came to doubt that classic placebo effects are powerful in depression. But in ordinary circumstances, a pill's symbolic impact and its inherent efficacy can't be pried apart by observation. That's why research on placebo is critical. If any random pill would work for her depressed patients, Viola's yardstick is off. A great deal rides on what we make of sham treatments.

Well, then, what does evidence-based medicine say? For researchers, the classic placebo effect—response based on expectations attached to a pill—is a unicorn: often described, rarely seen.

Placebo, as we ordinarily imagine it, is a bargain and a miracle. A person in pain is offered a capsule full of nothing, and the suffering ends. Or begins. Placebos can elicit nausea, somnolence, even skin rashes. In behavioral research, explorations of how expectancy causes an acute symptom constitute a cottage industry. But beyond parlor tricks, beyond tonic-water tipsiness, what is the classic placebo's potential?

Slight, it seems, when it comes to what doctors treat.

In 2001, Asbjørn Hróbjartsson and Peter Gøtzsche, Danish medical researchers with ties to the Cochrane Collaboration, looked at trials in which placebo pills or other sham interventions, such as sham surgery or sham acupuncture, had been contrasted with "no treatment" conditions. The analysis reviewed studies of forty disorders, including anemia, bacterial infection, epilepsy, and carpal tunnel syndrome. The intent was to isolate this factor, pretend treatment, and see whether it influenced medical conditions.

Hróbjartsson (think "Robertson"—the name is Icelandic) and Gøtzsche were seeking what Irving Kirsch wanted—and what Robyn Dawes said could not be found in conventional drug studies—a measure of the placebo pill's effect, but from trials in which a sham intervention was the active treatment, and something less hope-inducing, such as time on a wait list, was the control condition.

Hróbjartsson and Gøtzsche found that, for the most part, sham interventions conferred no extra benefit—none. Where placebo did outperform the wait list, the difference was small. The resulting article, in *The New England Journal of Medicine*, was titled "Is the Placebo Powerless?" The authors answered, "In conclusion, we found little evidence that placebos in general have powerful clinical effects."

Hróbjartsson and Gøtzsche were not denying the need for control arms in outcome trials. Their point was that in the grab bag of placebo effects, this one, expectancy tied to a pill or a procedure, played a trivial role. The passage of time might matter, and patients' eagerness to please. But in almost no instance did giving or withholding pills make a difference.

Hróbjartsson and Gøtzsche grouped studies various ways.

They looked at trials that used categorical measures, such as response and remission. Hróbjartsson and Gøtzsche called them binary outcomes. The patient is dead or alive, smoking cigarettes or abstaining, depressed or no longer depressed. For binary outcomes, it did not matter how you measured your ailment, whether through objective measures (death or blood sugar levels) or subjective measures (dizziness or Hamilton ratings). No classic placebo effect emerged. The sole exception was in the treatment of pain, where the brain's own opiates seem to come into play.

Pain studies aside, for binary—well or ill—outcomes, if patients on dummy pills got better, so did patients on the wait list. Hróbjartsson and Gøtzsche found no trials—none—in which a pill reliably produced more remissions or recoveries than "no treatment."

Hróbjartsson and Gøtzsche looked also at studies with continuous objective outcomes, such as blood pressure, and found no classic placebo responses. Hróbjartsson and Gøtzsche did see modest effects in trials using "continuous subjective outcomes," such as a change in Hamilton scores. The movement was on the order of that seen with psychotherapy or antidepressants in the less favorable analyses—effect sizes near 0.3. But even here, the researchers' likeliest scenario was that classic placebo effects made no contribution at all.

With continuous subjective outcomes, the only differences between placebo and no-treatment arms appeared in studies in which patients described their symptoms: seasickness or anxiety. Since no placebo effects appeared elsewhere—none where physicians observe directly, as with joint flexibility—the problem, Hróbjartsson and Gøtzsche speculated, might be the goodbye effect. Patients know when they are on a wait list. Wait-list patients don't come in to discuss "medication" side effects with staff and bond over the encounter. They are not tempted to give upbeat reports—but patients on pills might be.

Hróbjartsson and Gøtzsche made an additional argument. In this last bastion of sham treatment, the effects were largest in small trials, a pattern that suggests publication bias. Hróbjartsson and Gøtzsche theorized that because placebo has its proponents, when research showed that it failed to outperform the wait list, those data remained in the file drawer.

The Hróbjartsson and Gøtzsche paper—it has been updated twice—has been enormously influential. Of it, Ted Kaptchuk, a respected placebo researcher, has said, "At first when I read it, I worried I'd be out of a job . . . But frankly, [Hróbjartsson] was absolutely right." The study caused placebo advocates to moderate their claims. In a 2015 essay for *The New England Journal of Medicine*, Kaptchuk began the substance of his overview with this acknowledgment: "First, though placebos may provide relief, they rarely cure."

The "Powerless Placebo" paper included a handful of depression studies. Most concerned *maintenance*. Maintenance research looks at people who recovered in the course of a brief trial and are now free of depression. The subsequent outcome is binary: In a follow-up interval, does the remission last, or does depression recur?

When patients who had improved in a treatment trial entered a maintenance study, it did not matter whether they continued on a placebo pill or received no pill. They relapsed at the same high rate.

One criticism of maintenance trials stems from the view that antidepressants are habituating and that coming off them causes harm—so, of course, neither placebo nor "no treatment" will work. But Hróbjartsson and Gøtzsche's collection included an experiment involving patients who, in an antidepressant trial, had recovered on a sham pill. In the follow-up, the placebo responders were continued on placebo or switched to "no treatment." The patients had not been on an antidepressant and so had nothing to withdraw from. If being on a dummy pill had helped them, then staying on it should have kept them stable. It did not. "No treatment" was as good as dummy pills, and both were terrible. Over half of the patients in each group relapsed within six weeks.

What of the trials we have discussed most, drug versus placebo judged via average Hamilton scores? Hróbjartsson and Gøtzsche found only one with a "no treatment" condition.

In the early 1970s, a team of Indian scientists headed by a pioneering public health researcher, Dhirendra Nath Nandi, conducted a door-to-door survey in a rural village in West Bengal. They identified forty-one men and women with depression. None had ever been treated. These Bengalis earned average Hamilton scores just below 30—severe or very severe depression.

Nandi wanted to know whether tribal villagers would respond to antidepressants as urban clinic patients did. Enrolling every depressed person, all forty-one, he put half on a low dose of imipramine (100 milligrams) and a quarter on sugar pills. The remaining depressed patients were followed without treatment.

At two and four weeks the "natural course" group, on no pills, remained virtually unchanged.

In contrast, imipramine was effective. In the group on medicine, average Hamilton scores fell to 19 at week two and 13 (mild depression) at week four. Likely, the average patient on imipramine became a responder, losing half of his or her symptoms even on the low dose of medicine.

For those given sugar pills, the depression ratings dropped to 21 at week two but bounced back up to 27—severe or very severe depression—at week four. In Nandi's words, the patients "went back to more or less the depth of depression found before the administration of placebo." None enjoyed a response or remission.

The Nandi team had told the villagers that they would be taking "well-known" drugs. The procedure was designed to maximize classic placebo effects, yet by the four-week mark, the sugar pills were powerless.

Nandi concluded that rural and urban depressives respond to treatment identically. He made note of the course of response to the sugar pill: quick improvement that faded. If you ask doctors what placebo effects look like, most will describe that pattern, transient early improvement.

Frederic Quitkin, long a member of Donald Klein's team at Columbia, explored this phenomenon. He reported that about a quarter of depressed patients on placebo will experience rapid symptom loss but soon find themselves almost as depressed as they were at the start. The placebo response is quick and transient.

For patients on medication, too, marked early relief may vanish. But patients with the pattern we associate with medication "kicking in"—sharp change from week three on—do fine. One pattern is particular to medication and virtually unseen in the placebo group: improvement at three weeks followed by continued well-being at every subsequent point of observation. Antidepressants are stabilizing.

In my practice, occasional patients will respond quickly to medicine by turning bright and brittle, "putting a good face on it." This posture may be sustainable, if effortful. In a research center, a rater might score the presentation favorably. I see it as an aspect of the ongoing depression—and all the more if a patient cannot build on the response by making fresh efforts in love and work. It's hard to make hay in this cold sun. The antidepressant is failing. We will look elsewhere for help.

Lately, Peter Gøtzsche has become a forceful critic of medication use in the treatment of mental illness. For example, in a *BMJ* essay in 2015, he wrote, "I estimate we could stop almost all psychotropic drugs without causing harm." But regarding antidepressant trials in particular, he has held fast to the conclusion that pill-placebo effects are not in evidence. Writing about John Davis and Robert Gibbons's analysis of response to Prozac and Effexor, Gøtzsche notes, "What we see in a placebo group is not a placebo effect but mainly the spontaneous remission of the disease."

In the past decade, experiments seeking pill-placebo effects in depression have been few and flawed. One interesting small trial, out of UCLA, did find expectancy effects in patients on dummy pills—but not in patients on antidepressants. It was not just a matter of failing to reach statistical significance. In the medication arm of the trial, patients who said that they believed the treatment would not help enjoyed the same results as patients who anticipated great things.

If the analysis is on target, it may be that the more reliably medicines work, the more they arouse expectations that then inflate placebo responses in drug trials; meanwhile, little or none of that benefit transfers to drugs, which do their work on their own. In that case, to the extent that they exist, classic placebo effects, just like psychotherapy effects, are not additive and will cause researchers to understate what medication has to offer. In contrast, doctors like Viola will see clearly. In their clinical work, when they prescribe, they need not worry about missing a potential pill-placebo effect. With antidepressants, there is none.

Similarly for patients: if they attribute their improvement to the medicine—its inherent properties—and the good relationship with their doctor, they will not be mistaken. Spontaneous improvement will play its part as well; from their past experience (before ever taking medicine) of the course of their depression, patients may be able to gauge how much. In its small way, the UCLA study answers Nora's question, whether her recovery is due to her expectations. They make no contribution.

I don't want to put strong emphasis on an incidental finding in a preliminary study. In the end, Hróbjartsson and Gøtzsche's comprehensive survey is what best summarizes research on the classic placebo effect. In the mix of influences—hello and goodbye, time and circumstance, and, yes, uplift from the substantial support, emotional, social, moral, and economic, that clinical trials offer—hope attached to pill taking is at best a minor element.

29

Elaboration

I HAVE MENTIONED the theory that antidepressants restore resilience and permit recovery to proceed. Much of the support for this view comes from animal studies and parallel research on human brains. Depression seems to hamper the brain's ability to generate new nerve cells or elaborate connections between existing ones. Antidepressants reverse these impediments. But how does that renewed flexibility translate into people's becoming "unstuck"? What happens in the person?

For years, the official line was that antidepressants take two to four weeks to bring relief. Clinicians knew better. Kuhn spotted improvements in the first days of treatment. When I prescribed imipramine, I started with tiny doses and inched up to realistic levels; patients might notice nothing for some time. But with drugs such as Zoloft, where the initial dose can be the final, therapeutic dose, patients will report an immediate, if vague, response. The foreboding recedes. They're not slogging through molasses.

Thanks to the work of researchers such as Philip Cowen, an Oxford University psychiatrist, we know now that medications have a quick impact. In an experiment whose results appeared in 2009, Cowen gave either a placebo pill or a half dose of an antidepressant to patients with mild-to-moderate depression. Asked to assess emotional expressions in images of faces, patients on placebo had difficulty recognizing happiness. They were also slow to recall positive events in their lives. Patients on medication recognized happiness and recalled positive events—and the normalization was apparent *three hours* after the administration of the first pill. The early improvement predicted a fuller response down the road.

If their helpful effects can be detected immediately, why do medicines take weeks to calm depression? Cowen finds that antidepressants act right away to correct flawed emotional processing, counteracting negative slants in perception. Long before the depression remits, patients on antidepressants see themselves and their surroundings in a warmer light. Part of what happens next may be social and psychological. Cowen writes:

> According to this view, effects of antidepressants on emotional bias are seen rapidly, but the translation of these changes into improved subjective mood takes time as the patient learns to respond to this new, more positive social and emotional perspective of the world. An increased tendency to interpret social signals as positive may not immediately lead to improved mood but could reinforce social participation and social functioning, which over repeated experience improve mood and the other symptoms of depression.

This psychological sequence may not tell the whole story. Sometimes, antidepressants seem to act directly, ending a bout of illness. Occasional patients follow the "unique" pattern that Fred Quitkin observed. Three weeks in, they feel better abruptly and stay well. And as we shall see, certain medicines still being tested for depression seem to reverse the syndrome in hours or days.

Also, even where our current antidepressants act as catalysts, the change that they bring about goes beyond attitude. The medications induce actual resilience to stress—protecting cells from certain forms of biological injury—and allow for greater possibility of learning. Probably, antidepressants work on two levels, lifting despair and making the brain more responsive.

Either way, there's a multiplier effect. Antidepressants allow the adoption of new beliefs and behaviors, so that the drug action is enhanced by gains in social functioning and the benefit of what often follows, a more supportive environment.

If, sometimes against the evidence, I believe in the special virtues of combined treatment, antidepressants and psychotherapy, it's because when medication breaks the ice, patients become open to insight and productive activity.

Cowen's model raises questions about the "inherent efficacy" of medication. When it works promptly, freeing the brain, has an antidepressant been effective? We may be inclined to say no, not yet. Only if a patient does, in practice, elaborate early change into substantial symptom loss will we give credit.

Recently, researchers have reported that Botox, injected to paralyze frown muscles, can combat depression, especially in patients already on antidepressants. Probably the cure involves neurological feedback—the brain reads the relaxed forehead as an indicator of favorable circumstance. Social responses may play a role, too. People are friendlier to people who look relaxed. We would not applaud the nerve toxin (as an augmenter for antidepressants) if it only smoothed out wrinkles. The subsequent steps must occur and result in mood improvement.

It is not enough for us, then, that antidepressants alter emotional perception. Paradoxically, when we speak of inherent efficacy, inherent means immanent—unpacked, elaborated, present. Changed brain biology is only the beginning of a sequence. The patient's new willingness to phone a friend represents the drug's action. So does the friend's encouraging response. But we measure change only through diminished scores on the Hamilton scale. Analogously, we might give antihypertensives credit only if they prevent stroke; lowering blood pressure is not enough.

This standard (for what counts as inherent efficacy) is exacting, and it explains why the number needed to treat is never as low as we hope. At the level of brain cells, the medicine may do its job, and still we will not arrive at a result we call efficacy.

In this context, the placebo can do harm. Awareness that a study uses dummy pills may induce uncertainty and dissuade patients on active medication from capitalizing on the early improvement. Irving Kirsch has contributed important papers on this subject. Again, to my mind it is in this effort, elaborating the theory of the placebo, that he excels.

In 1993, Kirsch ran an experiment that involved lying to participants. He divided one hundred undergraduates into three groups. To one, he said that everyone would get coffee, the real thing, caffeinated. To another, he promised decaf. Students in the third group learned that they were in a double-blind study and might be given either caf or decaf. Each subject was then served strong coffee, once with and once without caffeine. One outcome measured was tension.

Among those told that they were getting caffeine, regular coffee produced high levels of tension and decaf did nothing.

For those told that they were getting decaf, the tension effect disappeared; even high-test did not give the jitters.

The interesting condition was the one where the students had been told that they were in a controlled trial. Those students, too, felt no rise in tension. When it came to tension, being told that you were in a trial was the equivalent of being told you were on decaf.

This result demonstrates an *instruction effect*. What an experimenter said shaped what subjects experienced. Their awareness that they might be on placebo (decaf) made an outcome based on chemistry and neurobiology—caffeine's inherent ability to arouse tension—disappear.

Kirsch commented that this result cast doubt on the "validity of current double-blind methods." If *instruction*—mere awareness that placebos are in play—matters, drug effects reported in controlled trials may be lower than real inherent drug effects enjoyed by patients treated through their doctor's prescribing.

Instruction's power to mask efficacy has been encapsulated in the coinage *lessebo*, a wince-inducing Teutonic-Latin mash-up that has the virtue of being memorable. According to the word's originators, *lessebo* refers to a reduced medication benefit "because the patient is uncertain as to whether his or her randomly assigned compound is truly active or not." Hopeful expectancy drives the classic placebo effect. With the lessebo effect, the motive force is corrosive doubt.

Researchers first made note of this phenomenon in the 1990s. A 2010 study confirmed that patients in a trial comparing two medications were more likely to respond than patients in a trial comparing one of those medications and placebo. Similar results have been found in the treatment of Parkinson's disease: drug trials with placebos showed lower efficacy. In the face of uncertainty, drug responses are muted.

Doubt is a major topic in psychology today. Studies in behavioral economics, conducted via game playing, show that humans dislike ambiguity. Even when an overall situation is unthreatening, uncertainty activates the amygdala, a part of the brain involved with fear and vigilance. Introduce doubt, and you produce change in the brain and then in perception and behavior.

In the case of depression, we can turn to Cowen's theory of elaboration. A patient takes an antidepressant. Three hours in, he feels stirrings of change. Knowing that he might be on a placebo, he mistrusts the sensation. He does not pick up the phone and so does not receive the encouragement a friend would offer. An instruction or lessebo effect prevents the full expression of the drug's powers, blocking the part that extends beyond the initial change in brain and body.

This point is important conceptually. If recovery from depression depends partly on elaboration of early changes in perspective, and if doubt interferes with elaboration, then placebo-controlled trials (by their nature, because of their design, and regardless of how well they are conducted) will be liable to a confound. They will produce overly conservative—spurious—results. Just as prescribing doctors have no easy way to tease out the influence of hopeful expectancy, so researchers cannot see past lessebo effects. They arise from the structure of these trials—from the use of placebo arms, informed consent, and blinding, which introduce uncertainty and weaken medication responses.

As Austin Bradford Hill warned, strict reliance on randomized trials can cause the field to underestimate the worth of treatments like antidepressants. Studies (like Lisa Ekselius's) that forgo placebos supply a useful counterbalance. Even the clinical setting has its advantages. In a doctor's office, like our imagined Viola's, there is no suggestion that drugs are not drugs. Patients freed up in the early going by antidepressants will think and do things that consolidate those gains. The doctor will take note and refine her estimate of the medications' worth. Her informal observation can serve as a partial corrective to distortions inherent in conventional outcome research.

30

Interlude
Slogging

IT'S NOT THAT my own clinical perspective is rosy. More than once, Freud wondered whether psychoanalysis might be an impossible profession, with unsatisfying results a given. In general-practice psychiatry, we still live with failure.

The sequence I have sketched, restored resilience leading to useful elaboration, occurs often enough. But few patients arrive simply "depressed." Many have depression in the context of paranoia, alcoholism, narcissism, social phobias, or Asperger's syndrome. And then the prospect is less sanguine.

If you have trouble reading social signals and communicating your own intentions, then an uptick in optimism may only lead to more rejection and disappointment. Complex patients have complex brains. One way or another—less restored resilience, less successful elaboration— medication is unreliable in patients with multiple diagnoses. Or perhaps the success is only less apparent. A patient's mood lifts, but impairments remain.

Two conditions related to major depression—psychotic depression and recurrent depression that represents a form of bipolar disorder— are unlikely to respond to antidepressants alone and may worsen in response to them. Those variants cover a lot of territory, which means that we can't always use these helpful tools or we need to employ them sparingly.

The bipolar subtype can be frustrating. Patients will experience severe depression, and the kernel of manic potential that remains active may make their suicidal impulses dangerous. Antidepressants may provide short-term relief but at the risk of inducing mania, the dyscontrol that encompasses impulsivity, euphoria, irritability, contempt, terror, and disastrous bad judgment. Doctors try to prescribe mood stabilizers first and then introduce antidepressants, but with excruciating depression we do not always have the luxury of time. We may feel impelled to act—and sometimes antidepressants simply make these patients worse.

The result is constant fiddling. I will be raising and lowering drug doses and monitoring responses through frequent phone conversations whose content will extend to advice, exhortation, and frank cheerleading. We're trying to avoid disaster.

In my time together with patients, face-to-face, I aim to create a quiet space. My intention is to prevent the enterprise from taking on a frenetic air reflective of aspects of the ailment.

These cases occupy a fair amount of any psychiatrist's mental real estate, which is why we often feel that we've exhausted the available therapeutic resources—why we don't protest the claims that antidepressants are ineffectual.

A tiny fraction of what doctors do finds direct representation in research. I have pointed to problems in candidate-drug trials. They collect an atypical group, needy people with time on their hands and an incentive to exaggerate, along with patients unresponsive to treatment. But even academic studies tend to be selective. They may exclude people with suicidal thoughts, drug-abuse histories, or ongoing depressive episodes that have been too prolonged or too brief. Some of my Brown colleagues interviewed 346 depressed patients in an outpatient practice and determined that, depending on the exclusion criteria, as few as 29 would qualify for entry into an outcome study.

All that the controlled trials with their select patients tell doctors is whether a given antidepressant is a tool suited to our use. It's practical observation that fills in the details.

It would be easy to create a false impression. Most of the clinical day is calm. I will see people who are pessimistic and reclusive. Here, antidepressants' shortcomings will be of a different sort. They will have helped by halves, interrupting, say, an acute episode, but leaving depressive personality traits in place. These patients may bear a heavy burden of history—abuse in childhood, recent losses. Psychotherapy looks like a good expedient, but the pace of change will be deliberate, much as it was when I entered psychiatry.

And then some patients need to come off medication. After six years on an SSRI, good years, years of blissful relief from battering by a recurrent mood disorder, a patient develops a condition that may be a late drug side effect. There are many, each uncommon, each worrisome. Patients have sleep disorders, hormonal disorders, blood-element disorders, movement disorders related to parkinsonism. Is the antidepressant to blame? We will not know, but we will taper it and perhaps not start another.

One patient says, "It's like being forced to move to a country with no electricity. It's not that humans never lived like that, but in our world, it's deprivation—no electricity, and it's not my house that was powered, it's my mind and body." The testimony is to efficacy, now lost. We will return to that time-tested remedy, psychotherapy. We will look to bright lights and daily exercise. All the same, the patient will feel deprived. She may suffer what recurrently depressed people do suffer, painful and disabling episodes.

The difficulties of the daily work make the occasional quick, complete, and lasting responses memorable. Antidepressants provide dabs of light in what remains a gray pointillist canvas.

31

Lowliness

ONE OF THOSE bright spots is work with mild major depression, which tends to do well with what psychiatrists offer, medication and psychotherapy, a wonderful truth, since "mild" is serious enough. The label *major depression* applies only to highly symptomatic episodes—intervals involving more intense suffering, more widespread impairment, than dysthymic patients experience on most days. Even in less severe cases, where some freedom of action remains, depressed patients will be hobbled by apathy, low energy, and dark views of the self and the world.

I think of a stuck writer, a long-form journalist, Maggie. It's not just that she can't make progress on the next chapter. She no longer believes that finishing will make a difference. She can't sit at the computer, is phobic about the office altogether. Research is no easier. She won't pick up the phone, much less travel. The miasma has spread to engulf her day job—teaching at a community college. Nothing matters. Besides, she's worthless.

How depressed is Maggie? She eats and sleeps. She drags herself to campus when she needs to and even attends committee meetings. By the numbers, she barely makes the diagnosis. But the fixed perspective leads her in circles, bumping her up against the same imagined obstacles. Can we be said to be doing psychotherapy?

Within days of taking an antidepressant, Maggie finds that she can approach her desk. She begins answering e-mails, then revising lectures. She turns to her manuscript in progress. Once more, Maggie thinks aloud in front of me, weighing competing means for shaping material. Soon we are on to more abstract issues: commitment, values, and goals. All that had been missing was the whole person. Who was this woman who foresaw only failure?

Before antidepressants—before I gained the courage to prescribe them—mild major depression might go on and on, leaving patients demoralized. I might ask, Didn't you win awards for teaching? In my hands, logical guidance rarely broke the logjam. Medication did.

No one doubts these observations. Antidepressants do well with the lesser forms of major depression. The problem is, placebos do, too, in some research. For all that critics cavil, there's little doubt that doctors should and will use medication to shorten profound depressive episodes. It's about less disabling presentations that serious people disagree.

The notion that antidepressants work best for grave forms of mood disorder is called the *severity hypothesis*. It dates to the earliest days of the psychopharmacologic era, when lesser depression was psychotherapy's domain.

But attempts to subdivide depression—neurotic and vital, psychogenic and biogenic, exogenous and endogenous—failed. Even if it begins in what looks like neurosis, as depression worsens or persists, it accretes symptoms that doctors think of as physical. It is hard to specify a subtype—a cluster of traits—that will not respond to medication.

Roland Kuhn had presumed that imipramine would prove effective for vital (biological) and not reactive (more psychological) depression. But when he prescribed for patients with "caused" depressions—with polio or after a criminal abortion—they responded. In Gerry Klerman and Jonathan Cole's collection of studies, medication did best for outpatients.

The severity hypothesis never died, but in practical terms the newer antidepressants cast it in shadow. Well tolerated, Prozac and Zoloft and the rest were prescribed for every level of illness. Because they mute the debilitating self-consciousness and social anxiety that accompany depression, the medicines were well suited to the lesser variants. Between the existing research and patients' experience, the question of usefulness in mild major depression answered itself.

If some experts retained misgivings, Irving Kirsch was not one of them, not at first. Responding to his "Emperor" paper, the one based on FDA data, readers complained that Kirsch had failed to separate out severe depression. Writing in 2002 and again in 2005, Kirsch replied that there was little reason to believe that efficacy follows severity. He had performed a quick analysis of the FDA studies and "found no relation between severity and antidepressant effect." In a 2003 overview, outpatient trials had shown larger drug benefits than inpatient trials. Kirsch referenced research by NICE, the British clinical-standards institute, in which patients with severe depression proved more responsive than patients with higher (very severe) or lower (moderate) grades of illness.

Depending on the selection of studies, you could find any pattern you pleased: uniform efficacy, more efficacy in severe depression, more in mild depression, or more in the middle.

As for the categories, Kirsch noted inflation in labeling. What was now called severe depression had once been moderate. Antidepressants' best use might be in the treatment of standard, midrange depression—if there was a pattern at all. Of course, Kirsch also argued that, in general, antidepressants' inherent efficacy was minimal.

Kirsch changed his opinion of the severity hypothesis. In 2008, after reanalyzing the FDA files, Kirsch wrote that antidepressants are useful only in very severe depression. Below Hamilton scores of 28, antidepressants no longer met the NICE standard: three points of extra benefit, drug over placebo.

Researchers using the same data but different methods pushed the cut point down to 26 or 24. The vast majority of trials in the FDA collection involved groups with average Hamilton scores of 24 and above, so where the drugs had been tested, they worked. Most patients with Hamilton scores below 24 had taken Serzone.

Severity turns out to be a tough issue to investigate.

Fewer Hamilton factors apply in milder depression. You can't reverse suicidality in someone who's not suicidal. When a medicine helps less ill patients on the *Is life worth living?* front, the scale will not register the change.

When a patient with very severe depression recovers fully, he can lose 25 or 30 Hamilton points. In a comparable trial of mild major depression, a patient who wipes the slate clean can contribute only, say, 12 points. Each patient who remits contributes little to the average number of points lost per patient.

The term of art for this problem is *floor effect*. When you start near the floor, you can't make great leaps down. For medications, like antidepressants, that bring strong benefits to certain individuals (rather than minor benefits to many), floor effects cause underestimates of the efficacy in the treatment of less ill patients.

One way to avoid this distortion is to look at categories. For instance, in each group how many people lose half their symptoms? That's what regulators from Sweden, England, France, and Holland did. Stung by critiques of trials submitted to the FDA, the Europeans reanalyzed all the data in their files, which were more complete and detailed than the FDA's.

Response rates were uniform. "There was no evidence of a diminishing magnitude of effect with lower severity at baseline," the regulators noted. "The responder criterion is a relative measure, and thus floor effects, which might contribute to the diminishing effect size observed with lower average [Hamilton] score at baseline, are avoided."

John Krystal's analysis of trajectories came from studies of patients with average Hamiltons of 20, typical in outpatient clinics. Krystal demonstrated important benefits for patients who, at the start of treatment, were nothing like severely depressed.

Using the same studies of Prozac, Paxil, Lexapro, and Cymbalta, Krystal asked about melancholic depression, in which patients experience impairment in energy, sleep, and appetite. Unexpectedly, nonmelancholic patients (with depressions that look less physiological) proved likelier, on medication, to enter a favorable trajectory. That's what clinical experience—what my experience—shows: antidepressants start neurotically depressed patients in the right direction.

To my mind, these explorations—of response, trajectory, and depression subtype—provide adequate answers to Kirsch's challenge. The apparent pattern, less efficacy for milder depression, reflects floor effects. Once you take into account how antidepressants work, holding some patients back and helping others a lot, then in data much like the FDA's, medications prove effective across the board.

The severity hypothesis looks like the antidepressant controversy overall—less worrisome once you consider people, rather than averages. But there remained a big problem with this debate, centered on drug-agency data. Hoping to keep placebo responses manageable, Pharma had run tests on very sick patients. With rare exceptions, trials excluded people with mild major depression. Conclusions about them were based on extrapolation, the extension of lines on graphs, guesswork.

Once again, Kirsch had set an agenda—putting the severity hypothesis back in play. His challenge made researchers hungry to look at files of individual patients, especially patients with lesser forms of major depression—and in more thoughtful trials, not ones run by drug companies to satisfy regulators.

32

Washout

THERE WERE TWO such studies. One, published in 2010, found that antidepressants work only for severe depression. The other, appearing two years later, found that they work well for mild-to-moderate major depression. The first study received extensive publicity. The second— we will turn to it in the next chapter—received none.

Again, we need to know. With antidepressants, primary-care doctors do most of the prescribing. They see less severe illness. Should they back off? Or does the growth of depression treatment in general practice count as an achievement for public health?

If you have doubts, likely they can be traced to one publication, a meta-analysis by the Penn-Vanderbilt group who had shown that Paxil mutes depressed patients' neuroticism. This team is highly accomplished. As befits the topic's and the authors' importance, their confirmation of the severity hypothesis received marquee publication, in *JAMA*. *USA Today* covered the report under the headline "Antidepressant Lift May Be All in Your Head." *The New York Times* led with "Popular Drugs May Help Only Severe Depression." When I spoke with my friend Alan's neurologist, the concerns he expressed contained echoes of the *JAMA* paper.

To settle the severity debate, the Penn-Vanderbilt group conducted a patient-by-patient analysis of a carefully curated set of data from out-side the FDA collection. They concluded that antidepressants' benefits are "substantial" for those with severe depression but "minimal or non-existent, on average, in patients with mild or moderate symptoms."

To evaluate that finding, we need to understand an additional ele-ment in the design of outcome trials. In most drug studies, after pa-tients sign on they get placebo for a week. Participants who improve markedly are dropped, and the real drug trial begins.

The "washout" or "run-in" phase addresses any number of problems. For our purposes—seeing whether medicine helps in mild depression—the important consideration is that washouts may counteract a highly distorting tendency in outcome trials, baseline score inflation.

Let's recall what happens. If raters have a sense of the minimum Hamilton score for admission to a study, and if they are under pressure to fill an enrollment quota, they will be inclined to tack on question-able Hamilton points. The boost will not be uniform. There's no need to raise ratings in the very ill. Scores for least afflicted participants will be most inflated.

If drug companies demand a Hamilton of 17 for entry, they will see many patients with scores of 17, 18, and 19. The rest of the ratings distribution may be unremarkable. This distortion has been noted even in trials run at centers like UCLA and Harvard. When off-site raters, with no stake in the pace of enrollment, analyze tapes of admission interviews, they find patients to be much healthier than the on-site Hamilton scores suggest. According to off-site assessments, many pa-tients admitted to drug studies simply are not depressed.

Baseline score inflation has various meanings. In my use, it stands for the bunching of scores near the entry level—low severity—of any trial. Arif Khan identified the pattern in fifty-one drug-company studies testing ten antidepressants. He concluded that raters "may arbitrarily assign minimally qualifying initial scores to borderline subjects to in-crease enrollment (baseline score inflation)." Similar distortions have been found in research on dementia and Tourette syndrome.

Without a run-in phase, the less ill patients whose scores have been inflated will go on to lose—that is, seem to lose—symptoms they never really had. Since placebo will "succeed" with these participants, even potent antidepressants will have trouble competing in the low range.

Because of this distortion, trials without washouts will be especially likely to find a severity gradient—less efficacy in mild depression—even where (in the real world, when patients are judged accurately) there is none.

That said, the *JAMA* authors mistrusted placebo washouts. Use them, and you dismiss the best placebo responders, the ones who, on pills, get better immediately. Without run-ins, a protocol mimics what happens if, at a first meeting, a doctor prescribes an antidepressant. In their own clinical research, the Penn-Vanderbilt team ran trials without washouts.

The Penn-Vanderbilt researchers investigated the severity hypothesis by gathering studies like their own. They amassed more than two thousand citations of randomized medication trials for depression. They eliminated those with placebo washouts. They eliminated studies of dysthymia. They eliminated trials where they could not obtain patient-by-patient data.

Six trials met the criteria. Three tested imipramine, and three, Paxil.

To my reading the collection was problematic. In it, some patients with moderate depression had received low doses of medication. Most patients at the mild end of the spectrum did not even have major depression. So, yes, in this idiosyncratic batch of research, medication might work best in severe illness, but because the dosing and diagnosing were uneven, the question of what standard drug treatment would do in nonsevere major depression remained open. Even this material contained indications that it might work well.

Certainly, the three imipramine studies were mismatched, and in ways that will be familiar to us.

The most straightforward trial tested severe depression and aimed to get patients on 200 milligrams of imipramine, a substantial dose. They benefited.

Next came our constant companion, the NIMH collaborative study. Whether it should be considered a drug trial is a matter for discussion, but the Penn-Vanderbilt researchers worked hard to use the material well. To make results comparable to those in standard studies, they relied on outcomes midway through the experiment, at the eight-week mark, and they included data from all participants. One researcher assured me that the team had checked for "dose skewing"—did healthier patients receive less medication?—and found none. That analysis remains unpublished, and given Donald Klein's concern ("It is quite possible the milder patients received ineffective, small doses"), it is hard not to wish for transparency about whether and when in the eight weeks patients with different levels of depression received plausible drug treatment.

But the real problem is with the third trial. Seemingly designed to showcase Saint-John's-wort, the herbal remedy for mood disorder, it used imipramine as a comparator. The imipramine was given at 100 milligrams, which the study's own authors acknowledged to be below the "recommended mean dosage for efficacy" and arguably "suboptimal." Imipramine succeeded, just barely, as a benchmark—but only if you made a slight adjustment to the Hamilton scale.

The participants in the Saint-John's-wort study had moderate levels of depression, so it was not surprising that the *JAMA* analysis would find poor outcomes in that range. By including results from patients on 100 milligrams of imipramine, the meta-analysis, which set out to test the severity hypothesis, seemed to have put a different question into play: whether depression responds best to full, recommended doses of medication.

The three Paxil studies only added complexity. Two were the Penn-Vanderbilt team's own. In all, the *JAMA* meta-analysis involved 307 patients from Penn-Vanderbilt trials and 411 from the rest of the research universe. Criticizing review articles, Gene Glass had complained that authors who define "adequate design" narrowly end up highlighting their own work. Perhaps meta-analysis is not immune to that tendency.

One Penn-Vanderbilt team trial tested two psychotherapies for depression and used Paxil as a comparator. Despite high dropout rates in the Paxil arm (apparently volunteers wanted psychotherapy), the drug outperformed placebo, but with better efficacy in more severe cases. The other of the team's trials involved only patients with severe depression, and Paxil had worked there, too, with a number needed to treat of 4. Those results were known in advance, prior to the development of the criteria for the *JAMA* meta-analysis. More symptomatic depression had a leg up before scores from any other doctors' patients were added in.

The third Paxil trial, one of those quirky small studies that carry their own interest, had the greatest potential to cause trouble. Conducted at Dartmouth and other sites, it tested a psychotherapy focused on problem solving and included medication and placebo arms. Here's the rub: the trial *excluded all cases of major depression.*

The Dartmouth team was investigating whether medication works for "minor depression." To meet the diagnosis, patients needed to have three or four symptoms from the list that includes sadness, difficulty experiencing pleasure, insomnia, and so on. Major depression requires between five and nine symptoms.

Looking at all the patients in the Dartmouth trial—patients with three or four depressive symptoms—the researchers found good responses to Paxil. The number needed to treat ran between 4 and 5. Quite low-level depression (depression yet milder than the mildest major depression) responded to medication about as well as severe major depression does. The Paxil data seemed to disprove the severity hypothesis or cast it in grave doubt.

The story would end here but for the way that minor depression is defined.

"Major depression" encompasses both acute and chronic cases. You may be in your first, brief episode, or you may be in a prolonged episode preceded by many like it—either way, if you have the required five symptoms, you have the diagnosis.

Minor depression is different. If the disorder is chronic or recurrent, it's called dysthymia—or was in the late 1990s, when the Dartmouth group did their diagnosing. In their protocol, dysthymia was considered first. If you had chronic low-level depression, you were dysthymic. If your low-level depression was not chronic, you had minor depression.

In drug trials, chronic depression tends not to respond to placebo, so drug effects show through. Most of the patients in the Dartmouth study had dysthymia. They did phenomenally well on Paxil. The remission rate—full recovery—was 80 percent, with a number needed to treat of 3. Chronic minor depression appears to be what Paxil treats *best.*

The *JAMA* analysis included only the remaining patients, those with (acute) minor depression. Paxil did not appear to work—but that's because the dysthymic patients, for whom Paxil was curative, were missing.

Because in the *JAMA* sample severe depression was often chronic depression and mild depression generally was not, it was clear, before running any numbers, that the weakest antidepressant effects would appear in patients who began with low Hamilton scores. We would expect that trend even if antidepressants work equally well up and down the line—as, in fact, they appear to do when we approach minor depression the way we do major depression, including all illness, acute and chronic.

The focus on washouts begins to look like a fetish, one that comes at a cost: the bias that arises from reliance on trials with high dropout rates, uneven prescribing, and a lack of uniformity in diagnosis.

As for minor depression, the Dartmouth study contained hints that Paxil helps after all. Using ratings like those employed in quality-of-life studies, the researchers tracked overall mental health. On that measure, the most impaired patients—those for whom the minor depression caused serious difficulty in thought and action—made gains on medication relative to placebo, and at a statistically significant level.

For mildly depressed patients who were actually doing poorly, then, Paxil provided relief that the Hamilton scale failed to pick up. As an approach to brief, minor depression, watchful waiting might be a reasonable strategy; where suffering impairs function, Paxil might be the preferred next step. This clinically relevant information disappears in the maw of meta-analysis.

Where should doctors seek guidance?

The individual trials appear informative. In all but one, the antidepressant succeeded in its assigned role, as comparator or as primary treatment. (In the Saint-John's-wort study, imipramine tested out better if you excluded one Hamilton item, "somatic anxiety"; apparently the raters had mistaken drug side effects, such as indigestion, for depression symptoms.)

Paxil is broadly effective. In severe and very severe depression, it sports a number needed to treat of 4. In dysthymia, 3. For patients impaired by brief, minor depression, Paxil brings quality-of-life benefits.

Meanwhile, imipramine soldiers on. Moderate doses treat grave depression. Even a suboptimal dose can serve, more or less, to validate a sample of patients with midrange illness.

That's before we take into account baseline score inflation, which can create a gradient of results even when, in reality, antidepressants work equally well everywhere.

The *JAMA* meta-analysis is no smoking gun—hardly the sort of evidence that would convince a doctor that when his less depressed patients do well on antidepressants, he is seeing placebo effects. To me, the paper illustrates a different moral: not to rely on a meta-analysis until you've perused the constituent trials.

Here, their lessons run counter to the thrust of the overview paper. They are: Ask about impairment. Yes, patients with severe symptoms may do well on antidepressants. But so will patients with chronic mood disorders and patients (whatever the symptom count) hobbled by hard-to-measure effects of illness. Where it impacts quality of life, depression tends to respond to medication. If low doses don't work, try full ones.

33

All Comers

CHARACTERIZING MILD MAJOR depression, I mentioned Maggie, who could barely drag herself to work until medication restored her morale. I think equally of Josh, whose chief complaint was a dulling of thought. After a minor business setback, one that should hardly have derailed him, he found himself unable to analyze alternatives or make choices. He had never before been in this state.

Psychotherapy with a psychologist whose work I admire had reached a standstill. But an antidepressant, Lexapro, lifted the impediment, and in short order.

These stories, Maggie's and Josh's, are among the commonest in psychiatry and, for that matter, in all of medicine. The *JAMA* paper's conclusion—minimal antidepressant efficacy in mild and moderate depression—is contrary to clinical experience. That meta-analysis, so particular in its inclusion criteria, should have left the field and the media hungry for a contrasting overview, one built around patients with mild-to-moderate major depression. Ideally, the research would test adequate doses of medication. Ideally, the enrollment design would encourage honesty and accuracy.

That study exists. In 2012, in the wake of the *JAMA* paper, researchers at the New York State Psychiatric Institute, mostly Columbia

University faculty, looked at thirty-two years' worth of research from the hospital's depression-evaluation service, where Donald Klein and Fred Quitkin, pioneers in outcome assessment, had worked.

Sifting through records on 1,440 patients, the Columbia group located 825 with nonsevere major depression, more patients in the relevant range than there were patients altogether in the *JAMA* collection. The average initial Hamilton score was below 14—mild. The files came from six randomized trials, testing four types of antidepressant, all in adequate doses. Imipramine was the drug most often tested, typically at 200 to 300 milligrams—realistic prescribing. Except that the trial designs included a run-in phase, this overview contained the research that the *JAMA* team had been seeking.

Here's the beauty part: In their entry criteria, five of the six studies had no lower limit to the Hamilton score—none—and no minimum symptom number. All were welcome. The sixth study, like the Dartmouth paper in the *JAMA* collection, required a Hamilton score of 10, what NICE called "subthreshold" depression. The Columbia researchers noted, "Clinicians should have had no incentive to apply diagnostic criteria loosely or inflate entry [Hamilton] scores."

Where baseline score inflation is not at issue, how do antidepressants measure up in the treatment of mild-to-moderate major depression? They work well. In trials that used the standard Hamilton scale, drug outperformed placebo with an effect size just over 0.5, medium. Looking at response rates, the number needed to treat was 4. On medication, typical patients ended up in remission, or close to it.

The Columbia meta-analysis has two important weaknesses.

Only forty-nine patients were on an SSRI—Prozac, at a high dose. This limitation is serious. But in head-to-head tests, SSRIs match imipramine, and the field has always believed that if imipramine outperforms the SSRIs anywhere, it is in the treatment of severe depression. SSRIs test out especially well with dysthymia. They mute neuroticism. They may affect people with no mood disorder at all. If other antidepressants treat mild-to-moderate major depression, almost certainly SSRIs do, too.

The second shortcoming—in some regards, it is a strength—is that the Columbia studies come from a single site, an urban university clinic. The trials tended to draw on a different population from the one recruited by drug-testing mills. Most had at least part-time jobs or sporadic employment and some college education. Patients might get vouchers for travel, but there was no van. And the experiment has the virtue of completeness. All relevant trials are included.

The central result is so strong that the severity hypothesis becomes moot. If antidepressants work yet better in sicker patients, then bless us all. But it may be that medication effects are uniform. In the Penn-Vanderbilt analysis, the number needed to treat for "very severe" depression was 4 or 5, effectively the same as the result for mild-to-moderate depression here. And we know that dysthymia responds at that level.

The Columbia results suggest that the problems we have been discussing—baseline score inflation, inadequate dosing, and inconsistencies in diagnosis—are substantial. Avoid the confounds, and uniform treatment effects emerge.

When the Columbia study appeared, no headlines read "Popular Drugs May Help in Mild-to-Moderate Depression" or "Antidepressant Lift Not All in Your Head." Yet, if one possible conclusion—no utility for most patients—is important, then so is the other: medications are broadly effective.

It would be nice if other studies of this type existed—university-based trials testing Zoloft, Lexapro, and the rest, studies where, at entry, patients' level of depression does not matter, studies that avoid baseline score inflation, studies that give us a shot at understanding whether low levels of depression respond to medication. If you think about it, we have heard mention of another sort of research that takes on all comers—in the discussion of my friend Alan and the usefulness of antidepressants for stroke survivors. There, everyone who suffers a certain sort of brain injury is invited to sign on. Patients don't need to be depressed to participate. No one, patient or staff, has an incentive to exaggerate mood symptoms.

With Alan, my concern was motor function, which is why I had searched for the *Lancet: Neurology* study. On Prozac, stroke victims recovered more arm and leg movement. But the French neurologists also tracked symptoms of depression. Compared to patients given Prozac, those on placebo were four times as likely to develop depression. The antidepressant dose was the standard one, 20 milligrams of Prozac. In the medication group, the average change in the depression rating over three months was zero—no new symptoms, despite the stroke. (A few patients gained enough symptoms to qualify for a diagnosis of depression, but many more patients lost whatever depressive symptoms they had arrived with.) Patients on placebo proved much more vulnerable.

These outcomes speak against the severity hypothesis. At entry, the average patient did not qualify as depressed. Medication helped at the lowest severity—no depression.

The stroke study is typical. If we look beyond psychiatry to fields such as neurology and cardiology, in numerous outcome trials the patients are real and we take them as they are. The ticket in is an affliction, like coronary artery disease, that has a strong association with depression.

In a similar category is research on a medicine, interferon, used to treat infectious diseases (often hepatitis) and certain cancers. Interferon tends to cause depression. Antidepressants can prevent that development or interrupt it just as it emerges. Most interferon trials take on all comers—people with and without depression. There's no incentive to exaggerate symptoms.

This research is important in its own right. In the face of medical illness, depression is destructive. To return to stroke for a moment: Think of two groups of patients, those who are depressed in the wake of a stroke and those who are not. Ten years later, more than three times as many in the first group will be dead. In life, patients with poststroke depression fail at "activities of daily living," such as dressing themselves. They demonstrate more cognitive impairment, like problems with memory, than would be expected based on their brain injury. They are less likely to return to work. Even when the depression does not persist, the disability does.

And depression is common in stroke survivors. In the early weeks following the brain injury, a third of the patients will be depressed. Over a five-year period, half of stroke survivors will suffer depression. Once it appears, the depression tends to continue or recur.

Even after antidepressants had come to be widely prescribed, neurologists were cautious about using them in stroke patients. The risks were substantial—seizures, falls, delirium, and perhaps even bleeding and further damage to the brain—and any harm caused by stroke might prove unchangeable, not subject to influence through medication. But the need was great, so doctors undertook the research. On antidepressants, patients had less depression and better brain health overall.

A similar story appears repeatedly in what is called psychosomatics, the study of the overlap between disorders of body and mind: urgent need, substantial risk, tentative research—and then the discovery of widespread benefits from antidepressants.

To generalize about a large literature: In trials where depression is not required for entry, the average patient arrives with mild or no depression. On medicine, patients who start with symptoms tend to lose them. For those who begin free of depression, antidepressants prove protective. Three, four, or five times as many patients on placebo will enter a new episode of depression. When patients on placebo become depressed, the prompt initiation of antidepressants (the intervention is called *rescue*) ends the emerging episode. Often, what is at issue are "first depressions," bouts of mood disorder in people who have never before had one.

The antidepressant controversy tends not to encompass these studies because psychosomatics is complex. For instance, SSRIs can act as blood thinners, enhancing heart health. Antidepressants may confer flexibility and resilience in the brain in ways that are only marginally related to depression. Perhaps medication succeeds with cardiac and neurologic patients for incidental reasons—because, mood effects (and side effects) aside, antidepressants protect body organs. As for interferon-induced depression, despite the similar list of symptoms, it may not be identical to run-of-the-mill, wear-and-tear, genetics-and-adversity depression. And preliminary evidence suggests that Prozac can enhance the antiviral effects of interferon—so fighting depression may not be the only action at issue. There's a lot to debate.

Still, these studies are of high quality. The patients are real and unselected—all comers to a stroke ward or cardiac catheterization lab or (with interferon) hepatitis or cancer clinic. No one's scouring single-room-occupancy hotels to corral candidates. The placebo conditions are vigorous, with everyone necessarily getting extensive medical attention. The targets for treatment include episodes of depression caught at the outset, as patients on interferon or placebo pills accumulate mood symptoms. SSRIs are the antidepressants most often used. They do not—at all—look like medicines that fail in the face of mild or acute illness.

Instead, it's the severity hypothesis that fails. The most plausible studies, the ones likeliest to enroll real patients, contradict it. Cast a broad net, and you find that in experimental settings, antidepressants act as they do in clinical settings, helping patients with a wide range of conditions.

34

Interlude
Cotherapy

THAT'S MY EXPERIENCE. I find antidepressants useful up and down the line. I have never had much truck with the distinctions the field has lived with: major depression, dysthymia, minor depression—and there are others.

For fifteen years, starting in the 1980s, I taught an introductory psychotherapy course for beginning psychiatry residents at Brown. For each meeting, as reading I assigned a case vignette—a description of interactions between a doctor and a patient—excerpted from a textbook on one or another school of therapy. In class, we reasoned back from practice to theory. What can we deduce about the account of mind that informs the treatment?

I fantasize about doing something parallel for my own work—sifting through old charts, rethinking sessions, in hopes of getting outside myself and pinpointing what drives me. When it comes to prescribing, I'm guessing that I'd find that it's *worry*.

Severe depression worries me. Patients risk losing their jobs and alienating loved ones. There's suicide to guard against, and concern about injury to brain, heart, glands, and the rest. I hope to display calm, but I'm in a rush.

Since the days of Ray Osheroff, it's been malpractice to let overwhelming depression fester. I throw the kitchen sink at it: antidepressants, yes, but also psychotherapy and bright lights, along with less proven remedies like exercise, vitamins, and fish oil. In the acute phase, I may move to multiple medications.

I'm not focused on numbers needed to treat. The patient and I will try this and that until we find a way through. We'll speak daily. I'll enroll family members. I may consult with colleagues. I'm reasonably confident that my patient will make progress—confident about prognosis, if we can get through the here and now. There are utterly untreatable depressions—but today, few.

My judgment about what demands assertive treatment does not rely on symptom counts.

I think of a patient, Troy, who sought no care for a bout of depression that led him to questionable decisions in his work life, kicking over the traces, jettisoning stressors. He wanted to be free, free to ruin his career if he chose. In one sense, he was right about delaying treatment: his depression resolved spontaneously. Only then did he consult me, at a friend's insistence. Over the years, I had run into Troy at public gatherings, and now, in my office, I could see a difference. He had been left with impaired concentration and a reclusive social style. I guessed that the residual state was "physical," or "brain based." I insisted on medication. I had noted only the two symptoms, but the picture was concerning. On antidepressants (and the kitchen sink), Troy emerged himself again. He reengaged, apologetically, with colleagues he had alienated.

Experiences such as this one make me mistrust symptom scores and value empathetic assessment. Randomized trials are good at counting. Practicing doctors are good at looking and feeling. Some "mild depression" is severe.

In tough cases, the decision to prescribe is easy. With more indolent depression, I like to give psychotherapy time, and here's where worry earns its keep. In a treatment that's seemed routine, I'll find myself newly uncomfortable, in session or after hours. The mood's too fixed, the lack of motivation too paralyzing, the self-doubt too corrosive, the obsession too consuming. Like Miss Clavel in *Madeline*, I wake in the night. Something is not right.

Years after a divorce that threw Olivia into prolonged depression, she allows herself to be coaxed into dating again. The new boyfriend,

Lyle, is a less successful, less imaginative colleague in her line of work. Contempt allows her to enter the relationship. Lightly committed, she will not be hurt. The problem is boredom. Olivia considers the timing of a breakup and the means. How can she let Lyle down gently?

Disengagement proves difficult. Lyle displays a depth of attachment that Olivia had not reckoned with. Unexpectedly, she is charmed after all. At the moment of Olivia's drawing near, Lyle breaks it off abruptly, decisively. He had imagined she would treat him better. He confesses to thoughts of joining someone, a specific someone, who will.

Olivia enters a state of diminishment. The constant feature is rumination about Lyle. How could he encourage her return to openness and then do her harm? In session, she is in tears.

The sequence cries out for psychotherapy, connecting the current abandonment to the prior divorce and, before it, the loss of her mother in Olivia's childhood. But Olivia scarcely has the resources to participate in conversation. She recycles recriminations against herself.

Olivia does not recall her ambivalence and condescension toward Lyle. In her memory, she was always adoring. She focuses on failures of strategy and execution: If only she had been—*something*—more open about her feelings, or more controlled. The topics I think need discussing—narcissism, mistrust, the fear of being unlovable—are never in the mix. Instead, Olivia ruminates over her word choice in minutely recollected conversations. She weeps.

Some psychologists would call Olivia's suffering grief. Others would reference a post-traumatic state. Depression is near enough.

Olivia complains that her friends misremember the course of the relationship. They seem to be pulling back from her, losing sympathy. How disastrous, I think, if she drives them away. Olivia is doing less well at work, too, but the pending social catastrophe—what if she loses her friends' support?—is what troubles my sleep.

Once in Paris, I met the editor of a book series called *Les empêcheurs de penser en rond*, "preventives for circular thinking." That is the effect I seek.

I turn to medication. Ruminative depression is where SSRIs excel. Lately, colleagues have suggested—I am agnostic, but I do not dismiss the claim—that weepiness is a useful marker. Antidepressants interrupt tearful episodes.

On Zoloft, Olivia is bereft but not consumed by loss. She can bear to encounter Lyle's friends. She can read a book.

Would I prefer that Olivia turn better than well? Some patients do. Olivia's response is favorable enough: we can talk again.

Often, I refer to antidepressants as cotherapists. They're the good cop to my bad. Zoloft provides calm, and a new freedom to explore. I gesture toward a difficult possibility: It's the humiliation that hurts, more than lost love. How could that jerk—so beneath her!—blow her off? Olivia considers. Doubts about Lyle filter back into memory. Friends express relief at Olivia's restored perspective.

I have no intention of keeping Olivia on medicine. I'm hoping for some months of stability and then a chance to taper. I would love a change in circumstance—the beginnings of a less defensive choice in romance. Perhaps we can come to see the time with Lyle as helpful, a good start in the renewed effort to let men in. The contretemps contains lessons about what relationships require.

As for Olivia's early progress: Was she moderately depressed? Has she "responded"?

I have no notion. Zoloft eases my worry. I can see a way back for Olivia.

Lots of doctors assess medications this way, and I think rightly so. The formal literature says—in some general sense, without precision about efficacy—that a drug works. In prescribing, we see how, according to our own needs, our needs for our patients.

I've harped on the response rate that Lisa Ekselius recorded for patients given antidepressants in primary-care practices: 90 percent of the great majority who follow through with treatment, with good results for 75 percent and more of those who start the drugs. They make dealing with mood disorders vastly easier, through the factors that Per Bech points to: improved mood, self-regard, and competence.

Antidepressants are handy tools. Because they potentiate psychotherapy, depression has become highly treatable. What appears useful is the whole package: medication, psychotherapy, and elaboration in the world.

35

How We're Doing

WHAT DO WE make of what psychiatrists provide? I mean, fiddling with drug doses, listening, interpreting, everything? Increasingly, researchers have tried to measure the benefits of expert care. We'll look at this effort from two angles, two takes on how psychiatry contributes to depression treatment.

One line of inquiry concerns psychosomatics. Depression is a common accompaniment to other illness, and public health advocates and cost cutters are intent on treating psychiatric disorders in medical settings. The result has been research on what is called collaborative care.

For example, the COPES project (for Coronary Psychosocial Evaluation Studies—run at Columbia University and elsewhere) asked whether improved psychiatric treatment makes a difference for depressed patients with heart disease. The program—it began in 2005—targeted patients who had suffered a recent heart attack or were experiencing unstable angina, pain that signals reduced blood flow to the heart. Those conditions put patients at high risk of further deterioration or death.

Discussing psychosomatics, we have considered research that takes on all comers. The COPES group used a different approach. They enrolled patients and then waited three months. Only those with persistent heart disease and persistent depression entered the experiment. The run-in guaranteed that everyone had real mood disorder, generally mild-to-moderate depression.

The cardiac patients came as they were, a few already in psychotherapy, a few more on antidepressants. The researchers randomized participants into two groups. One continued to receive their usual medical care. The other got enhanced treatment, either psychotherapy (focused on problem solving) or antidepressants administered by experts. The patients chose.

The researchers also followed a group of similar cardiac patients who were not depressed. There were almost 240 participants in all.

Periodically, patients in the enhanced-care group underwent reassessment. If they were not doing well, they could switch to a different intervention or add one—pharmacotherapy or, for those not yet in it, psychotherapy. The question was whether psychiatric care, done to an acceptable standard, matters.

In their usual care (the control condition), cardiac patients got plenty of assessment, attention, and pills. The grab-bag elements were present.

Over six months, collaborative care yielded an effect size of 0.6, medium-plus. With depressed cardiac patients who are already in good hands, more systematic treatment brings improvements at a level rivaling any found in the mental health arena.

The researchers also tracked "major adverse cardiac events," such as recurrent heart attacks. The attentively treated group had significantly fewer. Ten adverse events occurred in depressed patients receiving "usual care," five in the never-depressed group, and three in the group given enhanced psychiatric care. Yes, there was the usual confound: two of the five antidepressants offered were ones that may protect the heart. Still, treating eighty people for six months appeared to spare them seven major cardiac events, a level of benefit that, if it held up, would rival results for any known preventive cardiac intervention.

Comparable outcomes have been found from collaborative care for stroke survivors, women attending obstetrics and gynecology clinics, and less select groups: the elderly, adolescents, and primary-care-clinic patients. Some of these trials omit psychotherapy and offer more attentive pharmacology, on its own, as the experimental condition. The largest body of evidence, for diabetic patients, shows that the benefits of enhanced psychiatric attention begin with decreased depression and extend to better control of blood sugar.

These trials are not perfect—they can hardly be double-blind—but most have the advantage of inclusiveness, attracting a range of patients, many new to mental health care. In the treatment efforts, antidepressants play a prominent role. If they didn't work—and if skilled fiddling with them made no difference—the trials could hardly show efficacy.

Researchers have used a different approach to evaluate psychiatrists' care for their more customary patients, hard-to-treat depressives. Two large, lengthy studies, beginning in 2001 and 2002, have looked at prescribing and, to a lesser degree, psychotherapy, offered in ways that resemble what doctors provide in their offices.

The better-known effort is called STAR*D, Sequenced Treatment Alternatives to Relieve Depression. The trial was not controlled, a downside that had its good points. Depressed patients, recruited in primary-care and psychiatry clinics, could sign on with confidence that they'd get a proven treatment. Those with additional psychiatric or medical disorders were welcome. The intent was to attract a range of patients.

Only the sickest came. For nearly 80 percent of the participants (more than twenty-eight hundred were tested), the disorder was chronic. The average length of the *current* depressive episode was over two years, generally despite attempts at treatment. The average enrollee had lived with depression on and off for over fifteen years and was now in a seventh episode. Most patients were alcoholic or had other forms of mental illness. The average Hamilton score at entry was 22, moderate depression or, in the inflated nomenclature Kirsch criticized, "severe." STAR*D showed how psychiatry does with its failures.

In the first phase, patients were put on Celexa, managed by their own doctors. About 30 percent of patients achieved remission within weeks—virtually no symptoms. Responses (including remissions) ran at just under 50 percent.

Commentators considered this outcome disappointing, but is it? A decade and a half into a career of depression, during an episode that's lasted two years despite treatment, medically complex, sometimes alcoholic patients have a fifty-fifty chance of responding to the first drug they're offered. Does any specialty do better with its difficult cases?

It's unlikely that classic placebo effects played a role: these patients had failed on all sorts of pills. Effectively, what was being tested was enhanced care—adequate medication doses in a supportive environment.

In later phases of STAR*D, patients were offered different or additional medicines or psychotherapy. If they stuck with the trial, almost 70 percent of these difficult patients remitted—but the dropout rates were astronomical, and often patients who improved then relapsed. The patients who had been sickest at the start were likeliest to remain depressed.

Psychiatry was divided about the meaning of these results. While many patients remained symptomatic, the pace of STAR*D was deliberate, the treatments were not aggressive, and even so, with the first or second medication used, most participants emerged from depression. Participants who entered with months or years of mood disorder mostly responded within weeks, a sign, in my view, that psychiatric care can make an important difference.

Although STAR*D was more flexible than typical drug trials, it left room for a more interesting inquiry. What if psychiatrists are left to their own devices? Can they do better?

Here's where fascinating, underreported—and misreported—research from the same era comes in. The Penn-Vanderbilt team, joined by doctors at Rush, in Chicago, undertook a study of vigorous prescribing. Experienced pharmacologists were invited to push depressed patients hard, using any medication or combination of medications, and get them into remission. Jan Fawcett, who had helped design the NIMH collaborative trial and is now in his eighties, oversaw the prescribing.

Besides antidepressants, half of the patients (there were 452 in all) received intensive cognitive psychotherapy of a sort that, in prior research, had proved highly effective with depression. In the new study, psychotherapy would continue, sometimes twice weekly, for eighteen months or until patients' symptoms disappeared.

Once patients had enjoyed four weeks in remission (or substantial responses just shy of it), doctors worked to get them to recovery—six more good months. Because it focused on remission and recovery, I think of this trial as the R&R study.

The treatment was insistent. If a patient was already on an antidepressant, the pharmacologists raised it quickly to its upper limit. They waited only briefly for signs of progress. If none appeared, the doctors added a second medication or tapered the drug and chose a different one.

Not all the details have appeared in print, but between one article and a series of conference presentations, an overview has emerged. As in the STAR*D study, the patients were challenging, with severe or chronic depression, sometimes in conjunction with other conditions. As in STAR*D, the average starting Hamilton score was 22.

In R&R, the remedies used were diverse. Often, patients ended up on two or three drugs, including augmenters, like thyroid and lithium. Some patients needed antipsychotic medications. A few did well with older antidepressants, like imipramine. A handful responded to amphetamine or medicines like Valium, often in combination with conventional antidepressants. But many patients remitted on a single antidepressant. Selection and (full) dosage appeared to be important.

By the eighteen-month mark, about 80 percent of those who *started* the trial had made it to some level of remission. Many had gotten there much earlier. Almost everyone who remitted also stayed well for six months or more.

Psychotherapy played a limited role. In the R&R study, when 77 percent of patients remitted on medication, combined treatment pulled that figure up only to 80 percent. On its own, in prior research, perhaps with less ill patients, that same cognitive therapy had achieved a 40 percent remission rate in sixteen weeks. The R&R study stands as further evidence that the effects of psychotherapy and antidepressant medication are not additive. For symptom relief, most of what medication and talk accomplish together can be done by medication alone.

The press gave a blindered view of the R&R results. Most reports focused on a subgroup of participants who benefited from psychotherapy. It inoculated certain patients, those who arrived with "severe and nonchronic depression"—isolated intense episodes—against relapse.

But when you divide data all sorts of ways, all sorts of patterns emerge. Patients with more common levels of depression—Hamilton

scores below 22, typical for outpatients—seemed to do better on medication alone (82 percent remitted) than on combination treatment
(72 percent).

Looking at all patients with chronic depression, more (70 percent)
recovered on medicine alone than on medicine-plus-psychotherapy
(63 percent). That difference was not statistically significant, but even
if therapy did nothing to impair the effects of medication, the result
hardly made the case for combined treatment. No one was keen to
broadcast this finding, that for chronically depressed patients offered
vigorous prescribing, psychotherapy adds little.

Now, I don't believe that result, any more than I believe that psychotherapy has a special role for severe and nonchronic depression. It
may be that, on its own, skilled pharmacologic care is hard to beat.
Perhaps the prescribing doctors were so evidently expert that patients
invested little in the therapy. What happens in the office of a psychiatrist who does both jobs, talk and prescribing, may be a different
matter.

Still, the R&R study presents a challenge to evidence-based medicine and the press: Are we evenhanded in our consideration of test results? Where must we let numbers tell their story, and where may we
reserve room for judgment? In the treatment of chronic depression, to
favor combined treatment, psychotherapy augmented by medication, is
to favor common sense over formal evidence.

The psychotherapy findings aside, the R&R results are reasonably
encouraging. With the passage of time or intensive medication management, hard-to-treat patients emerge from depression, a result that
holds throughout the severity spectrum. The recoveries have substantial stability. (In a presentation, the researchers said that even patients
who "relapsed" tended not to return to their prior level of depression.)
Some of this depression would have remitted with no treatment; most
episodes end, give or take residual symptoms. But the unimpressive
effect sizes we've seen in brief drug-company trials translate into substantial effectiveness in practice.

Treated by the R&R pharmacologists, the vast majority of patients
made it to remission, and with low dropout rates. Almost all completers
got better and stayed better. If the study's participants were comparable
to those in STAR*D, then the exercise of judgment had made a

difference. We may wonder, What is it that a skilled psychopharmacologist might know?

There's a gap between what academics believe and what doctors act
on. Conventional wisdom has it that symptom patterns give no clue as
to which medicine will help whom. All the same, clinicians try to
match treatments to patients.

Here I want to edge myself out on a thin limb. I see indications that
the conventional wisdom is mistaken.

The commonest notion about drug selection runs along these lines:
Medicines like Celexa that work via serotonin will help patients whose
depression is colored by anxiety, where that term embraces timidity,
obsessiveness, social unease, and self-doubt. That was the group I offered Prozac when it became available. In contrast, medicines that have
mixed effects or work via norepinephrine—desipramine, Wellbutrin,
perhaps Effexor, and especially reboxetine—will most help patients
with lethargic depressions, where low energy is a distinguishing feature.

That's not to say that certain medicines treat only certain symptoms. Depression is a syndrome; as it remits, symptoms tend to lift in
concert. When anxious patients get better on Prozac, generally their
energy will return. When reboxetine works, it relieves anxiety as well
as lethargy. But perhaps symptom patterns can predict who will respond to what.

In 2005, a team from the University of Catania, in Sicily, published
a study of targeted prescribing. They had been working with depressed
stroke survivors. The prevailing view was that in poststroke depression,
brain pathways that use serotonin are disrupted, so that medicines like
Prozac work best. In a bold move, the doctors in Catania had evaluated
reboxetine, whose direct effect is on norepinephrine.

The twist was that they limited the trial to stroke patients with
depressions characterized by passivity, low energy, flattened facial
expression, drowsiness, and slowed speech and movement. If
norepinephrine-based antidepressants treat lethargic depression, perhaps reboxetine would help these stroke victims after all.

The Italian trial enrolled only thirty-one patients, but the results
were spectacular.

There were no dropouts. Psychosomatic research has that advantage. Stroke survivors attend checkups. Here, patients given placebo did not change at all. At zero, four, eight, and sixteen weeks, their average Hamilton scores ran 24, 24, 24, and 23—substantial depression. The figures for patients on reboxetine dropped steadily: 24, 15, 12, and finally 9—mild or subthreshold mood disorder. The identifiers (passivity and so on) had picked out reboxetine-responsive patients from a group thought to need drugs from a different class.

In another study, the same research team divided a larger sample of stroke survivors into two groups, those with anxious depression and those with lethargic depression. Half in each category got Celexa and half, reboxetine. The wrong drug (Celexa for patients with bodily slowing, reboxetine for anxious patients) did nothing. The right drug lowered Hamilton scores decisively.

Perhaps it is because they were conducted on neurological patients that these experiments have gotten no play. But the Sicilian research suggests that the clinical lore is right: the symptom picture offers hints about who will respond to what.

Later, Richard Metzner, a clinician at the Semel Institute for Neuroscience at UCLA, attempted a loose replication of the STAR*D trial, only matching patients, 117 in all, to antidepressants through a system similar to the one used in Sicily. He achieved a 59 percent remission rate at six weeks, about twice the benefit obtained with Celexa alone in the first phase of STAR*D.

The standard view remains that there is no reliable way to select antidepressants. But if, as these small and quirky studies suggest, prescribing is an art, then conventional drug trials, where random assignment determines the treatment, underestimate antidepressants' potential.

Whatever the truth about clinical expertise, psychiatrists will almost certainly improve at matching drugs to patients. Researchers have begun identifying genetic markers that correlate with response to one or another sort of antidepressant. In most studies, the predictive power is weak. You would need to genotype dozens of patients to produce one remission more than you would get through randomly choosing a medication.

But a recent trial found a genetic variant with a "number needed to screen" of 10: you would need to gene-test only ten patients to obtain one remission more than you would get by randomly assigning patients to take an SSRI (Zoloft or Lexapro) or, in contrast, an antidepressant that directly affects the brain's handling of serotonin and norepinephrine alike (a form of Effexor). This level of advantage might not be quite enough to be employed clinically, but even a little further progress might make insurers willing to pay for testing to avoid weeks of futile treatment efforts.

If the testing pans out, then even using today's drugs, efficacy results will rise and emperor's-new-clothes claims will fade. It is implausible that genetic markers are specifying responses to one placebo as opposed to another—which is also to say that even now it is absurd to deny that Zoloft, Lexapro, and Effexor are real antidepressants.

In the genetic studies, patients follow the pattern that David Healy, in Wales, had noticed. They do better globally, reporting fewer side effects, on their preferred antidepressant (the one that genotyping predicts will work for them) and experience adverse responses—low efficacy and numerous side effects—on nonpreferred ones. That's why average response rates in drug trials are misleading: the figures, weighed down by results from patients who worsen, mask marked improvement in those whom treatment helps.

We now have a better-rounded picture of antidepressants' potential. We've known that patients with uncomplicated mood disorders, the type treated by internists and family doctors, have high response rates on the first drug they're prescribed. With tough cases, it can take longer to find the right regimen, but with expert prescribing, over three-quarters of those who start treatment enjoy substantial improvement. This ability to make a difference—with difficulty, in time—with hard-to-treat patients is another reason that ours has been the antidepressant era.

36

Steady As She Goes

WE'VE REACHED THE end of our consideration of the antidepressant controversy—of the central question, whether antidepressants interrupt bouts of depression. I hope it's clear that they do. Practicing doctors witness antidepressants' efficacy daily, and the formal evidence supporting those observations is ample.

But once medicines work—what then? How long should treatment continue? Most Americans taking antidepressants have been on them for two years or more—30 percent for five years or more. This extended use creates intimate relationships with these medicines, for better and worse. Patients live unhappily, with side effects such as diminished sex drive, and contentedly, with a sense of security long absent in their lives.

Doctors rely on medication to stave off recurrence or prevent the worsening of partially treated episodes. In my practice, I have patients who pass in and out of depression, never shedding all their symptoms. Almost all these patients find benefits from antidepressants.

Libby is an unmarried special-education teacher, now in her sixties. Only occasionally, for intervals lasting months, is she fully free of depression. The difference that medications have made is in her functioning. Before seeing me, and in the years when we tried to sustain her (with talk, exercise, bright lights, and the rest) off medication, she had days and weeks when she could not drag herself to school. Now, on antidepressants "indefinitely," she is able to work steadily, doing summer sessions and taking on private clients.

Her life is different. In her down periods, she may have morbid thoughts—"as well off dead"—but is almost never suicidal. She travels on vacation. She golfs. She jogs. She has lunches with friends. She has a conventional middle-class existence. That scorned outcome that can be something of a miracle.

Do Libby and I worry that she is overexposed to medication? We do. I lower her doses in springtime and raise them in autumn. In time, antidepressants may fail her or produce intolerable side effects. For now, they enrich her life. So far so good, and thank goodness for that.

When chronic medication use constitutes best practice is complicated. We always prefer for patients to be off medication. But on the narrow question of efficacy, there is extensive research. It goes under the name *maintenance*, a term we encountered when discussing pill placebos.

For patients who have recovered on an antidepressant, what happens if they continue the regimen? What happens if they stop? Approaching the maintenance literature the way that psychiatry's critics approach the FDA data—considering effect sizes only—we'd call the case open-and-shut. *Every* randomized, controlled trial finds that staying on medicine protects against further episodes.

One layer down, discussions of maintenance become complex. The trials are liable to confounds—new ones, distortions we have not yet met. The result is endless debate about the consistent numbers.

As in the central antidepressant controversy, the fuss stands at a distance from patient care. In practice, it seems clear that antidepressants, once someone does well on them, are stabilizing. Often, that effect is what patients, both those who get full relief and those such as Libby who limp along, value most. Medications give the feeling of having a floor to stand on. At the least, intervals between setbacks are longer.

Antidepressants' reliability in maintenance is another quality that makes them transformative. Our discussion began with Nora, who had put together four good years on medicine. For patients to follow Nora's arc of improvement is something like the norm. They arrive dominated by depression. It controls their consciousness. When they are not depressed, they know that they might be. Small disappointments can cast them into the abyss. By muting apprehension, antidepressants allow these patients to act. At home, at work, they can make commitments. It is hard to overstate the importance of this contribution, from medication and from psychiatric care in general: making the future predictable. Confidence lets people pursue their dreams.

To investigate this potential, protection from mood disorder, scientists take patients who have done well in a brief drug trial and then assign them randomly to continue with that drug or switch to placebo. The research tracks relapses: Over time, how many patients in each arm of the trial become depressed? Generally, it is people with chronic or recurrent depression who enter these experiments.

I have said that the results are consistent. An integration involving more than nine thousand patients found that those switched to placebo were three times as likely to return to depression as those kept on medicine. In each of fifty-four individual trials, medication outperformed placebo. Few research collections in medicine are this uniform in their results. Few meta-analyses are likely to be as reliable. The effect size for prevention is in the 0.6 to 0.7 range, as sizable a benefit as we have seen.

In this field, too, there are FDA data. For over a quarter century, the agency has required that companies proposing to market an antidepressant submit a maintenance trial, registered in advance. There are fifteen, a complete set, no file drawer. Sadly, as with other drug-company trials performed for the FDA, most in this set are deeply flawed. The FDA scientists have published a technically impressive overview analysis, and still—complete sample and statistical expertise notwithstanding— we will need to take the results with a grain of salt. That said, they show that in every trial patients who stay on antidepressants suffer fewer and later subsequent episodes than patients switched to dummy pills. On placebo, the rate of relapse doubles.

Academic trials, like the R&R study, out of Penn, Rush, and Vanderbilt, give the same answer. That trial had a late phase in which patients who had recovered were kept on medicine or tapered off. Stopping medication more than doubled the rate of recurrence. Prior time spent in psychotherapy—months of treatment—offered no additional protection. All that mattered was continued prescribing.

For patients with long-standing mood disorders, once a bout of depression has ended, antidepressants are protective. The benefits hold for any interval that has been studied: weeks, months, or years. Continued treatment cuts the risk of recurrence by a half to two-thirds.

Despite this copious and consistent evidence, some experts doubt that maintenance is protective. Often, their objection stems from what happens when patients are taken off medication and switched to placebo pills. In early studies particularly, for patients put into the control arm, researchers sometimes stopped the drug abruptly, simply supplying placebo pills that looked like the antidepressant.

Quitting cold turkey can lead to discontinuation effects, like headache, dizziness, a sense of malaise, or "brain zaps," an unpleasant flash or shiver that feels like an electric shock. Those symptoms play out over days or, more rarely, weeks. But can quick discontinuation also hasten the return of depression? If so, then maintenance trials are comparing destabilized people (those taken off medication) with unharmed ones (still on drug), a terrible confound.

In an observational study—looking, for instance, at patients who simply decided on their own to quit—a Harvard psychiatrist, Ross Baldessarini, found that an abrupt transition increased the odds of relapse, particularly in the first six months. But patients who bolt and stop treatment may be different from patients who listen compliantly, tapering their medication at a time and in the fashion that their doctor recommends. Perhaps Baldessarini was only noting a contrast between methodical people and impulsive ones.

Randomized trials tell another story. When Baldessarini reviewed twenty-seven controlled studies, he had found no harm from abrupt cutoffs: "Contrary to prediction, gradual discontinuation . . . did not yield lower relapse rates." In that analysis, patients made to go cold turkey were *less* likely to enter a new episode of depression than patients taken off drugs slowly. Similarly, no disadvantage from quick tapers showed up in the large (nine-thousand-plus patients) meta-analysis, a *Lancet* study of more than four thousand patients, or the FDA synthesis.

I have spoken of my love for idiosyncratic studies. One of my favorites, conducted by French researchers, confronted the discontinuation issue head-on. In a heroic effort that involved the participation of eighty-three psychiatric centers, the team enrolled 371 patients who

met stringent and seemingly quirky criteria. The men and women enrolled were at high risk for depression. Each had suffered at least three
episodes in the prior four years. Each was now in remission. None had
used Zoloft to get there.

Now, if the patients were still on some other antidepressant, they
were taken off and observed for two to four months. The 288 participants who remained, those who had not dropped out and had continued
to do well, were randomly assigned to take Zoloft or dummy pills.

The beauty of this ambitious setup is how it addresses the problem
of discontinuation. All the research subjects have come off drugs. If,
months later, some patients remain at heightened risk of recurrence,
they will have equal odds of receiving Zoloft or placebo.

Also, the test is especially rigorous. Normally, patients who need
maintenance will continue with the medicine they did well with in the
first place. Here, to succeed, Zoloft had to protect patients who had
recovered on different drugs, including ones (such as reboxetine, in
David Healy's experiment in his own lab) where success might pick out
people likely to feel *worse* on a medicine, such as Zoloft, that affects
serotonin transmission primarily.

Given the stringency of the trial, the findings were striking. Over
eighteen months, among patients on placebo the recurrence rate was
double that of patients on medication, and with placebo the recurrences
came sooner. This difference appeared despite a highly supportive
study environment, involving "repeated contact with mental health
professionals"—minimal supportive psychotherapy. Once that factor is
in play, so is additivity. Maintenance—here, putting remitted depressed
patients on a new antidepressant—may be yet more stabilizing than the
numbers suggest.

The French trial proved too complex to inspire replication. Still, it
serves as a preliminary answer to the principal objection to the results
of maintenance trials. If the "harm via withdrawal" problem is a red
herring—if in maintenance trials, what you see is what you get—then
continued use of antidepressants really does cut the recurrence rate by
half to two-thirds.

Drug continuation is likely yet more protective. Maintenance studies suffer from an especially distorting form of (our old nemesis) differential dropout. As trials stretch on, patients stop showing up. Here

as elsewhere, exit questionnaires find that patients leave placebo arms because the "treatment" is not working. The dropout rate in the placebo arms of the FDA maintenance trials reached almost two-thirds, as opposed to less than half in the drug arms. The analyses tend not to count disappearance as relapse. When failures walk away and the data focus on the few who persist in taking dummy pills, placebo will get more credit than it should.

In the early going, then, drugs are doing better, and placebos worse, than the numbers suggest. After that point, all randomization has been lost, so the results become harder to interpret.

Let's look in on a trial at the six-month mark. Many patients assigned to take dummy pills will have relapsed or dropped out. Who's still participating? At this late stage, the placebo arm contains many people who do not require medication to stay well—people who are naturally resilient (or were misdiagnosed from the start). That's why they've gotten this far on inert pills.

Meanwhile, the medication arm is mixed. Besides the naturally resilient and the misdiagnosed, it will have held on to people with highly recurrent mood disorder who need antidepressants to stay afloat and are benefiting from them. Overall, it's a sicker group.

If we follow results for another six months, we're conducting an unfair experiment, one that compares naturally stable people (in the placebo arm) to less stable people (in the antidepressant arm). The better that antidepressants work in the first six months—the more that they protect fragile patients—the less reliable the remainder of the trial will be.

The term of art for this problem is the *differential sieve*. The placebo arm contains a fine sieve that (over six months) lets through only healthy people. The antidepressant arm contains a wide-gauge sieve that lets through sick people as well. This setup is precisely as bad as if our triage nurse had sent all the sicker patients to one arm of the trial.

The FDA authors made note of this confound: "The population, of course, changes over time. Presumably, by 6 months, most patients likely to relapse on placebo will have done so, and new relapses become less frequent. The overall drug-placebo difference in relapse rate, however, is maintained."

Beyond the half-year mark, the placebo arm contains few vulnerable people, so we would expect relatively more recurrences among patients still on antidepressants. That doesn't happen. Patients in both arms remain steady, and in some trials antidepressant continues to outperform dummy pills.

Because the differential sieve confound is so distorting—because at a certain point people in the control group are at low risk for depression—no one knows precisely how much extra stability antidepressants afford in long-term use. But in his overview of randomized trials, Baldessarini found a substantial ongoing advantage almost to the three-year mark. At that point, 60 percent of those on medication remained depression-free—but under 20 percent on placebo.

And before the differential sieve kicks in, the advantages of medication are undeniable. Baldessarini looked at the first ten or twelve months of maintenance for patients who had suffered several past episodes of depression. On an antidepressant, they did almost as well as patients with less history of mood disorder. On placebo, they were almost certain to relapse. The issue here is not severity but chronicity. In the patients with the most persistent illness, discontinuing medication may quadruple the risk. One of the clearest results in psychiatry is that, for patients with recurrent depression who respond to an antidepressant, continued use over a year offers substantial protection.

There's an additional reason that the clinical reality is likely to be better than the research implies. In the French trial, as in many others, if patients experienced deterioration that, in a clinician's judgment, called for a medication adjustment, they were counted as having suffered a recurrence, even if they were not depressed. In office practice, as a patient falters, her doctor can respond promptly, say, by raising the drug dose to forestall worsening or by briefly adding a second drug. If one antidepressant in a fixed dose is two or three times as effective as no treatment, ordinary medical care should be more protective yet.

But even the numbers that researchers present are impressive. Think about what it means for ongoing antidepressant treatment to spare patients half to two-thirds of the episodes they would otherwise succumb to—and for any length of time that has been studied. As preventatives, these medicines have remarkable range. They protect patients, like those in the French study, with highly recurrent depression. And antidepressants prevent the onset of mood disorder in people, such as stroke victims, who have never had it. The most and the least chronic cases benefit.

In the maintenance literature, the notion of medicine as glorified placebo loses meaning. There's nothing to glorify. Placebos don't prevent depression, and antidepressants do.

37

Interlude

Nightmare

THE MAINTENANCE LITERATURE is clear—antidepressants ward off depression—yet by itself that observation does not tell doctors what to do. Antidepressants may be stabilizing, and still we may not want patients on them indefinitely.

Wherever possible, I taper patients off. If they are not seeing me regularly, I will catechize them on self-monitoring for deterioration. If they slip, I will restart medication promptly, often with a refresher course of psychotherapy.

Why? Especially with recurrently depressed patients, why discontinue medication when maintenance is protective and mood disorder is harmful? I could answer in terms of antidepressants' side effects, which are many. Antidepressants may increase the rate of cataract formation in the eyes. Certain of the drugs have been associated with a change in electrical conduction in the heart. The drugs may affect calcium absorption into bone. Older patients on medication are at higher risk for automobile accidents and perhaps falls. (This last issue exercises Peter Gøtzsche the most; he believes that the rate of falls in medicated elderly patients has been underestimated.)

But in truth, I was as conservative a prescriber before these specific risks were identified, and at a time when estimates of the protective benefits of antidepressants were, if anything, higher.

No, I have always liked to keep drug exposure to a minimum because when medication is used chronically, bad things tend to happen. One of my child-psychiatry teachers, the late Donald Cohen, used to say, "I rarely have to sit down with a mother and tell her, 'You know that drug I've been prescribing for your son? We've just found that it makes children smarter.'" Actually, there have been reports along these general lines with antidepressants. I have mentioned evidence that the medications may protect memory in chronically depressed women. But the more usual pattern is for the late-appearing news to be bad. In *Listening to Prozac*, composed before long-term use of antidepressants was common, I wrote, "We know that some drugs, especially ones that are taken chronically, will have unknown or even late-appearing (tardive) side effects."

When I say that, in clinical decision making, experience balances research findings, part of what I mean is that doctors learn from practice altogether, from work with patients with many diagnoses. The influences may be mixed. I recall studies of antipsychotic medications for schizophrenic patients that found "drug holidays" to be counterproductive. If you took patients off medicine, they risked sharp relapses, requiring vigorous prescribing, so that the overall exposure—milligrams of drug taken—increased. I saw precisely that problem in my training years. In contrast, some research suggests that when people with a tendency toward manic depression are given antidepressants without accompanying mood-stabilizing drugs, even if the acute problem resolves, the rate of future episodes may increase. We're applying lots of not-perfectly-relevant knowledge to the case at hand.

In this context, I want to mention what I call the "nightmare scenario," the notion that antidepressants are counterproductive. Skeptics have expanded on Ross Baldessarini's concern over rapid withdrawal and asked whether the apparent benefits of maintenance speak to addiction. Might medicine make patients dependent on the cure? The extreme version of this concern is that in the very long term, treatment makes patients vulnerable. While they are on medication, they stay well. When they come off, they will be engulfed by depression.

If I find this claim implausible, it's because I take people off antidepressants all the time. A handful—they took antidepressants early in their treatment and later relied on psychotherapy alone—visit regularly, a few times a year. They do fine—better than they had done in the early going, before ever taking medicine. This experience has led me to read the "nightmare" literature critically.

It tends to arise from a particular sort of analysis. A researcher will contrast patients who have done well in the placebo arm of a drug trial to patients who have done well in the medication arm of a drug trial. How do they fare once the experiment has ended?

In a follow-up phase, the patients on placebo will remain on placebo, while the patients on medication will be switched to placebo. There will be more relapses in the group that discontinued the antidepressant. The skeptics conclude that medication merely postponed trouble and perhaps did harm. Recovering on placebo leads to a steady course; recovering on medication predicts instability once the antidepressant is withdrawn.

Having seen the differential sieve in action, we will object that this result—more relapses in follow-up from the antidepressant arm—will occur if medication is effective and placebo pills are not.

Through its nonaction, placebo identifies the least shaky participants in any trial: they recover even on dummy pills. The short-term trial serves as a sieve, separating out ill people and passing through (for further study) healthy ones. Patients who recover on antidepressants are a more vulnerable group. Some will have had serious illness and responded to the medicine. The treatment arm of the trial is a broad-gauge sieve that lets through sick people.

Patients who do well on placebo will continue to do well. That's what healthy people do. In contrast, off medication, people who responded to it may falter. That's what sick people do. They may nonetheless fare better than they would have without treatment. Because they are effective, the drugs carry ill patients, ones who don't respond to the placebo grab bag, through the original phase of treatment.

A trial in which some patients enter via response to placebo and some enter via response to medication is not randomized. It suffers from susceptibility bias.

I would be tempted to say that, on the continuum from randomized trials to storytelling, the nightmare reports stand at the anecdote end, except that anecdotes have the virtue of transparency. They are what they seem. But if we were to grant some such status, we might say that the nightmare calculations amount to a cautionary tale with this moral: There's simply too much that we don't know about the powerful medications.

I share that viewpoint, which is why, ample evidence of efficacy notwithstanding, I often find myself reluctant to prescribe. In particular, I am ambivalent about prescribing for young people, a category I extend through college age into the midtwenties. Some of the hesitancy is research based. A study has found that for adolescent monkeys, year-long Prozac treatment has a lasting impact on serotonin transmission in the brain. That nugget of evidence—of unknown significance—comes amid a host of vague concerns. It is worrisome to intervene directly in the developing nervous system. Beyond the wish to ease suffering here and now, what makes me prescribe—and, however hesitantly, I do it all the time—are counterbalancing concerns about the enduring effects of depression. It's important to interrupt progressive diseases. Depression now predicts recurrent depression down the road.

The situation is the reverse of the one we imagine if we listen to those who question the evidence base for antidepressant use. Well-documented hazards lead us to prescribe; unsubstantiated fears stay our hand—a balance that, to my mind, constitutes good judgment.

38

Interlude

For My Sins

I AM NOT prone to spirituality. We joke in my family that swimming is our religion. We must be in the open Atlantic, in Massachusetts, before Memorial Day and after Columbus Day, and not just for a second.

Religion goes beyond the regularity of observance. The ocean enforces a sense of proportion, awareness of our insignificance. It demands virtues, courage and perseverance. Swimming has an aesthetic, the up and down of it, the being in nature, primitive and sublime. Swimming has its ecstatic and contemplative aspects—in mind and being, the oscillation between focus and unself-consciousness. Swimming testifies to love of family, the family at play. Perhaps that's the real religion. Family is sacred.

I make this confession—for a secular person, I do seem to confess often—as a lead-in to saying that for me the clinical encounter is a sacrament. It would not be wrong to apply that (metaphorical, half-serious) term to the moment of prescribing. I want to be deeply aware of what I bring to it. The patient and I are vulnerable, in touch with great forces.

Here we are, Nora and I. Or the patient may be Stephan, Olivia, Caroline, or another. The time comes to choose. What I bring to bear is not narrow evidence, not one single dispositive research result. Better:

What bears on me is a life in psychiatry, a life within a tradition of thoughtful lives.

The experience is of being influenced by encounters with patients and interchanges with colleagues and teachers, all those observations, direct and indirect, of patients on medication and off. The experience reflects years of reading, of seeing antidepressants work in the consulting room and in the literature.

When I review medication's successes over a half century and more, it will sound, forgive me, like a litany—a litany of evidence.

But imipramine worked in Roland Kuhn's hands.

It worked in the randomized trials that followed hard upon his discovery.

Antidepressants worked in the first meta-analysis, by Gene Glass.

They worked in the major NIMH trial, benchmarked by imipramine.

By the numbers, antidepressants showed efficacy in the first major debunking study, "Hearing Placebo."

The first effort in evidence-based psychiatry, reviewing dysthymia treatment, found antidepressants effective at a high level.

If read carefully, even drug company research—shaky in more ways than one—demonstrates efficacy.

When the severity hypothesis resurfaced, researchers reviewed our largest collection of drug trials for mild-to-moderate major depression. Antidepressants worked there.

Antidepressants diminish neuroticism.

Antidepressants confer overall well-being. They show benefits, in quality of life, even in people who continue to suffer symptoms.

Antidepressants work for general medical patients, patients with neurological or cardiac ailments who are merely liable to depression— interrupting episodes promptly when they appear.

Antidepressants prevent the onset of depression in patients with few symptoms and the recurrence of depression in people with long-standing mood disorders.

For clinic patients, three-fourths of depressive episodes and more will respond to antidepressant treatment.

Even hard-to-treat chronic patients—almost all, if they hang in— will achieve remission on antidepressants, over time.

When depressed patients respond to medication, keeping them on it will spare them half or two-thirds of the episodes they would other-wise be liable to—for any length of time that's been studied.

That list may give a distorted picture of how information arrives. It comes piecemeal. Since the seventies, I've seen antidepressants in ac-tion and then read journals for guidance. I seek out a study, or it crosses my desk: Should it cause me to revise my views? What are the details? What confounds is it subject to?

There can be seismic shifts in medical knowledge. Peptic ulcers were long thought to be caused by temperament, stress, and spicy foods. In the 1980s, research confirmed an unlikely competing hypothesis, that bacterial infection plays a leading role.

The antidepressant story has not been like that. Information has accreted, most of it supportive of prevailing opinion. There has been no emperor's-new-clothes moment—no revelation of *myth*, to use Per Bech's word, regarding the efficacy of antidepressants.

As for *how well* antidepressants work, in the numbers needed to treat, we've heard a drumbeat of 4s or 4-to-5s. I see those numbers needed to treat—and even occasional higher ones—as tickets in, indi-cators of overall efficacy.

That's because, with the efficacy estimates, there's headroom. Drug trials are no longer run on the people medicine helps most reliably. Our rating scale is at once too inclusive and too narrow, emphasizing bodily symptoms and missing effects on neuroticism and overall well-being. In the design and conduct of our trials, incidental factors, good and bad—minimal supportive psychotherapy, baseline score inflation—pump up the response rate in the control arms, while lessebo effects and the use of low doses make medications look less robust than they do in office practice. That's all before we consider problems with additivity.

Think of Allison, in her interviews with Verna, the research subject who endorsed every item on the Hamilton scale. Contrast Allison's vantage to our internist's—Viola's—in her observation of a patient like Verna. Who contributes better information to our impression of what drugs do?

Formal research has its role: to pick out treatments that are inher-ently effective. But for telling us *how much*, overviews of randomized trials will not always have the advantage over doctorly experience. The doubts about antidepressants' worth simply don't seem *serious*.

The notion that depression is highly responsive to placebos—responsive in any important way, over time—strikes me as implausible. Here I rely on the feel of the disorder, its ponderousness. I rely on hours spent with Adele and others like her, patients whose depression does not budge in response to promising dramatic treatments but that eases with antidepressants.

It's true that psychiatrists are agnostic priests. We are aware that the Pharma trials are shameful, ethically and scientifically. We are aware that our understanding of medications is incomplete. We feel obliged to protect our patients from unknown harms—not demonstrated but still imaginable. That's the contribution of papers on the nightmare scenario, papers that, however limited in scientific merit, give name to dark fears that are unavoidable in psychiatric practice.

Yet there are issues about which I am not agnostic. I do not want to go back to the days of Ray Osheroff and Irma and, when his treatment was psychotherapy only, Robert Liberman. I think of Moira, gloomy, reclusive, and prone, despite psychotherapy, to recurrent low-level depressive episodes. Moira's life is better for her having discovered medication, and in a psychiatrist's memory, there will be many Moiras.

39

Interlude

Practicing

THINKING ABOUT MY PRACTICE—doing a quick version of the inventory I proposed when I discussed *worry*—I see that I often stray from standard recommendations, the ones that emerge from formal evidence.

The best research suggests that antidepressants must be used in full doses, the equivalent of 200 milligrams of imipramine or more. It finds that residual symptoms predict recurrent depression; medication should be pushed until patients no longer suffer the least hint of insomnia or low self-worth. In chronic or recurrent depression, which is most of what I treat, formal evidence points to the need for long-term maintenance with the medication regimen that broke the back of the most recent episode—high doses, indefinitely.

In contrast, the evidence supporting psychotherapy in depression is relatively weak. One analysis of high-quality studies found an effect size of 0.2, low efficacy. The case for adding psychotherapy to medication is slimmer yet.

As for alternative modalities: Bright lights on dark mornings test out well, especially as adjuncts to antidepressants. So do most measures to improve sleep—combating apnea, normalizing the timing of the sleep-wake cycle, and so on. Other remedies we would be happy to see as effective—exercise, meditation, yoga, and diet change—have less support than most people imagine.

The exercise literature in particular is rife with confounds. It turns out that people who are willing to exercise are also less emotionally vulnerable, and the association—so research on many thousands of twins and their family members suggests—is partly inborn. Genes for exercise tolerance and mood resilience travel together.

When they are assigned to the (sedentary) control condition in a workouts-for-depression trial, people who enjoy exercise are likely to walk, or jog, away. As a result, the research suffers from a crippling form of dropout bias: the exercise arm retains emotionally healthy people, while only those most prone to depression stay to sit through the lecture-and-slide-show arm.

For years, the British quality overseer, NICE, has pushed doctors to withhold prescribing for mild and moderate levels of depression, proposing exercise as an alternative. In 2011, the guideline was enshrined as a quality standard, a measure by which doctors' practices would be judged. When the initiative was evaluated—in a controlled trial patients were (or were not) offered individually tailored counseling to encourage physical activity—those in the program exercised more but gained no mental health benefit, not at four months, not at eight, and not at a year.

Evidence-based practice would, as I read the literature, require reliance on high doses of medicine, supplemented by bright lights and good sleep hygiene—and little else. Psychotherapy would see limited use, and exercise, less.

My practice fails on many of these fronts, by which I mean that it does not follow the published evidence. I rely heavily on psychotherapy, often postponing prescribing until I hit a roadblock. Even then, I tend, relative to the literature, to undermedicate patients, and in every way—lower doses at shorter duration, with less scrambling to eradicate stray symptoms. I don't mean that I never push hard. For patients who have improved but still consider themselves to be in the grip of depression, I may rely on multiple drugs at substantial doses. Even in those cases, in time I may back off.

Sometimes, I will throw the kitchen sink at depression. I've been influenced by a patient, Chloe, whom I met early in my practice, in

imipramine days. A disorganized young woman, Chloe had dug herself
a deep hole of the sort you want not to find yourself in. We were going
in circles when Chloe proposed a "month of power." She would do everything right: quit street drugs, stop hooking up with uncaring guys, wake
with the lark, eat healthy foods, unplug the television, practice yoga,
attend church, take her prescribed medicine regularly, and speak hon-
estly with me.

Chloe had appeared vague and passive, with no inclination for self-
protection, yet she pulled off her program. My thought was of ski lessons, how you can follow most of what you're taught—set the shoulders
down the hill, bend from the ankles, resist stemming into the turn—
and do one thing wrong, push your butt back, and find that you've still
got your weight up the mountain. No, you need to be fully in balance.
That's what Chloe aimed for. She became much less depressed and a
bit less spacey, and in these matters, a little goes a long way.

Treating patients with chaotic lives, I may suggest—not in these
words—a month of power. Declaring the intention and, more, pulling
it off can be remoralizing, never mind whether any particular element
makes a difference.

For better-organized patients, I may recommend one or another adjunctive treatment: bright lights, exercise. Patients seek out yoga or
acupuncture on their own, and I do not discourage them.

About much of what I do, there are no trial results to bring to bear.
My observation is that, for depressed patients, cutting out alcohol can
make a difference. Patients will not realize how much a routine that
they consider minimal—a bourbon before dinner and a half bottle of
wine at table—affects their sleep, their equanimity, and their functioning in their marriage. Depressives tolerate that disruption poorly.

And so on. I rely on efforts unsupported by evidence, and where
there is evidence, I follow it selectively.

I have mentioned having patients back off on medication. Not
because the research says so—as we have seen, the data (for instance,
Ross Baldessarini's) are mixed—but because of what I've seen work, I
go slow. Aiming to have someone off drugs on the summer solstice, in
late June, I may start cutting the dose on the equinox in March, in
hopes that lengthening daylight will get the discontinuation off to an
easy start. While the sun shines, we'll make hay, stabilizing relation-

ships at home and in the workplace. For patients who have been on antidepressants for years, we may taper over fifteen months or more. For the sort of patient I'm thinking of, standard practice would demand medication for life.

In a slow taper, we may come to a point of rest, a dose below which symptoms threaten to break through. After restabilization and more good months, we may taper further. No controlled trial can afford the patience I employ.

As I say, I may pull back on dosages, even in the face of chronic or recurrent depression. My work with Caroline—I mentioned her when I discussed the introduction, in this country, of Prozac and Zoloft—might serve as an example. In my practice, with responsible, verbal patients watched over by responsible, verbal family members, I can catch slippage early and institute "rescue." I see less full-blown recurrence than the research literature predicts, very little altogether, and I imagine that conservative dosing spares patients some of the risk and harm that accompany all medication use.

For my patients, mostly competent and motivated, however disabling their illness, this expedient, the pushing and pulling back, tends to work well in this important sense: those who have been stuck resume important activities. I have said that antidepressants work ordinarily well, but the phrase applies equally to how patients do. They regain capacities that allow them to lead the lives that they were leading, or imagined they would lead, before depression intervened.

I make no brief for the way I practice. Often, I mistrust my approach because I find it so gratifying. Doctors should be skeptical of treatments they enjoy administering. I am aware that others succeed with other methods. If patients do poorly under my care, I may refer them to doctors who prescribe more vigorously. But employed in my way, sparingly, antidepressants are genial cotherapists. Reading the more hostile overviews, you would conclude that antidepressants are remarkably dangerous substances. I have not found them so.

My patients, and I with them, do encounter side effects, but fewer than you might think, given the excitement over them in the media. I deal with weight gain sometimes, and with apathy (an occasional result of long-term SSRI use) rarely. Like all doctors, I recommend diet and physical activity. I lower doses, switch drugs, or try an interval without. The media often treat antidepressants' shortcomings as if they were eerie, as if antidepressants were strange invaders of the body rather than typically flawed medications, treatments that require oversight, as treatments do. I wonder whether stigma is not at issue, or taking sides, for psychotherapy and against pharmacology. The clinical issues regarding side effects—how to inform, how to follow, how to mitigate—resemble those accompanying treatment for any medical condition.

I don't mean to overstate the diffuseness or the dynamism of my approach. I have not moved far from where I began. Mostly, I'm doing psychotherapy, not pushing meditation or fish oil. Although I have emphasized dose adjustments, often my patients who are on antidepressants do well on relatively constant regimens. Much of the up-and-down involves minor modification in times of stress. A good number of patients in my practice have been and likely will remain on a stable regimen "indefinitely."

I wonder whether my methods spare my patients some of the popularly discussed downsides to medication. Take withdrawal effects. Doctors have always known—the writings on imipramine say as much—that as people discontinue an antidepressant, they may experience stray symptoms. My patients sometimes report jitteriness on the way down, or a malaise that mimics a mild viral syndrome, but rarely for more than a few days.

In blogs and online chats, patients complain about protracted withdrawal effects, sometimes a dulling of thought that lasts months. Perhaps because of my deliberateness, I rarely—actually, never—see that result. Ronald Pies, a colleague who treats complicated cases of chronic depression, has written about his similar practice—ultraslow tapers—and gives the same report, no serious withdrawal effects.

I seem also to avoid other problems, related to loss of efficacy.

Psychiatrists' great fear is of what used to be called *tachyphylaxis*, a sudden return of depression full force, in a form that's hard to treat—free fall—while a patient is taking a dose of medication that has worked for years. I mentioned this problem in *Listening to Prozac*. A drug—classically, lithium or a monoamine oxidase inhibitor (MAOI)—suddenly stops working. Nothing helps, not raising the dose, not adding other medicines. These episodes can be excruciating. Sometimes, discontinuing the original drug and, weeks later, reintroducing it restabilizes the patient.

I never see classic tachyphylaxis. My guess—pure speculation—is that it is likeliest when a treatment cocktail flogs the brain, with high doses of drugs hitting multiple sorts of nerve receptors. MAOIs have this effect. Certain aggressive combined treatments—polypharmacy—do, too. Perhaps my tendency to undermedicate spares my patients this terrifying event. Anyway, classic tachyphylaxis is rare, and my guess is that I'm mostly not putting my patients in harm's way.

More generally, the total-exhaustion response must be uncommon because lately the term *tachyphylaxis* has been downgraded to refer to any relapse in the face of ongoing treatment. In drug studies, the definition can be loose. One standard has it that if, after entering remission, a patient regains 70 percent of the symptoms—70 percent of the Hamilton score—she had when she entered a drug trial, she has relapsed. A patient who begins with moderate-to-severe depression, recovers, and then becomes mildly depressed while still on an antidepressant is said to be in tachyphylaxis. In other studies, if in her doctor's judgment a patient needs an antidepressant dose increase, she is in relapse. These criteria lead to reports of high rates of tachyphylaxis, 30 percent a year or more for patients in ongoing treatment. People call this lesser drop-off in efficacy "Prozac poop-out."

I have cited numbers, but finally it is hard to know whether even the lesser sort of failure is common. Chronic illnesses wax and wane, generally worsening over time. In the face of scrupulous insulin treatment, diabetes can progress; patients apparently in good control, with normal blood sugar levels, lose eyesight or kidney function. It's not that insulin fails at its job, it's that it doesn't do everything. Something comparable may occur with antidepressants in depression: they help whatever brain system they are helping, but the underlying illness will break through, so that more or different help is needed.

Published data notwithstanding, my patients, those on medication, seldom suffer a marked loss of efficacy—or perhaps it's only that I see matters idiosyncratically. As I have said, I am not beyond fiddling with antidepressant doses, increasing them in the face of new stressors or symptoms and pulling back in balmier times. If one antidepressant, at a full dose, fails, I may add a low dose of a second—and then, perhaps, later pull back.

I don't doubt that in any year a third of my patients on medication receive attention to their drug regimens. But it's unusual for me to see episodes of full-blown depression at the level that brought a patient to treatment. Raising a medication dose does not mean that something dire has happened—nor that whatever is going wrong is drug-related. We're working together to mitigate a chronic, fluctuating (and some-times, sadly, progressive) condition.

My practice has also been spared the dangerous turns toward sui-cidality that have been written about since shortly after Prozac became available. In 1990, Martin Teicher of McLean Hospital and Harvard, in collaboration with Jonathan Cole, reported six cases in which pa-tients experienced new and intense suicidal preoccupations after hav-ing been put on medication. Based on what I had seen in my own practice and heard from colleagues, I concluded, in *Listening to Prozac*, that Teicher's observation was likely to prove valid—that the SSRIs, and older antidepressants as well, can cause paradoxical worsening of symptoms, and in dramatic fashion.

Parenthetically, Teicher's report illustrates the virtue of clinical ob-servation—of anecdote. What caught the McLean group's attention was the quality of the impulse, "intense suicidal preoccupation." Over-all, SSRIs prevent suicides, so this risk—of, infrequently, fomenting preoccupations with self-harm—would have been hard to identify or confirm statistically. In that context, the case series, a collection of vignettes, is invaluable.

Once the risk was identified, it became manageable. When I first prescribe, I warn patients to watch for deepened depression, new or intensified suicidal thoughts, and any increase in agitation, irritability, or impulsivity. (Teicher's signal contribution was occasioning that con-versation.) Patients do, rarely, phone to discuss adverse responses. We may discontinue a drug, mark time, then try another. Occasionally, a patient and I together have judged to wait out a period of serious dis-comfort. Sometimes this patience has been rewarded—the medication goes on to work—and sometimes not. Mercifully, there have been no disasters.

I don't mean that suicide is not at issue in my practice. I have lost patients. They are with me constantly. But no case, not one, has looked like those Teicher described, drug driven, with an upsurge of urgency. And often, remarkably often, I have seen antidepressants pull patients from the brink and hold them steady.

On antidepressants, commonly, suicidal thoughts become less intrusive and less compelling. Patients compare the result to the effect of morphine on pain: it is no longer at the forefront of consciousness. And of course, when depression lifts, many patients consider their past suicidal impulses alien.

I read the literature—public health surveys and randomized trials alike—as reflecting the benefits of SSRIs as preventives against self-harm. The controversial area involves children, adolescents, and young adults. There, some of the data have trended the other way, although authoritative studies correlate increased prescribing with decreased adolescent suicide.

If I do not obey formal evidence, I do attend to it. Am I seeing the failure rates that appear in published reports? If not, perhaps my use of medication is accurate enough. Do antidepressants act as the literature says they should, tending to core depressive symptoms, mitigating neuroticism, opening the door to elaboration in love and work? Mostly, patients do well, in the near and long term. I don't see myself as working with drugs that fail catastrophically, early or late.

Would my patients fare better if my work were evidence based? Having posed the question, I find I cannot make sense of it. Could a doctor rely on randomized trials only and treat real people? What would that practice look like?

40

We Are the 38 Percent

WHEN I PRESENT my own approach to depression, intentional underprescribing, it may seem that I am ducking an important part of the
antidepressant controversy, the argument over whether medication is
handed out promiscuously. I share the concern. As antidepressant use
has accelerated—as drug residue becomes detectable in our water
supply—it has been hard not to imagine that some of it is excessive.

Overprescribing can prove hard to document. I know as much from
my work with Gerry Klerman. In the early 1980s, he tasked me with
composing a reply for the signature of the surgeon general, Julius Rich-
mond, on whether "mother's little helpers" such as Valium were being
overprescribed for women. Experts on my working group found that
women got more mental health treatment in general, starting with
psychotherapy. Patients prescribed for arrived with high levels of impairment. Anxiolytic-related suicides had dropped. So had recent prescribing. And so on. Despite widespread unease at the level of drug
use—it looked excessive—without research "on the ground," surveys
that asked doctors why they had acted in each case, fault was hard to
pinpoint.

The objective research on antidepressant prescribing has been similarly short on detail. Surveys find that many patients on medication

have no relevant diagnosis in their charts, but do busy GPs record the justification for each treatment they offer?

My own experience gave no special cause for worry. In my office, I had not seen anyone arrive medicated for indications I considered trivial or cosmetic, not a single case in decades of practice. Correspondence and phone calls I had fielded, a steady stream, for years, told the same tale, substantial need. Meanwhile, I continued to hear from and be referred patients treated with psychotherapy only, and no medication, despite long intervals of debilitating depression.

That is not to say that when medicine was prescribed, I agreed with every choice made. Some of the new patients who arrived on antidepressants I might have treated longer in psychotherapy alone. Certain regimens alarmed me: too many drugs, or unlikely combinations. Still, every patient had a condition that seemed to call for treatment. Sometimes when I tried tapering an implausible fourth medication, depression recurred. I came to respect the out-of-town "cowboy," the aggressive prescriber who had discovered what worked.

My practice was privileged. Most patients had seen topflight doctors in the past. Still, I imagined that if there were massive unjustifiable prescribing, I would have encountered at least one example.

Lately, the quality of research on prescribing has improved. Probably the best data come from a household survey of people willing to discuss their medical histories. The questionnaire used ignores some mental illnesses and underdiagnoses others. In interviews, respondents may not disclose symptoms that they complained of to their doctors in times of distress. Still, the results present a revealing picture of the match between treatments and ailments.

One widely publicized analysis, from 2014, looked at residents of Baltimore who had been followed with periodic interviews for twenty years. Thirteen percent were using antidepressants. Only 31 percent of those on medicine had ever met diagnostic criteria for major depression. Another 31 percent had been diagnosed with one of four serious anxiety disorders known to respond to antidepressants. But (according to diagnoses arrived at through answers to survey questions) 38 percent had never had any condition where, by the researchers' standards, high-quality evidence justified prescribing.

Having "ever met" sounds like a liberal criterion. It covers doctors

treating current episodes and preventing future ones. Even among patients who fit that description, some may be using medicine unnecessarily. In that light, the figure for the remaining patients, 38 percent, is
alarming. Is it almost the rule that people taking antidepressants are
on them for no good reason?

The press treated the data that way. The usual news lede declared
that two-thirds of patients on antidepressants were not depressed. The
website for HLN, the *Dr. Drew* cable network, ran the headline "Antidepressants Use Being Abused, Study Suggests." But to my reading, the
Baltimore analysis is less about overprescribing than about evidence-
based medicine, narrowly taken, and the concern that doctors fail to
practice to it.

We know enough about antidepressants to ask whether five diagnoses cover the territory. The researchers believed that research on
dysthymia was insufficient and so excluded it as a proper cause for
treatment. Likewise, they questioned the efficacy of antidepressants as
sleep aids. (Trazodone, a precursor of Serzone, is often used, in low
doses, as a sedative. Because it is thought not to be addictive, trazodone
is especially popular in the drug-treatment community.) The figures
ignore antidepressant use for smoking cessation, premenstrual syndrome, post-traumatic stress disorder, and many other indications. Minor
depression was specifically excluded. (We may recall the Dartmouth
study, which contained hints that in minor depression antidepressants
can be helpful for patients who suffer few but disabling symptoms.)
Seven percent of those interviewed were stroke survivors.

The Baltimore analysis was not about whether doctors had prescribed thoughtfully, it was about whether the prescribing went beyond
what strict standards of evidence could justify—or rather, it assumed
that thoughtfulness meant accepting rigorous constraints on evidence.

By way of contrast, it is instructive to see how other researchers,
from Harvard and elsewhere, approached the national version of this
same data. The group was examining a different question, whether
Americans use mental health services unnecessarily. The investigators
created an ever-broadening series of categories to detect reasons for
seeking care.

In a given year, over a quarter of those who sought help had never
qualified for a diagnosis of mental illness. But an additional 10 percent

had revealed "some other indicator of possible need," such as a history of hospitalization for mental illness or a report of a recent substantial stressor like rape. (It is a commentary on the limitations of the interviews that a number of people who had spent time in a mental hospital had, on the basis of symptoms they disclosed, been categorized as never having suffered a mental illness.) Many of those in treatment fell one symptom shy of a full diagnosis. And so on. In the end, the analysis was left with 8 percent of respondents who had received services for no apparent reason—and many of them had been seen in "alternative" settings, for interventions like prayer. It may be that almost everyone who consults a doctor for mental health care arrives with substantial need.

I am not suggesting that needing mental health services is the same as needing antidepressants. I mean only that survey data can be utilized in different ways. You can propose strict standards and report on instances in which caregivers fail to meet them. Or you can consider indicators of distress and disability to estimate how much treatment may be, in a broad sense, warranted. The first method asks whether doctors follow certain rules. The second is more generous: Do the data hint that doctors and patients may be acting sensibly in the face of disorders for which treatment is always, finally, empirical?

Let's imagine a Baltimore householder who will (shortly, when interviewers arrive) land in the 38 percent. This patient shows up at a mental health clinic. He has, perhaps, a history of recent stroke or of dysthymia. Or he has achieved sobriety and now finds his stability threatened by insomnia—sleeplessness that has not responded to what the doctor recommended at a prior visit, attention to sleep hygiene. He has, our hypothetical patient, disabling minor depression—persistent, despite weeks of pastoral counseling. He arrives seeking relief from a medical problem, a typical psychiatric problem.

What should his doctor do?

Evidence-based medicine offers scant guidance. Regarding dysthymia and much else, the Baltimore researchers judge the pharmacology trials inadequate and would be bound to consider psychotherapy trials less convincing yet. What is at issue is not the psychiatric equivalent of routinely dispensing antibiotics for the common cold. Instead, when doctors prescribe antidepressants, often we are seeing the resolution of clinical dilemmas in the face of limited research.

In almost all cases, the need will be substantial—and scattered, imperfect evidence will suggest that antidepressants can help. A fair proportion of that ominous 38 percent may represent thoughtful patient care.

From a clinician's standpoint, the 38 percent figure stands as a judgment on the research base, which should be broadened and, equally, against the notion that strict adherence to evidence-based medicine is possible—a judgment against the requirement that, failing validation by randomized trials, doctors must not act. Practice on that principle is impossible. Most of what patients arrive with stands beyond the reach of well-researched treatment, and for some conditions doctors nonetheless have a fair notion of what might be worth trying.

The evidence on trazodone as a sedative is mixed, and yet, prescribing, I have had the occasional gratifying success. A patient with chronic insomnia begins to sleep through the night, and as a bonus, she finds relief from the chronic low-level anxiety that had been with her on waking. I have had patients whom I weaned off complex medication combinations and who continued to do well with, as their sole treatment, a low dose of trazodone at bedtime.

Nothing about the try-this-then-that approach to, say, disabling minor depression is unusual. Consider the treatment of headache. With a migraine sufferer, a neurologist will run a series of practical trials, each using a medicine of limited efficacy, until one does the trick, interrupting attacks, decreasing their frequency and intensity, or preventing them outright. Knowing more would be better—what's likely to work for whom and why. But there's no shame in employing expedients that don't, on a population basis, yield highly favorable numbers needed to treat. That an intervention works decisively for some people is evidence, too.

Our wishes stand as a fair test of our commitment to narrow-gauge evidence. Thinking of members of that ill-defined group, the 38 percent, do we wish that many of them had received psychotherapy?

If so, should we disown the wish? Not every figure that finds its way into print (that low effect size for psychotherapy!) should shape doctors' practices.

Whatever our wishes, the reality is hardly generous. In a given year, almost a third of American adults with major depression receive no medical attention for it.

No one knows how often antidepressants are misused. If we were to study the "health-care delivery" question better, through having specialists rediagnose patients treated in the regular course of things, we would still need standards. Regarding appropriateness, there is substantial disagreement. We may differ even (thinking of Doris Mayer) about what counts as a favorable outcome. Is lessening symptoms always for the best?

I don't doubt, finally, that antidepressants are overprescribed, prescribed inaccurately and unthinkingly, prescribed with poor follow-up, prescribed for too long, and the rest. There are medical horrors I never see—results of treatment in Medicaid mills, for instance, horrors that extend beyond mental health care. Nursing home physicians seem to overuse psychotherapeutic drugs. I worry a great deal about an area of practice I have little access to, the treatment of children. My impression is that antidepressants work unreliably in children and carry serious risks—known ones and, more frighteningly, unknown ones hinted at by our knowledge about the vulnerability of the developing brain.

But thinking about the different takes on the door-to-door survey data: doctors are prescribing for people in distress and generally with plausible reasons for doing so. I take minor comfort from what I have seen personally, judicious use of medication in adults. I confess to faith in my colleagues; with infrequent exceptions, I respect their work. And always, I worry about stigma. How much of our concern do we expend on that unfortunate remnant, the third of sufferers who receive no attention at all for this highly treatable affliction, depression?

41

What We Know

DEPRESSION TREATMENT WILL change, and we have reason to hope that breakthroughs will come soon. In the meanwhile, we practice psychotherapy and prescribe our current antidepressants. We know, I am guessing, most of what conventional outcome trials will ever tell us about their efficacy.

More high-quality academic research, like the STAR*D and R&R studies, might conceivably inch us forward, but it's not in the cards. In 2013, Thomas Insel, then director of the NIMH, signaled that the agency was done with that sort of effort. He was investing in basic brain sciences, on the theory that until we understand more about depression, improvements in treatment will likely remain incremental.

Meanwhile, the pharmaceutical industry has largely abandoned drug development in psychiatry. The drubbing, however well deserved, that Pharma took in the past decade must have played a role, but other reasons include the problems we have seen in randomized trials. Ever-rising placebo response rates make the arithmetic work against the enterprise. By chance, some effective antidepressants will test out poorly. And the conditions for vetting me-too drugs—variants of what's already available—must be distressing even to industry. Finally, no one can think it's right to scour homeless shelters for "volunteers."

Despite the drop in research funding, psychiatrists are optimistic. One reason is ketamine, an anesthetic that is being repurposed as an antidepressant.

Although drug companies have taken an interest lately, the ketamine story developed independent of industry. For decades, researchers have sought new brain targets for depression treatment—receptors and nerve pathways involving chemicals other than serotonin or norepinephrine. A quarter century back, a team at Yale began looking at drugs that influence the brain's handling of a neurotransmitter called glutamate. By 1994, John Krystal (we have discussed his research on trajectories of recovery) had begun working with low doses of ketamine, an anesthetic that affects a particular type of glutamate receptor. In 2000, Krystal and his colleagues reported that seven depressed patients had responded to an intravenous infusion of ketamine with quick relief—within hours or days—from core symptoms.

Ketamine is also a recreational drug and can cause hallucinations or a dissociative state, a sense of not being oneself. Research on ketamine abusers had raised red flags about risks to the brain from long-term exposure. Follow-up to Krystal's study came slowly. In 2006, NIMH researchers—one, Dennis Charney, had migrated from Yale—reported on the response to ketamine, mostly favorable, of eighteen patients with treatment-resistant depression. This study is of the sort that can still be run well: it is always possible to recruit real patients who have proved unresponsive to available medications. Further confirmations followed. Meanwhile, in advance of additional research, many people have been treated in clinicians' offices. It looks as if ketamine infusions end depressive episodes promptly.

Key clinical questions remain unanswered: how long the relief lasts, how often the treatment can be repeated, whether extended use has a downside. (Although ketamine has not been offered chronically to many patients, already colleagues have told me of two instances of serious tachyphylaxis to ketamine—dramatic loss of efficacy after repeated doses.) Meanwhile, researchers have tried to tame ketamine, looking for variants that can be given in pill form or as nose sprays and that avoid the transient unpleasant effects.

Some efforts have failed. Ketamine seems more effective than other drugs that target glutamate, a development that has caused researchers to wonder whether ketamine does after all work through its effects on glutamate receptors. Perhaps it acts via some other, distinctive means, so that the discovery of its usefulness for depression, if that pans out, will have been serendipitous. If so, ketamine may open the door to unexplored approaches to mood disorder.

It is the rule rather than the exception for proposed antidepressant drugs that work through novel mechanisms to fail in the late going. Because it has been around for fifty years, because many people have taken it recreationally or as an anesthetic, ketamine seems likelier than most to survive scrutiny, but you never know.

If ketamine or a near variant does succeed, we may wonder what role our current antidepressants will assume. As new medications become available, older drugs for the same indication have varied fates. With the advent of the SSRIs, imipramine faded into the background. In contrast, digitalis or close analogues survived decades of competition from newer heart medicines and have only lately fallen in rank.

Let's take *ketamine* now as our word for an imagined drug, the next Prozac, the antidepressant that takes the field by storm. What happens to Zoloft and Lexapro will depend on what practicing doctors discover about ketamine. Writing about Prozac, I referred to its "personality." Prescribing, observing, hearing from patients, clinicians learn whether a drug is harsh or mild, brash or subtle, difficult or easy to live with. These informal impressions contribute to experience, the observations that doctors add to lessons from the formal literature. The sum guides the application of treatments. Medication use is always crowdsourced, through crowds of experts. Not because of controlled trials, but through what emerged in the course of practice, doctors learned to reserve Serzone and trazodone for special purposes; Zoloft and Lexapro became go-to treatments for depression.

If our imagined ketamine is highly effective but hard to live with or liable to cause harm over time, it may be used to jump-start recovery from depression, with SSRIs retaining a role in maintenance. We halt an episode with nose spray; then we turn to Celexa.

Ketamine may come with so many adverse effects that its use is confined to severe depression. SSRIs might—this development would have its amusing aspect—become the treatment of choice for less symptomatic states. Why not? Our current medicines work well for low-level chronic conditions, stabilizing the emotionally fragile. The SSRIs' effect on neuroticism might keep them in business.

Perhaps inhaled ketamine will handle the whole job. Patients employ it, find relief, and put the sprayer on the medicine-cabinet shelf, to be turned to as needed for "rescue." In the face of this routine, recurrence loses its threat. Depression becomes intermittent, a nuisance treated as migraine headache sometimes is, through medication taken when an episode threatens.

Say that the relief is predictable, the effect size high. Will we have conquered an old foe, a disabling disease? Or changed what it is to be human? Those questions were ones I posed in *Against Depression*. How serious are we in our quest to vanquish mood disorders? I'd love to see that drama play out—to have access to a highly effective antidepressant drug in my lifetime—and perhaps I will have the chance.

Many interventions are vying for the role I have called ketamine. The NIMH is funding a program, titled Rapidly-Acting Treatments for Treatment-Resistant Depression, meant to offer prompt testing for medications that might interrupt depressive episodes quickly. Right now, academic centers are testing brief courses—under a week—of a "kappa-opioid receptor antagonist." Some opium receptors in the brain affect pain perception, but others appear to regulate mood, and the new drug is meant to target them.

A quite different drug has shown promise in early tests. It is designed to influence the brain's capacity to make new cells and new connections between cells in a region relevant to depression—and to do so without first affecting the brain's use of serotonin or norepinephrine.

Researchers have been looking at nonstandard approaches to depression from the most superficial (Botox injections into forehead frown muscles) to the most profound (chemicals that alter the functioning of molecules within nerve cells). There's early interest in pheromones, ultra-low-dose chemicals that work not through being absorbed into the bloodstream but by influencing receptors in the nose, unrelated to smell, that signal to mood centers in the brain. An area that has looked intriguing for decades, the use of anti-inflammatory drugs, such as Celebrex and Aleve, in depression treatment has gotten new play, although scattered findings also suggest that the drugs may interfere with the action of SSRIs. Groups interested in the brain effects of gut flora—bacteria in the bowel—are investigating their own approaches to depression. Natural herbal remedies have their advocates. That's before we consider the many variants of magnetic or electrical influence on the brain, safer and less demanding variants of ECT. Ours may be the era of tinkerers and putterers—of garage-laboratory innovation in mental health care. The exit, however temporary or partial, of Big Pharma may have its upside. I am more confident now of seeing a truly novel effective medication for depression than I have been at any other time in my career, including the lead-up to the introduction of Prozac.

We may soon be able to select treatments more thoughtfully. I have mentioned the use of genetic profiles. More generally, extensive effort is going into the identification of biomarkers—indicators in cells or body fluids that may allow doctors to pair treatment and patient. It's all very well to consider gross categories—anxious or lethargic. How much more useful it would be if a laboratory value gave direction: psychotherapy for this patient, ketamine for that one, and—unexpectedly, in the rare instance—stimulant medication for another.

For treatment outcomes, much of the new knowledge may come from research that forgoes randomization. We have learned that our standard trials can have disturbing downsides. The "blinding" requirement often means that treatments are not offered in their optimal form. The inclusion of placebos introduces problems with instruction effects and additivity. Recruitment issues are horrendous. After all that effort, we fail at the *How much?* question. It's no wonder that researchers are looking beyond controlled trials.

Some are working to cull information from natural settings. A team at Massachusetts General Hospital is building a resource bank for fifty thousand "citizen scientists," men and women with mood disorder who consent to serve as "data donors," contributing the contents of their electronic medical records. Patients can volunteer while still taking guidance from their doctors, following what they consider the best course of treatment.

The MGH collection is the main mental health component of the Patient-Centered Outcomes Research Institute, a structure, created under the Obamacare legislation, that will include records on many millions of insurance subscribers. Scientists and patients alike will propose research topics.

A data donor can ask, "If I add Advil to a full dose of Effexor, what are the odds that my depression will respond? Might it worsen? What is the risk that I will suffer serious bleeding?" Researchers will locate records of depressed patients who tried a given strategy, define a rough control group, and compare outcomes. Statisticians are scrambling to develop data-mining techniques that give valid answers. If the effort succeeds, psychiatry research will have what it lacks now, large numbers representing the experience of patients in routine care.

One paper along these lines has already appeared, on weight gain in more than nineteen thousand patients started on antidepressants. After a year, patients on Wellbutrin gained less than did patients on Celexa—and so on. The results were not impressive, but the size of the research sample was.

Weight is low-hanging fruit. Doctors weigh patients regularly. Researchers have looked at how doctors encode mental health visits in electronic records and found material that statisticians can work with, indirect indicators of the severity of mood disorders. Our next insights into antidepressants' risks and benefits—our tests of clinical wisdom— may well come from analyses of massive data sets.

Or it may be that we will come to understand antidepressants better when we arrive at a clearer understanding of what depression is. That's the NIMH method, to start with brain biology. The leading theory has it that depression will turn out to be many discrete conditions.

The model is autism, which seems to arise from a variety of genetic abnormalities. It needs to be said that we don't know what autism is either. Different causes may lead to a common downstream effect that then produces problems with empathy, intimacy, and language use. But autism is looking diverse—like cancer. Almost certainly, there will be many autisms.

In *Against Depression*, I took a position contrary to the prevailing view. My thought was that the diagnosis—depression—might prove reasonably coherent. I was influenced by the failure of past attempts to subdivide the category into more biological and more psychological variants. I still think that depression may have a coherent core, that many upstream causes will pass through a biological bottleneck, a limited set of abnormalities that cause the syndrome. Perhaps all mood disorders entail an impairment of resilience functions in the brain. That's why there's hope for ketamine, the real and ideal forms—because depression looks like one thing, a painful form of stasis.

I may be wrong. There may be many depressions, each in need of targeted treatment. We will come to know—and then, incidentally, we will understand what contribution the SSRIs and, before them, the tricyclics made when they were the drugs of choice.

I doubt that there will be great surprises. Through diverse sorts of research, through extensive clinical experience, we know our current antidepressants well. They alleviate depression. The level of efficacy sits in the territory bounded on the bottom by the numbers generated in imperfect trials and on the top by the absolute response rates encountered in practice—likely in the middle ground, with numbers needed to treat in the 3-to-6 range, where most medical interventions fall. Those figures sound right to me, based on how I see depression respond to medication, based on how I've seen it respond to psychotherapy, thyroid treatment, and the rest. My bet is that the higher—less favorable—numbers in some trials reflect bad research design and execution.

The *How do we know?* question turns out to be immensely complicated and reassuringly familiar. Knowing embraces a history and a heritage. It comes from seeing depression resolve faster than it once did, and from seeing patients lead fuller lives. It comes from research that has access to realistic groups of patients—early (1950s and '60s) research, research in cardiology and neurology, research in psychiatry that takes on all comers.

The notion that there's some grander take on reality strikes me as delusion. Our statistics are skewed by confounds. The results require interpretation. And what better perspective to bring to bear than the clinical?

Evidence-based medicine is not without its own downside. In the case of my good friend Alan, the influence was informal. A general impression—antidepressants' reach is limited—had made its way from shaky meta-analysis into popular reporting and then a neurologist's practice.

But EBM has been institutionalized. Exponents publish guidelines,

and they constrain practice. Insurance companies decline reimbursement for treatment at odds with the rules. Hospitals create standards
and punish doctors who fail to color within the lines. Training programs use the guidelines for teaching and testing medical students and
residents.

We've run into one case where this sequence made mischief—
when the British oversight group NICE recommended that for nonsevere depression, including mild and moderate major depression, doctors
forgo further prescribing in favor of alternatives like exercise.

That directive was based on the results of meta-analyses like
those we have looked at together, but it is hard not to think that taste
played a role as well—that, in a broad sense, the quality standard re-
flected Doris Mayer's sentiment about preferred ways for meeting
life's challenges. Meanwhile, the group ignored the confounds that
plague research on exercise. Regarding NICE's directive, critics writing in the *BMJ* noted "a lack of high quality evidence to support such
a recommendation."

Research testing of the NICE policy found that "facilitated physical activity" had no measurable effect on depression at any point in a
year. What if instead of attention to exercise—or in addition—NICE
had recommended attempts to optimize prescribing, the sort of enhanced care shown to help cardiac and neurologic patients? Participants in the study, many of them, might have enjoyed a year of good
life.

We're left with the suspicion that NICE's recommendation, to postpone further attention to prescribing, caused suffering and harm, to
brain, mind, patient, family. As for the many more patients not in the
study but in the clinics of Britain's National Health Service, the guideline does allow for them to be treated with further medication or psychotherapy once low-intensity treatments fail. But how much failure
should we tolerate? And how ironic for EBM to postpone treatments
for which evidence is strong in favor of one for which it is lacking.
Today, that quality standard is still in place, although NICE has signaled that it is revisiting its recommendations for depression treatment.

More generally, it seems to me that when it passes into policy,
evidence-based medicine risks hubris. EBM's methods have rarely been

subjected to its own standard: proof of efficacy. When we rein doctors in, do patients benefit? Think of the Canadian study of operating-room checklists. To cite one from a short list of statistically significant outcomes, when teams used the checklist, ambulatory patients experienced more complications. Perhaps there's a cost to upsetting surgeons' established routines. I don't want to put weight on an incidental finding—except to say that it's not obvious that we always do worse when we leave doctors to their own devices.

These examples—exercise, checklists—are the most innocuous. I ask my patients to exercise, although I am careful not to shame those too apathetic to begin. And I am sympathetic to experts who point to well-run small trials that contradict the conclusions of the Ontario checklist study. Perhaps surgical "time-out" should be enshrined through rules. The problem then becomes, where does the rule-making end? Based on EBM experts' reading of the meta-analyses, shall we have a policy: no antidepressants for mild and moderate major depression? We would fail our patients.

The damage would extend beyond the effects of that one guideline. Because our symptom-based diagnoses are imprecise and antidepressants are imperfect, prescribing is an art. When I consult colleagues, what I hope for is a special expertise, one that allows them, as Jonathan Cole did, to reach out of category and match drug to patient, never mind the diagnosis. As applied by insurers and health-care systems, evidence-based medicine punishes that skill. When I prescribe a medication and a drug plan denies authorization—Why is this depressed person on Ritalin?—I am rarely convinced that my patient has been afforded protection.

It's not just that EBM can get questions wrong and then make the answers into a rule. Like medication, EBM may have side effects. Will training young physicians to follow a guideline lead to better medicine than training them to read critically, observe closely, choose strong mentors, and aim to adapt treatments to cases? I would respect EBM more if its guidance included this requirement for trainees: *Make note of what you see.*

As for the antidepressant controversy, in retrospect it can be understood as one of those social phenomena that arise when long-standing grievance meets an opportunity for pushback. For partisans of psycho-therapy, openings to resistance arose in the form of flawed outcome stud-ies and the drug industry's egregious overreaching. Pharma's missteps came in the context of stalled drug development and—a factor easily underestimated—the culture's discomfort with technical approaches to problems of mind. These same circumstances primed journalists and the public for the antidepressant-as-placebo reports, however implausible.

If we get new and highly effective antidepressants—our "ketamine"—the debate will lose urgency. Before it does, I feel impelled to say that in its late phases, the debunking of antidepressants assumed an unat-tractive tenor. In the early going, the opposition felt like counterculture pushback. Later, it became triumphalist—and implausible.

Think of what imipramine and Prozac and the others achieve. In primary-care patients who stay on the first drug they're offered, the response rate may be 90 percent. No one—almost no one—believes that hopeful expectancy and the natural waning of symptoms produce anything like that level of improvement. If depression were that pla-cebo responsive, every civilization should have had access to effective remedies, and we in our time would have more types than we do.

Smug implausibility has a bad track record in psychiatry and psy-chology. The professions' stumbles often involve ideas that are at once unlikely and in accord with the zeitgeist. I am thinking of castration anxiety and penis envy, understood, in the time of Freud's dominance, as deep motive forces producing personality traits and mental illnesses. I wrote about those concepts in my brief Freud biography. They arrived in a Vienna proud of its new openness about sexuality. Freud's con-structs were at once outrageous and complicit, stirringly counterin-tuitive and cozily conventional. Danger arises when the implausible becomes the obvious. Think of the offhand ease with which a Chest-nut Lodge doctor said, of Ray Osheroff's career, "This business that he created was a giant breast."

Denying the efficacy of antidepressants may begin well enough, with a love of psychotherapy and a respect for human complexity. But in time, the position becomes stigmatizing, too much in accord with the notion that depression is something other, something less than what research and practice find it to be: a progressive, destructive multisystem disorder fully worthy of medical attention. Denial becomes forgetting—of Paula J.F., Irma, Robert Liberman, and endless others, Troys and Moiras, exposed to depression without antidepressants as a remedy.

Antidepressants don't look to be placebos. Consider the research on maintenance, with fifty-four trials all favoring medication. Only in psychiatry would there still be debate about whether the treatment is protective—whether the drugs are glorified dummy pills. Yes, there are concerns about a genial confound (antidepressants' possible benefits for various aspects of health), but finally the psychosomatic literature, the trials that find antidepressant efficacy for patients with stroke or heart disease or exposure to interferon, should put paid to the placebo canard.

Consider—how bold, how transgressive, in the era of straitlaced EBM, it feels to put this item on the list—consider what patients say: On medication, they have come back to life. Oh, we are mistrustful, but that testimony is not wholly without evidentiary value. To dismiss it, research results to the contrary would need to be solid. We would need to see that antidepressants do little and that depression is highly placebo responsive. Instead, our studies show drug efficacy for depression—mild, moderate, and severe—while the placebo story is suspect.

We have not—not yet—moved beyond our current classes of antidepressants, but we have come this far: achieving the ability, unique in human history, to treat depression reasonably well with medication. At the start of this journey, I asked, Do antidepressants work, and how do we know? It may be time to ask, How do we embrace our answers?

It's wondrous for humankind to have the use of treatments for that antique scourge, melancholy. Wondrous for a time, until the good news is absorbed and we turn our focus to the bad. Not everyone is helped, and not everyone helped is helped fully.

Perhaps an equal problem is that medications succeed and make melancholy look medical. Antidepressants can assume the role of partisans in an old struggle, about mind and brain, meaning and symptoms. Must that contest persist? Antidepressants and psychotherapy mesh so well.

Still, it's true: we discount the miracle because sometimes antidepressants fail; and then sometimes we discount it because they succeed.

A treatment that tests out as well as treatments in the rest of medicine is not enough. A treatment that works on the wrong basis—without prior growth in self-understanding—is too much.

We long for more and better—until we take perspective. As when the end of treatment nears, there comes a time to say, Look how far we've traveled.

Certainly, I have enjoyed the journey. The company has been good. I mean my patients, of course, and my teachers, ones you've met here and others I've thanked in prior books and more yet unnamed, and colleagues I consult and socialize with, along with those I know through their writing. But it would be wrong not to tip a hat in the direction of imipramine, the SSRIs, and lithium and the rest. Think of the difference between practicing in the course of my career and practicing in other eras—any, besides that heady one when modern psychotherapeutic drugs first came into use. To get to meet Prozac and then to work in concert—what unexpected reach, for a clinician trained exclusively, all but exclusively, in psychotherapy. I am conscious of the privilege.

How wrong, too, it would be to conclude on a solemn note. Practicing doctors live amid anecdote.

Just yesterday, I had a follow-up visit with a patient troubled by chronic mild depression. Zach is serious, deliberate, and painstaking. He had preferred to work with me in psychotherapy and then—some weeks ago—finally asked me to prescribe. Presently, the antidepressant kicked in. He functioned, he thought, somewhat better at work. Then Zach made note of an additional improvement, changed perspective:

"I'll tell you what was absent in the bad months: appreciation of what I have. I'd lost touch with what a good person my wife is. She'd sensed my dissatisfaction and turned resentful."

He said, "I must have been more depressed, and for longer, than I'd known. It's been since forever that I appreciated winter. I felt the oppression of the darkness. I missed the sunlight on the snow."

Over time, in session I've heard repeatedly how depression dampens responses to love and beauty. When medication works, the world does its bit. Patients are freed to notice what's precious in their lives. That's why doctors prescribe. They see how symptomatic relief adds dimensions to patients' consciousness. In retrospect, doctors—no, I— regularly I discover that I had failed to appreciate the extent of my patients' impairment.

In ways large and small, depression burdens lives. Combating it, psychiatry has been in stasis. But it would be shameful not to show gratitude for our imperfect tools. We're lucky to have them. Progress in mental health care may be slow, but make no mistake: for clinicians, for depressed patients, ours are still extraordinary times.

Notes

Judgment-based medicine demands choice: embracing some potential sources of insight and setting others aside. In the spirit of curating, in compiling these notes I have chosen to err on the side of leanness. Generally, I offer a reference or two on each topic: studies referred to in the text, leading articles, and small trials or analyses that I consider especially trustworthy or interesting. The citations should be read as if preceded by the phrase *for example*. They stand as representatives of an extensive literature.

Where I take statements of fact to be understood and agreed upon, often I supply no documentation. Regarding depression, more extensive referencing is available in my 2005 book, *Against Depression*. Much of the pre-1993 material on antidepressants appears in *Listening to Prozac*.

Epigraphs
vii *No one dares:* The text is my tweaking, using the original Spanish, of the translation in the English-language version: Marías, J., *Your Face Tomorrow: Fever and Spear*, vol. 1, trans. M. J. Costa (NY: New Directions, 2005), 241; from Marías, J., *To rostro mañana: 1 Fiebre y lanza* (Madrid: Santillana, 2002), 297.

Preface
xii The Lancet: Neurology: Chollet, F., Tardy, J., et al., "Fluoxetine for Motor Recovery after Acute Ischaemic Stroke (FLAME): A Randomised Placebo-Controlled Trial," *Lancet Neurol* 10 (2011): 123–30.

xii *commonly suffer:* Estimates of depression prevalence after stroke range from 20 percent to over 70 percent, with a consensus figure around 40 percent.

Jorge, R. E., Robinson, R. G., et al., "Mortality and Poststroke Depression: A Placebo-Controlled Trial of Antidepressants," *Am J Psychiatry* 160 (2003): 1823–29; and Price, A., Rayner, L., et al., "Antidepressants for the Treatment of Depression in Neurological Disorders: A Systematic Review and Meta-analysis of Randomised Controlled Trials," *J Neurol Neurosurg Psychiatry* 82 (2011): 914–23. For an update, see Robinson, R. G., Jorge R. E., "Post-Stroke Depression: A Review," *Am J Psychiatry* (posted online 2015), in advance of publication.

xii *prevent depression*: Rasmussen, A., Lunde, M., et al., "A Double-Blind, Placebo-Controlled Study of Sertraline in the Prevention of Depression in Stroke Patients," *Psychosomatics* 44 (2003): 216–21; and Robinson, R. G., Jorge, R. E., et al., "Escitalopram and Problem-Solving Therapy for Prevention of Poststroke Depression: A Randomized Controlled Trial," *JAMA* 299 (2008): 2391–400.

xii *think clearly:* Cognitive functions: Jorge, R. E., Acion, L., et al., "Escitalopram and Enhancement of Cognitive Recovery Following Stroke," *Arch Gen Psychiatry* 67 (2010): 187–96.

xii *likely to survive:* Jorge, Robinson, et al. 2003. See also this preliminary study showing that prompt administration of antidepressants may decrease deaths substantially in the first month: Mortensen, J. K., Johnsen, S. P., et al., "Early Antidepressant Treatment and All-Cause 30-Day Mortality in Patients with Ischemic Stroke," *Cerebrovasc Dis* 40 (2015): 81–90. See also Robinson and Jorge 2015.

xiii *Robert Robinson:* Personal communication, May 2011.

xiii Newsweek: Begley, S., "Why Antidepressants Are No Better Than Placebos," January 28, 2010.

xiii USA Today: Rubin, R., "Study: Antidepressant Lift May Be All in Your Head," January 5, 2010.

xiii Listening to Prozac: NY: Viking, 1993.

xiv *session with Nora:* See my discussion of case vignettes on pages xxi–xxii.

xiv *mood disorder:* In this book, I have retained a convention I used in *Against Depression* (NY: Viking, 2005). *Mood disorder* means depressive disorders: major depression, minor depression, and dysthymia. When discussing bipolar disorder or anxiety disorders, I name them specifically.

xv *World Health Organization:* The original studies are Christopher J. L. Murray and Alan D. Lopez's, *The Global Burden of Disease: A Comprehensive Assessment of Mortality and Disability from Diseases, Injuries, and Risk Factors in 1990 and Projected to 2020* and *Global Health Statistics: A Compendium of Incidence, Prevalence, and Mortality Estimates for over 200 Conditions.* Both were published in 1996 by the Harvard School of Public Health on behalf of the World Health Organization and the World Bank and distributed by Harvard University Press. There have been periodic updates: Global Burden of Disease Study 2013 Collaborators, "Global, Regional, and National Incidence, Prevalence, and Years Lived with Disability for 301 Acute and Chronic Diseases and Injuries in 188 Countries, 1990–2013: A Systematic Analysis for the Global Burden of Disease Study 2013," *Lancet* 386 (2015): 743–800.

xv *In the United States:* The one-in-eight figure is new: Kantor, E. D., Rehm, C. D., et al., "Trends in Prescription Drug Use Among Adults in the United States from 1999–2012," *JAMA* 314 (2015): 1818–31. The estimate for women ages forty to fifty-nine (23 percent) comes from prior reports and likely will rise when the 2012 data are broken out. For detailed but slightly older figures, see, http://www.cdc.gov/nchs/data/hus/2012/092.pdf, and the National Health and Nutrition Examination Survey (NHANES), principally October 2011, http://www.cdc.gov/nchs/data/databriefs/db76.pdf; also Olfson, M., Marcus, S. C., "National Patterns in Antidepressant Medication Treatment," *Arch Gen Psychiatry* 66 (2009): 848–56.

xv *"Hearing Placebo":* Kirsch, I., Sapirstein, G., "Listening to Prozac but Hearing Placebo: A Meta-analysis of Antidepressant Medication," *Prev Treat* 1, no. 2 (1998).

xv Should You Leave?: NY: Scribner, 1997.

xv *TED:* "Self-Definition" (TED9 Conference, Monterey, CA, February 18, 1999).

xvi *"sarcophagus of his image":* *The Armies of the Night: History as a Novel, the Novel as History* (NY: New American Library, 1968).

xvi *roundup review:* Angell, M., "The Epidemic of Mental Illness: Why?," *New York Review of Books,* June 23, 2011; and Angell, M., "The Illusions of Psychiatry," *New York Review of Books,* July 14, 2011.

xvii *"Defense":* Kramer, P. D., "In Defense of Antidepressants," *New York Times* Sunday Review, July 10, 2011, SR1.

xvii *to the editor:* "Letters: Sunday Dialogue: Seeking a Path Through Depression's Landscape," *New York Times,* July 17, 2011, SR10.

xviii *his column:* Beam, A. "Battling over Happy Pills: A Scholarly Tug of War over Treating Mental Disorders Boils Down to One Question: Do Antidepressants Work?" *Boston Globe,* July 26, 2011.

xviii *University of Iowa:* "Self-Esteem as a Social Value and Quasi-biological Trait," College of Medicine Lecture (University of Iowa Clinical Epidemiology Symposium, Iowa City, IA, October 12, 1994).

xix *Gawande's writing: Complications: A Surgeon's Notes on an Imperfect Science* (NY: Metropolitan Books, 2002).

xix *Groopman's: How Doctors Think* (NY: Houghton Mifflin, 2007).

1. The Birth of the Modern

3 *Roland Kuhn:* For this history, I have relied heavily on interviews conducted by David Healy in *The Psychopharmacologists* (London: Chapman and Hall, 1996); *The Psychopharmacologists II* (London: Chapman and Hall, 1998); and *The Psychopharmacologists III* (London: Arnold, 2000). The main interview of Roland Kuhn took place in 1996; of Alan Broadhurst, in 1994. Unless otherwise specified, extensive quotations are from those volumes or from T. A. Ban, D. Healy, et al., eds., *The History of Psychopharmacology and the CINP, as Told in Autobiography: From Psychopharmacology to Neuropsychopharmacology in the 1980s and*

the Story of CINP (Budapest: Animula, 2002). See also Lopez-Munoz, F., Alamo, C., "Monoaminergic Neurotransmission: The History of the Discovery of Anti-depressants from 1950s Until Today," *Curr Pharm Des* 15, no. 14 (2009): 1563–86; Cahn, C., "Obituary: Roland Kuhn, 1912–2005," *Neuropsychopharmacology* 31 (2006): 1096; and Kuhn's original papers: Kuhn, R., "Über die Behandlung depressiver Zustände mit einem Iminodibenzylderivat (G 22355)," *Schweiz Med Wochenschr* 87 (1957): 1135–40; Brown, W. A., Rosdolsky, M., "The Clinical Discovery of Imipramine," *Am J Psychiatry* 172 (2015): 426–29; and Kuhn, R., "The Treatment of Depressive States with G 22355 (Imipramine Hydrochloride)," *Am J Psychiatry* 115 (1958): 459–64.

3   *entry in the medical record:* Ban, Healy, et al. 2002, 334–35.

4   *Thorazine:* Chlorpromazine. Regarding brand versus generic names, I opt for the familiar. I use brand names for medications commonly known by them. I also use them (as here) in instances where experts quoted employ brand names. I use generic names, such as imipramine, for medications whose brand names have faded from memory.

5   *"strictly non-biological":* Healy 1996, 116.

6   *"fatigue, lethargy":* Kuhn, R., "The Imipramine Story," in *Discoveries in Biological Psychiatry*, ed. F. J. Ayd, B. Blackwell (Philadelphia: Lippincott, 1970), 207.

8   *Kuhn was the person:* Healy 2000, 366.

3. Random Thoughts

14   *planned a trial:* "Streptomycin Treatment of Pulmonary Tuberculosis," *Brit Med J* 2 (1948): 769–82.

14   *a new design:* Yoshioka, A., "Use of Randomisation in the Medical Research Council's Clinical Trial of Streptomycin in Pulmonary Tuberculosis in the 1940s," *BMJ* 317 (1998): 1220–23. Once more, priority is relative. Randomization had been employed before in medicine, once in the 1860s and, more notably, in 1905 in a trial of a brown-rice diet for protection against the vitamin-deficiency disease beriberi. (Randomization had been used extensively in the nineteenth century in the testing of telepathy and other psychic phenomena: Hacking, I., "Telepathy: Origins of Randomization in Experimental Design," *Isis* 79 (1988): 427–51. Hacking suggests that the superiority of randomization to balancing or matching was never established on intellectual/statistical grounds.) See also Ghaemi, S. N., *A Clinician's Guide to Statistics and Epidemiology in Mental Health: Measuring Truth and Uncertainty* (Cambridge, UK: Cambridge UP, 2009); and Benedek, T. G., "The History of Gold Therapy for Tuberculosis," *J Hist Med Allied Sci* 59 (2004): 50–89.

15   *bed rest matched:* An error in the original paper gives a different impression, but in the late going the differences were no longer significant: four of fifty patients on streptomycin died versus four of the remaining forty on bed rest alone.

17   *editorialist:* "The Controlled Therapeutic Trial," *Brit Med J* 2 (1948): 791–92.

18 *patients knew:* Apparently, patients were not informed of the details of the trial; some patients on bed rest alone might not have known that other participants were getting injections.

18 *Group psychotherapy:* Rackemann, F. M., "Joseph Hersey Pratt, 1872–1956," *Trans Assoc Am Physicians* 69 (1956): 24–27.

18 *outperformed:* Pratt, J. H., "Results Obtained by the Class Method of Home Treatment in Pulmonary Tuberculosis During a Period of Ten Years," *Boston Med Surg J* 176 (1917): 13–15; and Pratt, J. H., "The Class Method in the Home Treatment of Pulmonary Tuberculosis: An Account of Its Development During the Past Nineteen Years," *Boston Med Surg J* 194 (1926): 146–52.

19 *"until it hurts":* Cochrane, A. L., *Effectiveness and Efficiency: Random Reflections on Health Services* (London: Nuffield Provincial Hospitals Trust, 1972).

4. As Max Saw It

20 *depression rating scale:* Hamilton, M., "A Rating Scale for Depression," *J Neurol Neurosurg Psychiatry* 23 (1960): 56–62.

21 *"needs to realize":* Healy 1998, 99. Regarding Kuhn, see the first note to chapter 1 above.

22 *typical outpatient:* Zimmerman, M., Mattia, J. I., et al., "Are Subjects in Pharmacological Treatment Trials of Depression Representative of Patients in Routine Clinical Practice?," *Am J Psychiatry* 159 (2002): 469–73.

22 *a thousand patients:* Klerman, G. L., Cole, J. O., "Clinical Pharmacology of Imipramine and Related Antidepressant Compounds," *Pharmacol Rev* 17 (1965): 101–41.

5. Interlude: The Antithesis of Science

24 *a thousand patients:* Klerman and Cole 1965.

24 *1961 paper:* Liberman, R., "A Criticism of Drug Therapy in Psychiatry," *Arch Gen Psychiatry* 4 (1961): 131–36.

25 *private practitioner:* Lemere, F., "Negative Results in the Treatment of Depression with Imipramine Hydrochloride (Tofranil)," *Am J Psychiatry* 116 (1959): 258–59.

25 *systematic study:* Keup, W., Apolito, A., et al., "Inpatient Treatment of Depressive States with Tofranil (Imipramine Hydrochloride)," *Am J Psychiatry* 116 (1959): 257–58.

25 *cited an article:* Wolf, S., "The Pharmacology of Placebos." *Pharmacol Rev* 11 (1959): 689–704.

25 *telephoned:* February 27, 2012.

25 *published interviews:* Among others, Durgin, J., "Robert Liberman, M.D., '60: Agent of Change," *Dartmouth Medicine*, Winter 2009.

27 *outlying data:* Moncrieff, J., Wessely, S., et al., "Active Placebos Versus Antidepressants for Depression," *Cochrane Database Syst Rev* (2004): CD003012. See also Quitkin, F. M., Rabkin, J. G., et al., "Validity of Clinical Trials of Antidepressants," *Am J Psychiatry* 157 (2000): 327–37. In the Quitkin calculation,

active placebo fails to outperform conventional placebo even when the outlying study is discarded. More generally, the paper rebuts the active-placebo argument. One side note is that if, when patients in an antidepressant trial respond to treatment, they and observing clinicians guess that antidepressant rather than placebo is at work, they will be right most of the time. Treatment response (rather than perception of side effects) helps to break the blind.

With the advent of second-generation antidepressants, much of the air went out of the "active placebo" balloon. Lexapro and Zoloft, arguably the SSRIs with the subtlest side-effect profiles, tested out the best, when the active-placebo hypothesis would have predicted the reverse.

27 *"broadly accepted"*: Angell, June 23, 2011.

28 *two-to-one*: Confirmed recently in Undurraga, J., Tondo, L., et al., "Re-analysis of the Earliest Controlled Trials of Imipramine," *J Affect Disord* 147 (2013): 451–54.

28 *short list*: Cochrane 1972.

6. Off the Hook

29 *mental health research*: Hill, A. B., "Reflections on the Controlled Trial," *Ann Rheum Dis* 25 (1966): 107–13. See also Hill, A. B., "The Environment and Disease: Association or Causation?," *Proc R Soc Med* 58 (1965): 295–300.

30 *"ridiculous to scorn"*: Cromie, B. W., "The Feet of Clay of the Double-Blind Trial," *Lancet* 2 (1963): 994–97.

30 *flexible combination*: Hill cites Sargant, W., "Antidepressant Drugs," *Brit Med J* 1 (1965): 1495.

30 *mistrust of rating scales*: Healy 1998. The Kuhn quotes are from this second volume of interviews.

32 *no longer distinguish*: Bech, P., Gram, L. F., et al., "Quantitative Rating of Depressive States," *Acta Psychiatr Scand* 51 (1975): 161–70. See also Bagby, R. M., Ryder, A. G., et al., "The Hamilton Depression Rating Scale: Has the Gold Standard Become a Lead Weight?," *Am J Psychiatry* 161 (2004): 2163–77.

32 *Broadhurst conceded*: Healy 1996.

32 *Danish group*: Bech et al. 1975; and Bech, P., *Clinical Psychometrics* (Oxford, UK: Wiley-Blackwell, 2012).

33 *Max Hamilton traveled*: "The Clinical Validity of Rating Scales for Depression: Copenhagen, 1977," in Bech 2012.

33 *numerous successes*: Regarding the virtues of the scale, see Danish University Antidepressant Group (DUAG), "Clomipramine Dose-Effect Study in Patients with Depression: Clinical End Points and Pharmacokinetics," *Clin Pharmacol Ther* 66 (1999): 152–65, and correspondence with Per Bech, January 3, 2013: "In this DUAG study (DUAG 4 1999) we could demonstrate that the HAM-D$_6$ items were responsible for a dose-response relationship whereas the other HAM-D items [were] merely side-effects." See also Faries, D., Herrera, J., et al., "The Responsiveness of the Hamilton Depression Rating Scale," *J Psychiatr Res*

34 (2000): 3–10; and Bech, P., Fava, M., et al., "Factor Structure and Dimensionality of the Two Depression Scales in STAR*D Using Level 1 Datasets," *J Affect Disord* 132 (2011): 396–400.

33 *cleaner account:* Bech, P., Boyer, P., et al., "HAM-D17 and HAM-D6 Sensitivity to Change in Relation to Desvenlafaxine Dose and Baseline Depression Severity in Major Depressive Disorder," *Pharmacopsychiatry* 43 (2010): 271–76.

33 *early in trials:* Rasmussen, A., Lunde, M., et al., "A Double-Blind, Placebo-Controlled Study of Sertraline in the Prevention of Depression in Stroke Patients," *Psychosomatics* 44 (2003): 216–21.

33 *inconclusive:* Bech, P., "Meta-analysis of Placebo-Controlled Trials with Mirtazapine Using the Core Items of the Hamilton Depression Scale as Evidence of a Pure Antidepressive Effect in the Short-Term Treatment of Major Depression," *Int J Neuropsychopharmacol* 4 (2001): 337–45.

34 *serotonin-based:* Bech, P., "Is the Antidepressive Effect of Second-Generation Antidepressants a Myth?," *Psychol Med* 40 (2010): 181–86.

7. Interlude: My Sins

38 *We still see psychotic depression:* Rothschild, A. J., Winer, J., et al., "Missed Diagnosis of Psychotic Depression at 4 Academic Medical Centers," *J Clin Psychiatry* 69 (2008): 1293–96.

39 *Anorexia has fluctuated:* Lucas, A. R., Beard, C. M., et al., "50-Year Trends in the Incidence of Anorexia Nervosa in Rochester, Minn.: A Population-Based Study," *Am J Psychiatry* 148 (1991): 917–22; and Hoek, H. W., "Incidence, Prevalence and Mortality of Anorexia Nervosa and Other Eating Disorders," *Curr Opin Psychiatry* 19 (2006): 389–94.

39 *more robust:* Sheline, Y. I., Gado, M. H., et al., "Untreated Depression and Hippocampal Volume Loss," *Am J Psychiatry* 160 (2003): 1516–18.

8. Permission

41 *Cole's career:* See Katz, M. M., "Obituary: Jonathan O. Cole," *Neuropsychopharmacology* 35 (2010): 2647; and Schooler, N. R., "Jonathan O. Cole, MD (1925–2009): Innovator in Clinical Psychopharmacology and of the ECDEU/NCDEU Tradition," *J Clin Psychiatry* 72 (2011): 286–87.

41 *"green thumb":* Katz 2010.

42 *admixed with anxiety:* Johnson, D. A., "A Double-Blind Comparison of Flupenthixol, Nortriptyline and Diazepam in Neurotic Depression," *Acta Psychiatr Scand* 59 (1979): 1–8; and Van Megen, H.J.G.M., Van Vliet, I. M., et al., "Anxiolytics as Antidepressants," in *Depression: Neurobiological, Psychopathological and Therapeutic Advances*, ed. A. Honig, H. M. van Praag (Chichester, UK: Wiley, 1997), 427–44, cited in Bech 2001: "In studies on the potential antidepressive effect of benzodiazepines the decrease in the HAMD was found to be mainly on the improvement of items such as somatic anxiety, agitation, and sleep disturbances, and not on the amelioration of the core symptoms of depression."

43 *odd line of argument:* For example, Shorter, E., *Before Prozac: The Troubled History of Mood Disorders in Psychiatry* (Oxford, UK: Oxford UP, 2008). *Listening to Prozac* contains a riff on the "wrong" drug phenomenon.

9. Interlude: What He Came Here For

46 *"not psychotherapy versus":* Cited in Oldham, J. M., "Psychodynamic Psychotherapy for Personality Disorders," *Am J Psychiatry* 164 (2007): 1465–67.

46 *Writing in 1990:* Klerman, G. L., "The Psychiatric Patient's Right to Effective Treatment: Implications of *Osheroff v. Chestnut Lodge*," *Am J Psychiatry* 147 (1990): 409–18. The material in this chapter comes from Klerman's essay, the various replies to it, and my conversations and correspondence with Ray Osheroff in February and March 2012. The initial *O* in *Osheroff* is long.

48 *clinical lore:* Nelson, J. C., Bowers, M. B., Jr., "Delusional Unipolar Depression: Description and Drug Response," *Arch Gen Psychiatry* 35 (1978): 1321–28; Nelson, J. C., Bowers, M. B., Jr., et al., "Exacerbation of Psychosis by Tricyclic Antidepressants in Delusional Depression," *Am J Psychiatry* 136 (1979): 574–76; and Spiker, D. G., Weiss, J. C., et al., "The Pharmacological Treatment of Delusional Depression," *Am J Psychiatry* 142 (1985): 430–36.

10. Anti-Depressed

49 *commentary:* Mayer, D. Y., "Psychotropic Drugs and the 'Anti-Depressed' Personality," *Br J Med Psychol* 48 (1975): 349–57.

49 *stage play:* Yankauer, D., Mayer, H., *The Question Before the House,* 1935, referenced in the *Poughkeepsie Eagle-News* of March 4, 1935.

49 *fieldwork:* Fortes, M., Mayer, D. Y., "Psychosis and Social Change Among the Tallensi of Northern Ghana," in *Psychiatry in a Changing Society,* ed. S. H. Foulkes, G. S. Prince (London: Routledge, 1969, 2013), 33–74.

50 *1971 drug-use:* Editorial: "International Use of Tranquilizers," *BMJ* 3 (1974): 300.

50 *in the States:* Balter, M. B., Levine, J., et al., "Cross-National Study of the Extent of Anti-Anxiety-Sedative Drug Use," *N Engl J Med* 290 (1974): 769–74; Parry H. J., Balter, M. B., et al., "National Patterns of Psychotherapeutic Drug Use," *Arch Gen Psychiatry* 28 (1973): 769–83; and personal communication, Mark Olfson, 2011–2015. See also Kramer, P. D., Klerman, G. L., et al., "Women and the Abuse of Prescribed Psychotropic Medication," signed and distributed by U.S. Surgeon General's Office, April 1981. The Valium-era data serve as a reminder that our current concerns are less distinctive than we are likely to imagine. Of course, today, beyond the percentage of adults on medication, we worry about polypharmacy (multiple drugs for one patient) and prescribing for children.

51 *Cole revisited:* Cole, J. O., Davis, J. M., "Antidepressant Drugs," in *Comprehensive Textbook of Psychiatry,* ed. A. Freedman, H. L. Kaplan (Baltimore: Williams and Wilkins, 1974).

11. Interlude: Transitions

53 *portfolio:* Parron, D. L., Solomon, F., et al., eds., *Behavior, Health Risks, and So-cial Disadvantages* (Washington, DC: National Academy Press, 1982).

53 *proposed legislation:* Marshall, E., "Psychotherapy Works, but for Whom?," *Science* 207 (1980): 506–8.

53 *first substantial trial:* Klerman, G. L., Dimascio, A., et al., "Treatment of Depression by Drugs and Psychotherapy," *Am J Psychiatry* 131 (1974): 186–91.

53 *equally well:* Weissman, M. M., Prusoff, B. A., et al., "The Efficacy of Drugs and Psychotherapy in the Treatment of Acute Depressive Episodes," *Am J Psychiatry* 136 (1979): 555–58.

54 *250 schools:* Parloff, M. B., "Psychotherapy Research Evidence and Reimbursement Decisions: Bambi Meets Godzilla," *Am J Psychiatry* 139 (1982): 718–27. Here, Parloff sets the limits for the number of trials needed at between 6,800 and 4.7 million.

55 *"double depression":* Keller, M. B., Shapiro, R. W., "'Double Depression': Superimposition of Acute Depressive Episodes on Chronic Depressive Disorders," *Am J Psychiatry* 139 (1982): 438–42; and Klerman, G. L., "Long-Term Outcomes of Neurotic Depressions," in *Human Functioning in Longitudinal Perspective: Studies of Normal and Psychopathic Populations,* ed. S. B. Sells, R. Crandall, et al. (Baltimore: Williams and Wilkins, 1980), 58–70.

12. Big Splash

57 *Eysenck reviewed:* Eysenck, H. J., "The Effects of Psychotherapy: An Evaluation," *J Consult Psychol* 16 (1952): 319–24; Eysenck, H. J., "The Effects of Psychotherapy," *Int J Psychiatry* 1 (1965): 99–178; Eysenck, H. J., "The Effects of Psychotherapy Discussions," *Int J Psychiatry* 1 (1965): 317–25.

58 *contemporary commentator:* Rosenzweig, S., "A Transvaluation of Psychotherapy; a Reply to Hans Eysenck," *J Abnorm Psychol* 49 (1954): 298–304.

58 *young psychologist:* Glass, G. V., "Meta-analysis at 25," January 2000, http://www.gvglass.info/papers/meta25.html; Smith, M. L., Glass, G. V., "Meta-analysis of Psychotherapy Outcome Studies," *Am Psychol* 32 (1977): 752–60; and Smith, M. L., Glass, G. V., et al., *The Benefits of Psychotherapy* (Baltimore: Johns Hopkins UP, 1980).

58 *"common method":* Glass, G. V., "Primary, Secondary and Meta-analysis of Research," *Educational Researcher* 10 (1976), 3–8. Glass makes the case for poorly designed studies as useful sources of information and finally endorses the statement, unexpected from a statistician, "Knowledge exists in minds, not in books."

59 *Jacob Cohen:* Citations are from Cohen, J., *Statistical Power Analysis for the Behavioral Sciences,* 2nd ed. (Hillsdale, NJ: L. Erlbaum Associates, 1988).

60 *Standard medical treatments:* Leucht, S., Hierl, S., et al., "Putting the Efficacy of Psychiatric and General Medicine Medication into Perspective: Review of Meta-analyses," *Br J Psychiatry* 200 (2012): 97–106.

13. Alchemy

62 *admirers of Hans:* Prioleau, L., Murdoch, M., et al., "An Analysis of Psychotherapy Versus Placebo Studies," *Behav Brain Sci* 6 (1983): 275–310.

62 *"A good review":* Eysenck, H. J., "Meta-analysis and Its Problems," *BMJ* 309 (1994): 789–92. See also Eysenck, H. J., "Meta-analysis: An Abuse of Research Integration," *J Spec Educ* 18 (1984): 41–59.

62 *"scarcely any less":* Italics in the original. Smith, Glass, et al. 1980, 188.

63 *range encompasses:* Later, we will consider Irving Kirsch's "Emperor" paper, Erick Turner's reworking of the FDA data, and John Davis's and Per Bech's overviews of particular antidepressants; the research features effect sizes between 0.3 and 0.6. Results in the early trials of imipramine, before Kuhn's curse came into action, yielded effect sizes around 0.6, which may well be right for antidepressants in a drug-naïve population. Pym Cuijpers's review of high-quality trials of psychotherapy for depression finds an effect size of 0.2: Cuijpers, P., van Straten, A., et al., "The Effects of Psychotherapy for Adult Depression Are Overestimated: A Meta-analysis of Study Quality and Effect Size," *Psychol Med* 40 (2009): 211–23.

63 *hormone replacement:* The *Wikipedia* entry "Women's Health Initiative" serves as a good starting point.

63 *use of streptokinase:* Lau, J., Antman, E. M., et al., "Cumulative Meta-analysis of Therapeutic Trials for Myocardial Infarction," *N Engl J Med* 327 (1992): 248–54.

64 *contrasted meta-analysis:* LeLorier, J., Gregoire, G., et al., "Discrepancies Between Meta-Analyses and Subsequent Large Randomized, Controlled Trials," *N Engl J Med* 337 (1997): 536–42.

64 *alchemy:* Feinstein, A. R., "Meta-analysis: Statistical Alchemy for the 21st Century," *J Clin Epidemiol* 48 (1995): 71–79.

65 *allegiance bias:* Stegenga, J., "Is Meta-analysis the Platinum Standard of Evidence?," *Stud Hist Philos Biol Biomed Sci* 42 (2011): 497–507.

65 *celebrated meta-analysis:* Haynes, A. B., Weiser, T. G., et al., "A Surgical Safety Checklist to Reduce Morbidity and Mortality in a Global Population," *N Engl J Med* 360 (2009): 491–99.

65 *subsequent study:* Urbach, D. R., Govindarajan, A., et al., "Introduction of Surgical Safety Checklists in Ontario, Canada," *N Engl J Med* 370 (2014): 1029–38.

65 *defend checklists:* Leape, L. L., "The Checklist Conundrum," *N Engl J Med* 370 (2014): 1063–64; and Gawande, A., "When Checklists Work and When They Don't," *Incidental Economist*, March 15, 2014, http://theincidentaleconomist .com/wordpress/when-checklists-work-and-when-they-dont/.

14. Interlude: Providence

67 *hepatitis vaccines:* Bodenheimer, H. C., Jr., Fulton, J. P., et al., "Acceptance of Hepatitis B Vaccine Among Hospital Workers," *Am J Public Health* 76 (1986): 252–55; and Fulton, J. P., Bodenheimer, H. C., Jr., et al., "Acceptance of Hepa-

titis B Vaccine Among Hospital Workers: A Follow-Up," *Am J Public Health* 76 (1986): 1339–40.

68 Moments of Engagement: NY: W. W. Norton, 1989.

69 *"Curing Depression"*: *New York Times*, May 14, 1986, A1, A17.

15. Best Reference

70 *Collaborative Research*: Elkin, I., Shea, M. T., et al., "National Institute of Mental Health Treatment of Depression Collaborative Research Program. General Effectiveness of Treatments," *Arch Gen Psychiatry* 46 (1989): 971–82; and Elkin, I., Parloff, M. B., et al., "NIMH Treatment of Depression Collaborative Research Program. Background and Research Plan," *Arch Gen Psychiatry* 42 (1985): 305–16.

72 *"better, faster"*: Klein, D. F., "Preventing Hung Juries About Therapy Studies," *J Consult Clin Psychol* 64 (1996): 81–87.

72 *Psychologists argued*: Jacobson, N. S., Hollon, S. D., "Cognitive-Behavior Therapy Versus Pharmacotherapy: Now That the Jury's Returned Its Verdict, It's Time to Present the Rest of the Evidence," *J Consult Clin Psychol* 64 (1996): 74–80; Elkin, I., Gibbons, R. D., et al., "Science Is Not a Trial (But It Can Sometimes Be a Tribulation)," *J Consult Clin Psychol* 64 (1996): 92–103; and Klein 1996, 81–87.

72 *listed false symptoms*: As "professional patients" supplement their income with participation in outcome trials, this problem has worsened across all of medicine: Resnik, D. B., McCann, D. J., "Deception by Research Participants," *N Engl J Med* (2015) 373: 1192–93. The editorial raises concerns that symptom fabrication can lower effect sizes in outcome trials and interfere with the promulgation of useful treatments.

16. Better, Faster, Cheaper

74 *Jan Fawcett*: Conversations, March 26, 2012, and July 29, 2015.

75 *so far as I know*: Conversation with M. Tracie Shea, March 26, 2012.

75 *"therapeutic window"*: For instance, Perry, P. J., Zeilmann, C., et al., "Tricyclic Antidepressant Concentrations in Plasma: An Estimate of Their Sensitivity and Specificity as a Predictor of Response," *J Clin Psychopharmacol* 14 (1994): 230–40; and Perry, P. J., Wehring, H. J., et al., "Clinical Psychopharmacology and Other Somatic Therapies," in *The Medical Basis of Psychiatry*, ed. S. H. Fatemi, P. J. Clayton (Totowa, NJ: Humana, 2008), 600–601. The textbook indicates that the standard daily dose of imipramine is 150–300 milligrams.

75 *concerns*: Klein, D. F., Ross, D. C., "Reanalysis of the National Institute of Mental Health Treatment of Depression Collaborative Research Program General Effectiveness Report," *Neuropsychopharmacology* 8 (1993): 241–51.

76 *anticipated*: Hill 1966.

76 *differential dropout*: See, for example, Claghorn, J. L., Feighner, J. P., "A Double-Blind Comparison of Paroxetine with Imipramine in the Long-Term Treatment

of Depression," *J Clin Psychopharmacol* 13 (1993): 23S–27S. It is worth observing the process in miniature in a trial that Kirsch included in the main analysis in his "Hearing Placebo" paper: Davidson, J., Turnbull, C., "Isocarboxazid: Efficacy and Tolerance," *J Affect Disord* 5 (1983): 183–89. Medication shows phenomenal efficacy that loses significance in the completer sample because patients on placebo leave for inefficacy and patients on medicine leave when they feel better.

77 *NIMH researchers:* Collins, J. F., Elkin, I., "Randomization in the NIMH Treatment of Depression Collaborative Research Program," in *Randomization and Field Experimentation,* ed. R. F. Boruch, W. Wothke (San Francisco: Jossey-Bass, 1985).

77 *does not reward:* Intention-to-treat analyses can disadvantage medications when they cause side effects early: Greenland, S., Robins, J. M., et al., "Confounding and Collapsibility in Causal Inference," *Statistical Science* 14 (1999): 29–46. Although he attaches a different meaning to the result, in one of his major papers Kirsch finds that in drug-company trials submitted to the FDA, completer analyses, compared to intention-to-treat analyses, yield narrower differences between antidepressant and placebo: Kirsch, I., Moore, T. J., et al., "The Emperor's New Drugs: An Analysis of Antidepressant Medication Data Submitted to the U.S. Food and Drug Administration," *Prev Treat* 5 (2002).

77 *help some patients a lot:* Thase, M. E., Larsen, K. G., et al., "Assessing the 'True' Effect of Active Antidepressant Therapy v. Placebo in Major Depressive Disorder: Use of a Mixture Model," *Br J Psychiatry* 199 (2011): 501–7.

17. Interlude: Tolerably Good

80 *typical overview:* Sommi, R. W., Crismon, M. L., et al., "Fluoxetine: A Serotonin-Specific, Second-Generation Antidepressant," *Pharmacotherapy* 7 (1987): 1–15.

80 *column:* Kramer, P. D., "Metamorphosis," *Psychiatric Times,* May 1989; and Kramer, P. D., "The New You," *Psychiatric Times,* March 1990.

81 *Early in 1993:* Song, F., Freemantle, N., et al., "Selective Serotonin Reuptake Inhibitors: Meta-analysis of Efficacy and Acceptability," *BMJ* 306 (1993): 683–87.

81 *switched to Zoloft:* Thase, M. E., Rush, A. J., et al., "Double-Blind Switch Study of Imipramine or Sertraline Treatment of Antidepressant-Resistant Chronic Depression," *Arch Gen Psychiatry* 59 (2002): 233–39.

83 *antidepressant maintenance:* See chapter 36 below.

84 *health-related well-being:* For a thought-provoking overview, see Norman, G. R., Sloan, J. A., et al., "Interpretation of Changes in Health-Related Quality of Life: The Remarkable Universality of Half a Standard Deviation," *Med Care* 41 (2003): 582–92.

84 *so burdensome:* Ferrari, A. J., Charlson, F. J., et al., "Burden of Depressive Disorders by Country, Sex, Age, and Year: Findings from the Global Burden of Dis-

ease Study 2010," *PLoS Med* 10 (2013): e1001547. More recent updates have begun to appear in *The Lancet*.

84 *quality-of-life:* Bech, P., "Social Functioning: Should It Become an Endpoint in Trials of Antidepressants?," *CNS Drugs* 19 (2005): 313–24. See also Bech, P., "Role of Psychotropic Drugs in Quality of Life Improvement in Psychiatric Patients: Historical Aspects," in *History of Psychopharmacology*, 3rd ed., Lopez-Munoz, F., Alar, C., et al. (Ann Arbor, MI: NPP, 2014).

It is interesting to consider Doris Mayer's "anti-depressed" complaint in light of findings that medication confers vitality and social engagement.

84 *one study:* Kocsis, J. H., Schatzberg, A., et al., "Psychosocial Outcomes Following Long-Term, Double-Blind Treatment of Chronic Depression with Sertraline vs. Placebo," *Arch Gen Psychiatry* 59 (2002): 723–28.

18. Better than Well

87 *no mental disorder:* In *Listening to Prozac*, I did not always differentiate *cosmetic psychopharmacology* from *better than well*. In subsequent writing, I have tried to be more consistent in maintaining the distinction.

87 *essays:* Kramer 1989, 1990.

87 *Cole recalled:* Healy 1996.

87 *Arvid Carlsson:* Ibid.

88 *University of Wales:* Tranter, R., Healy, H., et al., "Functional Effects of Agents Differentially Selective to Noradrenergic or Serotonergic Systems," *Psychol Med* 32 (2002): 517–24.

88 *"prosocial":* Crockett, M. J., Clark, L., et al., "Serotonin Selectively Influences Moral Judgment Behavior Through Effects on Harm Aversion," *Proc Natl Acad Sci USA* 107 (2010): 17433–38; and Crockett, M. J., Siegel, J. Z., et al., "Dissociable Effects of Serotonin and Dopamine on the Valuation of Harm in Moral Decision Making," *Curr Biol* 25 (2015): 1852–59.

88 *Swedish researchers:* Ekselius, L., Von Knorring, L., "Changes in Personality Traits During Treatment with Sertraline or Citalopram," *Br J Psychiatry* 174 (1999): 444–48. See also Ekselius, L., Von Knorring, L., et al., "A Double-Blind Multicenter Trial Comparing Sertraline and Citalopram in Patients with Major Depression Treated in General Practice," *Int Clin Psychopharmacol* 12 (1997): 323–31. For depression, responses were first seen at two weeks and rose steadily. The response rate at twelve weeks ran from just under 70 percent (intention to treat) to around 80 percent (completers).

89 *replicated:* Brody, A. L., Saxena, S., et al., "Personality Changes in Adult Subjects with Major Depressive Disorder or Obsessive-Compulsive Disorder Treated with Paroxetine," *J Clin Psychiatry* 61 (2000): 349–55.

89 *dysthymia:* Hellerstein, D. J., Kocsis, J. H., et al., "Double-Blind Comparison of Sertraline, Imipramine, and Placebo in the Treatment of Dysthymia: Effects on Personality," *Am J Psychiatry* 157 (2000): 1436–44. See also Kocsis, J. H., Zisook, S., et al., "Double-Blind Comparison of Sertraline, Imipramine, and Pla-

cebo in the Treatment of Dysthymia: Psychosocial Outcomes," *Am J Psychiatry* 154 (1997): 390–95; and Kocsis, J. H., Schatzberg, A., et al., "Psychosocial Outcomes Following Long-Term, Double-Blind Treatment of Chronic Depression with Sertraline vs. Placebo," *Arch Gen Psychiatry* 59 (2002): 723–28.

90 *Finnish:* Jylha, P., Ketokivi, M., et al., "Do Antidepressants Change Personality?—a Five-Year Observational Study," *J Affect Disord* 142 (2012): 200–207.

90 *Canadian:* Quilty, L. C., Meusel, L. A., et al., "Neuroticism as a Mediator of Treatment Response to SSRIs in Major Depressive Disorder," *J Affect Disord* 111 (2008): 67–73.

90 *painstaking:* Tang, T. Z., DeRubeis, R. J., et al., "Personality Change During Depression Treatment: A Placebo-Controlled Trial," *Arch Gen Psychiatry* 66 (2009): 1322–30.

90 *the greater change:* DeRubeis, R. J., Hollon, S. D., et al., "Cognitive Therapy vs. Medications in the Treatment of Moderate to Severe Depression," *Arch Gen Psychiatry* 62 (2005): 409–16. The effects corresponded to a number needed to treat between 4 (for medication) and 5.5 (for psychotherapy). The Paxil (versus placebo) effect on personality corresponded to a number needed to treat of 3.

19. Interlude: Old Dream

94 *sociology text:* Scheper-Hughes, N., *Saints, Scholars, and Schizophrenics: Mental Illness in Rural Ireland* (Berkeley: University of California Press, 1977, 1982, 2001).

20. Spotting Trout

97 *"Listening to Prozac":* Kirsch and Sapirstein 1998.

97 *twit authority:* While in graduate school, Kirsch had done satire in collaboration with the *National Lampoon*, producing a comedy audio recording about various missing Nixon White House tapes. https://en.wikipedia.org/wiki/The_Missing _White_House_Tapes.

98 *Two critics:* Klein, D. F., "Listening to Meta-analysis but Hearing Bias," *Prev Treat* 1 (June 1998); and Dawes, R. M., "Commentary on Kirsch and Sapirstein," *Prev Treat* 1 (June 1998).

98 *recent Cochrane:* Leucht, C., Huhn, M., et al., "Amitriptyline Versus Placebo for Major Depressive Disorder," *Cochrane Database Syst Rev* 12 (2012): CD009138.

98 *Wellbutrin trials:* Zung, W. W., "Review of Placebo-Controlled Trials with Bupropion," *J Clin Psychiatry* 44 (1983): 104–14.

98 *TDCRP:* Elkin, Shea, et al. 1989.

99 *outrageous:* Joffe, R. T., Singer, W., et al., "A Placebo-Controlled Comparison of Lithium and Triiodothyronine Augmentation of Tricyclic Antidepressants in Unipolar Refractory Depression," *Arch Gen Psychiatry* 50 (1993): 387–93. It is interesting to note that the "placebo" in this experiment is imipramine or desipramine plus a placebo pill. In important calculations, Kirsch used an average

placebo effect, across all nineteen experiments in his collection. We can see that some of those "placebo" results occurred in patients taking full doses of antidepressants. And then, in this sense, his collection included active placebos, with side effects.

100 *glimmer:* Klein 1998.

100 *Thoreau:* Diary, November 11, 1850.

101 *antidepressant properties:* Van Megen and Van Vliet 1997; and PHARMA, "Discovers Award 2004," *Special Publications*, April 2004, 31. (See the 1989 award for adinazolam's developer, Jackson Hester.)

101 *rebound:* Rickels, K., London, J., et al., "Adinazolam, Diazepam, Imipramine, and Placebo in Major Depressive Disorder: A Controlled Study," *Pharmacopsychiatry* 24 (1991): 127–31.

101 *amylobarbitone:* Blashki, T. G., Mowbray, R., et al., "Controlled Trial of Amitriptyline in General Practice," *Br Med J* 1 (1971): 133–38.

102 *"not considered antidepressants":* Kirsch, I., "Are Drug and Placebo Effects in Depression Additive?," *Biol Psychiatry* 47 (2000): 733–35; Kirsch, I., "Medication and Suggestion in the Treatment of Depression," *Contemporary Hypnosis* 22 (2005): 59–66; and Kirsch, I., "Antidepressants and the Placebo Response," *Epidemiologia e Psichiatria Sociale* 18 (2009): 313–22. While this book was in press, Kirsch repeated the claim: Kirsch, I., "Antidepressants and the Placebo Effect," in *Placebo Talks: Modern Perspectives on Placebos in Society*, ed. A. Raz, C. S. Harris (Oxford: Oxford UP 2016), 17–32.

102 60 Minutes: Interview with Lesley Stahl, produced by Richard Bonin, February 19, 2012.

21. Hypothetical Counterfactual

104 *Dawes's complaint:* Dawes 1998.

104 *back-and-forth:* Kirsch 1998; and Kirsch, I., "Reducing Noise and Hearing Placebo More Clearly," *Prev Treat* 1 (June 1998).

105 *better-than-usual:* In this discussion, I do not consider interactive effects. It might be that when external circumstances are favorable, antidepressants deliver yet more help—that good fortune and medication are synergistic. In that case, medication may be performing especially well in the very case in which placebo seems to be doing proportionately more.

105 demand characteristics: Orne, M. T., "On the Social Psychology of the Psychological Experiment: With Particular Reference to Demand Characteristics and Their Implications," *Am Psychol* 17 (1962): 776–83. The seminal paper for an extensive literature.

106 *"package of placebo":* Klerman, G. L., "Scientific and Ethical Considerations in the Use of Placebo Controls in Clinical Trials in Psychopharmacology," *Psychopharmacol Bull* 22 (1986): 25–29.

106 *"75% of the response":* Kirsch and Sapirstein 1998.

106 *echo:* Angell, June 23, 2011.

22. Two Plus Two

108 *standard way:* The example is of the usual sort, and I hope that it is clear enough. I am not confident that tonic water would work in this fashion—not inclined to believe that placebo is powerful even in this domain. See Hull, J. G., Bond, C. F., Jr., "Social and Behavioral Consequences of Alcohol Consumption and Expectancy: A Meta-analysis," *Psychol Bull* 99 (1986): 347–60.

110 *"At the extreme":* Dawes 1998.

110 *interpersonal psychotherapy:* Klerman, Dimascio, et al. 1974. The early trials take on added importance because prior to the NIMH Collaborative study in the 1980s, research subjects were not routinely offered extensive emotional support. The drug arm tested "medication alone"—and still, in the combined treatment arm, psychotherapy added scant extra benefit.

110 *all-star team:* Zajecka, J., Amsterdam, J. D. (chairs), "Cognitive Therapy and Medications in the Treatment of Depression and the Prevention of Subsequent Recurrence" (symposium, Annual Meeting, American Psychiatric Association, New York, NY, May 7, 2014); and Hollon, S. D., DeRubeis, R. J., et al., "Effect of Cognitive Therapy with Antidepressant Medications vs. Antidepressants Alone on the Rate of Recovery in Major Depressive Disorder: A Randomized Clinical Trial," *JAMA Psychiatry* 71 (2014): 1157–64.

111 *the contrary:* For extensive overviews, see Cuijpers, P., Sijbrandij, M., et al., "Adding Psychotherapy to Antidepressant Medication in Depression and Anxiety Disorders: A Meta-analysis," *World Psychiatry* 13 (2014): 56–67; Cuijpers, P., Dekker, J., et al., "Adding Psychotherapy to Pharmacotherapy in the Treatment of Depressive Disorders in Adults: A Meta-analysis," *J Clin Psychiatry* 70 (2009): 1219–29; and (suggestive of limited additivity) von Wolff, A., Hölzel, L. P., et al., "Combination of Pharmacotherapy and Psychotherapy in the Treatment of Chronic Depression: A Systematic Review and Meta-analysis," *BMC Psychiatry* 12 (2012): 61.

111 *from UCLA:* Leuchter, A. F., Cook, I. A., et al., "Changes in Brain Function of Depressed Subjects During Treatment with Placebo," *Am J Psychiatry* 159 (2002): 122–29.

111 *predict responsiveness:* McGrath, C. L., Kelley, M. E., et al., "Toward a Neuroimaging Treatment Selection Biomarker for Major Depressive Disorder," *JAMA Psychiatry* 70 (2013): 821–29.

112 *bed rest:* Strictly speaking, whether bed rest helped patients in the pre-antibiotic era remains unknown; for those treated with antibiotics, bed rest adds nothing. Hirsch, J. G., Schaedler, R. W., et al., "A Study Comparing the Effects of Bed Rest and Physical Activity on Recovery from Pulmonary Tuberculosis," *Am Rev Tuberc* 75 (1957): 359–409.

112 *Elsewhere:* Kirsch and Moore 2002.

113 *undercut:* Moerman, D. E., "The Loaves and the Fishes," *Prev Treat* 5 (July 15, 2002).

23. In Plain Sight

114 *current*: American Psychiatric Association, *Diagnostic and Statistical Manual of Mental Disorders: DSM-5* (Arlington, VA: American Psychiatric Publishing, 2013).

115 *manifesto*: Evidence-Based Medicine Working Group, "Evidence-Based Medicine: A New Approach to Teaching the Practice of Medicine," *JAMA* 268 (1992): 2420–25. I use the word *manifesto* largely because of the paper's first sentence: "A new paradigm for medical care is emerging." To my (admittedly idiosyncratic) ear, the clarion call has the ring of "A spectre is haunting Europe . . ."

116 *"integration"*: Adapted from Institute of Medicine, *Crossing the Quality Chasm: A New Health System for the 21st Century* (Washington, DC: National Academy Press, 2001); and Sackett, D. L., Straus, S. E., et al., *Evidence-Based Medicine: How to Practice and Teach EBM*, 2nd ed. (Edinburgh: Churchill Livingstone, 2000). Regarding patient values, see Ubel, P. A., "Medical Facts Versus Value Judgments—Toward Preference-Sensitive Guidelines," *N Engl J Med* 372 (2015): 2475–77.

116 *disqualify*: This point, that a core function of evidence-based medicine is to exclude most evidence, is a favorite of the practicing dermatologist Jonathan Rees, who writes trenchantly on the subject. See, for example, Rees, J., "Why We Should Let 'Evidence-Based Medicine' Rest in Peace," *Clin Dermatol* 31 (2013): 806–10.

116 *EBM-based study*: De Lima, M. S., Hotoph, M., et al., "The Efficacy of Drug Treatments for Dysthymia: A Systematic Review and Meta-analysis," *Psychol Med* 29 (1999): 1273–89. I have noted the number needed to treat of just below 4 for response. Regarding remission, the data were less plentiful, but each individual study that made the calculation likewise found a number needed to treat of around 4.

117 *typical group*: Many patterns—an infinite number—produce a number needed to treat of 4. If all four patients did well on medication, but three did well on placebo, we would also have needed to treat four patients to get one additional response. In real drug trials, more than half of patients will respond to medication and over a quarter to placebo. For a recent overview, see Andrade, C., "The Numbers Needed to Treat and Harm (NNT, NNH) Statistics: What They Tell Us and What They Do Not," *J Clin Psychiatry* 76 (2015): e330–e33.

117 *standard textbook*: Sackett, D. L., Richardson, W. S., et al., *Evidence-Based Medicine: How to Practice and Teach EBM* (Edinburgh: Churchill Livingstone, 1997); and Sackett and Straus 2000. See also Leucht and Hierl 2012.

118 *treatment of headache*: Migliardi, J. R., Armellino, J. J., et al., "Caffeine as an Analgesic Adjuvant in Tension Headache," *Clin Pharmacol Ther* 56 (1994): 576–86.

119 *columnist*: Beam 2011.

119 *easily accessed*: Levkovitz, Y., Tedeschini, E., et al., "Efficacy of Antidepressants for Dysthymia: A Meta-analysis of Placebo-Controlled Randomized Trials," *J Clin Psychiatry* 72 (2011): 509–14.

119 *Cochrane Collaboration:* De Lima, M. S., Moncrieff, J., et al., "Drugs Versus Placebo for Dysthymia," *Cochrane Library,* April 20, 2005.

In June 2015, this review was withdrawn. Subsequently, I contacted Rachel Churchill, coordinating editor of the Cochrane Depression, Anxiety and Neurosis Group, which was responsible for the publication and, later, the withdrawal of the review, and Mauricio Silva de Lima, the lead author. Both have assured me that there is no scandal and no scientific ambiguity. The withdrawn paper remains posted on the Cochrane website.

In 2002, de Lima cowrote the original review with Joanna Moncrieff. At that point, he was a full-time academic. De Lima then headed the group, still including Moncrieff, that updated the review in 2005. By that time he was working at Eli Lilly. In 2007, a close colleague informed de Lima that, because of policy changes at Cochrane, as a Pharma employee he would no longer be included on the distribution of Cochrane's research-overview material. Since without that legwork updating reports would be more difficult, de Lima withdrew from the Collaboration.

No one else volunteered to update the dysthymia review. (Based on conversations that I have had in the preparation of this book, I have come to wonder whether dysthymia was orphaned in part because, in an era of skepticism about antidepressants, researchers involved in the politics of EBM were reluctant to be associated with a semiofficial report, on drug treatment of dysthymia, that would likely show substantial efficacy.) In 2015, based on further policy changes regarding reviews and employment in industry, as well as the lack of recent updates, Cochrane withdrew the dysthymia report.

Meanwhile, a 2013 overview by psychologists with no drug company ties found results similar to those in the Cochrane review: von Wolff, A., Hölzel, L. P., "Selective Serotonin Reuptake Inhibitors and Tricyclic Antidepressants in the Acute Treatment of Chronic Depression and Dysthymia: A Systematic Review and Meta-analysis," *J Affect Disord* 144 (2013): 7–15.

Information on Cochrane review withdrawal: correspondence with Rachel Churchill, August 2015, and correspondence and conversation with Mauricio Silva de Lima, July and August 2015.

119 *2011 follow-up:* Levkovitz, Tedeschini, et al. 2011.

120 *research group:* Ibid.

120 *Wampold:* Imel, Z. E., Malterer, M. B., et al., "A Meta-analysis of Psychotherapy and Medication in Unipolar Depression and Dysthymia," *J Affect Disord* 110 (2008): 197–206. See also Cuijpers, P., van Straten, A., et al., "Psychotherapy for Chronic Major Depression and Dysthymia: A Meta-analysis," *Clin Psychol Rev* 30 (2010): 51–62; and von Wolff, Hölzel, et al. 2012. Some evidence suggests that psychotherapy has its own severity gradient and, against expectations, works least well for the healthiest patients. Driessen, E., Cuijpers, P., "Does Pretreatment Severity Moderate the Efficacy of Psychological Treatment of Adult Outpatient Depression? A Meta-analysis," *J Consult Clin Psychol* 782 (2010): 668–80.

This research may be subject to some of the same confounds that plague the severity controversy regarding medication.

120 *psychotherapy outcome:* Wampold, B. E., *The Great Psychotherapy Debate: Models, Methods, and Findings,* 2nd ed. (London: Routledge, 2015).

120 *appear later:* McCullough, J. P., "Psychotherapy for Dysthymia: A Naturalistic Study of Ten Patients," *J Nerv Ment Dis* 179 (1991): 734–40.

24. Trajectories

122 *editorial:* "Just How Tainted Has Medicine Become?," *Lancet* 359 (2002): 1167; and Wright, I. C., "Conflict of Interest and the *British Journal of Psychiatry*," *Br J Psychiatry* 180 (2002): 82–83.

122 *Memoirs multiplied:* Kramer, P. D., "The Anatomy of Melancholy," *New York Times Book Review,* April 7, 1996, 27.

123 *quadrupled:* Mojtabai, R., Olfson, M., "National Trends in Long-Term Use of Antidepressant Medications: Results from the U.S. National Health and Nutrition Examination Survey," *J Clin Psychiatry* 75 (2014): 169–77; and Mojtabai, R., "Increase in Antidepressant Medication in the US Adult Population between 1990 and 2003," *Psychother Psychosom* 77 (2008): 83–92.

123 *topped 100 million:* Figures from CDC, 2007; IMS Health, 2009.

123 *exclusive company:* Lenzer, J., Brownlee, S., "Naming Names: Is There an (Unbiased) Doctor in the House?," *BMJ* 337 (2008): a930.

124 *salvo:* Kirsch and Moore 2002.

124 *reanalysis:* Kirsch, I., Deacon, B. J., et al., "Initial Severity and Antidepressant Benefits: A Meta-analysis of Data Submitted to the Food and Drug Administration," *PLoS Med* 5 (2008): e45.

124 *health authority:* National Institute for Clinical Excellence, *Depression: Management of Depression in Primary and Secondary Care* (London: National Institute for Clinical Excellence, 2004), cited in Kirsch, Deacon, et al. 2008.

124 *Other psychiatrists:* Horder, J., Matthews, P., et al., "Placebo, Prozac and PLoS: Significant Lessons for Psychopharmacology," *J Psychopharmacol* 25 (2011): 1277–88; and Vohringer, P. A., Ghaemi, S. N., "Solving the Antidepressant Efficacy Question: Effect Sizes in Major Depressive Disorder," *Clin Ther* 33 (2011): B49–61.

124 *commonplace:* Preston, A., "Does Prozac Help Artists Be Creative?," *Guardian,* May 18, 2013.

126 *looked past:* FDA Drug Approval Documents: Nefazodone, December 1994, http://digitalcommons.ohsu.edu/cgi/viewcontent.cgi?article=1022&context =fdadrug.

126 *watchdog group:* Preziosi, P., "Science, Pharmacoeconomics and Ethics in Drug R&D: A Sustainable Future Scenario?," *Nat Rev Drug Discov* 3 (2004): 521–26. See box within article: "History Repeats Itself: Bendectin and Nefazodone."

126 *three Hamilton points' worth:* Doing my own arithmetic and using Horder's account of the Hamilton ratings, I arrive at a Hamilton point differential of 2.98 for the three remaining antidepressants.

127 *abandon:* See, for example, Hall, H., "Antidepressants and Effect Size," *Science-Based Med*, July 19, 2011, https://www.sciencebasedmedicine.org/antidepressants-and-effect-size/.

127 *unbiased medical experts:* Lenzer and Brownlee 2008.

127 *Davis and colleagues:* Gibbons, R. D., Hur, K., et al., "Benefits from Antidepressants: Synthesis of 6-Week Patient-Level Outcomes from Double-Blind Placebo-Controlled Randomized Trials of Fluoxetine and Venlafaxine," *Arch Gen Psychiatry* 69 (2012): 572–79.

127 *John Krystal:* Gueorguieva, R., Mallinckrodt, C., et al., "Trajectories of Depression Severity in Clinical Trials of Duloxetine: Insights into Antidepressant and Placebo Responses," *Arch Gen Psychiatry* 68 (2011): 1227–37.

128 *typical patient:* Kirsch and Sapirstein 1998.

25. No Myth

131 *justly influential:* Turner, E. H., Matthews, A. M., et al., "Selective Publication of Antidepressant Trials and Its Influence on Apparent Efficacy," *N Engl J Med* 358 (2008): 252–60. For an overview of file-drawer bias throughout medicine, see Song, F., Parekh, S., et al., "Dissemination and Publication of Research Findings: An Updated Review of Related Biases," *Health Technol Assess* 14 (2010): iii, ix–xi, 1–193.

131 *express concern:* Turner, E. H., Rosenthal R., "Efficacy of Antidepressants," *BMJ* (2008): 516–17.

131 *exceptions:* In studies of Prozac involving more than eleven hundred patients, Turner found one offending trial: results on forty-two subjects were not separated out but had been amalgamated with other data; one way or another, all the Prozac results had appeared in the published literature.

133 *run of trials:* Correspondence with Thase, Khan, and James Faucett, April 2012 and throughout 2012–13. In the successful trials, not only did placebos do less well than in failed trials; the antidepressants performed better, too. It looked as if the benchmarking antidepressant was doing its job, identifying a representative group of depressed patients—who also responded to the (later-approved) candidate drug.

134 *corresponds:* Kraemer, H. C., Kupfer, D. J., "Size of Treatment Effects and Their Importance to Clinical Research and Practice," *Biol Psychiatry* 59 (2006): 990–96; and personal correspondence, Helena Kraemer, January 2013. The translation of effect sizes into categorical outcomes causes controversy among statisticians. Kraemer maintains that the equivalences she calculates are robust among types of studies. In her tables, an effect size around 0.45 corresponds to a number needed to treat of 4.

134 *Davis:* Correspondence with Davis and Timothy Ryan, 2013–15.

135 *Bech examined:* Bech, *Psychol Med* 2010; and Bech 2012. For Prozac, some trials came in at 0.38 and some at 0.40. See also Entsuah, R., Shaffer, M., et al., "A Critical Examination of the Sensitivity of Unidimensional Subscales Derived

from the Hamilton Depression Rating Scale to Antidepressant Drug Effects,"
J Psychiatr Res 36 (2002): 437–48.

26. *Interlude: Pitch-Perfect*

146 *homeless shelters:* Elliott, C., "The Best-Selling, Billion-Dollar Pills Tested on Homeless People," *Matter,* July 28, 2014, https://medium.com/matter/did-big -pharma-test-your-meds-on-homeless-people-a6d8d3fc7dfe.

146 *"inevitable":* Elliott, C., "Guinea-Pigging," *New Yorker,* January 7, 2008. See also Elliott, C., "What Happens When Profit Margins Drive Clinical Research?," *Mother Jones,* September/October 2010.

28. **Sham**

154 *Danish medical researchers:* Hróbjartsson, A., Gøtzsche, P. C., "Is the Placebo Powerless? An Analysis of Clinical Trials Comparing Placebo with No Treatment," *N Engl J Med* 344 (2001): 1594–602. See also Hróbjartsson, A, Gøtzsche, P. C., "Placebo Interventions for All Clinical Conditions," *Cochrane Library* 3, no. 1 (2010).

155 *effect sizes near 0.3:* Debating Hróbjartsson and Gøtzsche, Wampold argued that in studies with continuous subjective outcomes, placebo showed a number needed to treat of 7. Wampold, B. E., Imel, Z. E., et al., "The Placebo Effect: 'Relatively Large' and 'Robust' Enough to Survive Another Assault," *J Clin Psychol* 63 (2007): 401–3.

156 *"out of a job":* Feinberg, C., "The Placebo Phenomenon," *Harvard Magazine,* January–February 2013, 36–39.

156 *"rarely cure":* Kaptchuk, T. J., Miller, F. G., "Placebo Effects in Medicine," *N Engl J Med* 373 (2015): 8–9.

156 maintenance: Klerman, G. L., Dimascio, A., et al., "Treatment of Depression by Drugs and Psychotherapy," *Am J Psychiatry* 131 (1974): 186–91; Frank, E., Kupfer, D. J., et al., "Three-Year Outcomes for Maintenance Therapies in Recurrent Depression," *Arch Gen Psychiatry* 47 (1990): 1093–99; and Rabkin, J. G., McGrath, P. J., et al., "Effects of Pill-Giving on Maintenance of Placebo Response in Patients with Chronic Mild Depression," *Am J Psychiatry* 147 (1990): 1622–26.

156 *sham pill:* Rabkin and McGrath 1990.

157 *door-to-door:* Nandi, D. N., Ajmany, S., et al., "A Clinical Evaluation of Depressives Found in a Rural Survey in India," *Br J Psychiatry* 128 (1976): 523–27. The Hamilton scores reported in the article are the sum of two raters' evaluations; I have halved the reported scores and rounded to the nearest integer.

157 *rapid symptom loss:* Quitkin, F. M., Rabkin, J. G., et al., "Heterogeneity of Clinical Response During Placebo Treatment," *Am J Psychiatry* 148 (1991): 193–96; and Quitkin, F. M., McGrath, P. J., et al., "Different Types of Placebo Response in Patients Receiving Antidepressants," *Am J Psychiatry* 148 (1991): 197–203. Quitkin's and Nandi's work gives context to a report, out of the University of

Michigan, published while this book was in press: Peciña, M., Bohnert, A.S.B., et al., "Association Between Placebo-Activated Neural Systems and Antidepressant Responses: Neurochemistry of Placebo Effects in Major Depression," *JAMA Psychiatry* 72 (2015): 1087–94. In the study, patients who manifested even minor improvement on one week of placebo proved likelier to respond to antidepressants in a subsequent ten-week trial. Early improvers on placebo showed brain-image changes resembling patterns later found in medication responders.

Commentators saw these results as indicating that placebo response plays a large role in antidepressant response. But Nandi's and Quitkin's research shows that even dramatic initial symptom loss on placebo cannot guarantee a placebo response weeks later. The Michigan trial did not test whether early improvers remain well (or show ongoing brain changes) on placebo.

The experiment's placebo instructions were vigorous. Patients were told that they were on a fast-acting antidepressant; later, they were given what they likely believed to be an intravenous infusion of an antidepressant. Patients who cannot shed even one symptom in the face of those instructions may indeed prove hard to treat. The early part of the experiment looks like a test for a dense absence of resilience, which is also to say that the favorable brain changes may simply be markers of the ability to respond to subsequent treatment.

This study cannot say whether a classic placebo response forms part of the antidepressant response or whether the two share a biological substrate. We have encountered research (Leuchter, Cook, et al., 2002) that points in the opposite direction—suggesting that placebo and drug responses differ in their neurobiology.

158 *forceful:* Gøtzsche, P. C., Young, A. H., et al., "Does Long Term Use of Psychiatric Drugs Cause More Harm Than Good?," *BMJ* 350 (2015): h2435. In his discussion of efficacy, Gøtzsche accepts results from the *JAMA* paper discussed above in chapter 22. He also believes that antidepressants cause many more falls in the elderly than conventional calculations suggest.

158 *expectancy effects:* Leuchter, A. F., Hunter, A. M., et al., "Role of Pill-Taking, Expectation and Therapeutic Alliance in the Placebo Response in Clinical Trials for Major Depression," *Br J Psychiatry* 205 (2014): 443–49. Even though expectancy shows activity only in the placebo arm, this paper has been advanced as showing expectancy effects for antidepressants. (See, for instance, Harrison, P., "Patient Expectations Largely Dictate Antidepressant Response," *Medscape,* September 15, 2014, http://www.medscape.com/viewarticle/831689.)

It should be said that this study measures expectancy by asking people how helpful they think medication or treatment in general will be in relieving their symptoms. The method bypasses the issue of unconscious expectations.

This same study raises questions about supportive psychotherapy effects in drug trials, but as the lead author has said (Harrison 2014), it seems that participants had signed on to get medication and dropped out when they did not get pills. Only twelve participants finished the course of psychological support, a sign of something gone awry. The support provided was less extensive than that offered in other UCLA trials, such as Leuchter, Cook, et al. 2002.

29. Elaboration

160 *Cowen gave:* Harmer, C. J., O'Sullivan, U., et al., "Effect of Acute Antidepressant Administration on Negative Affective Bias in Depressed Patients," *Am J Psychiatry* 166 (2009): 1178–84. See also Tranter, R., Bell, D., et al., "The Effect of Serotonergic and Noradrenergic Antidepressants on Face Emotion Processing in Depressed Patients," *J Affect Disord* 118 (2009): 87–93; and Harmer, C. J., Goodwin, G. M., et al., "Why Do Antidepressants Take So Long to Work? A Cognitive Neuropsychological Model of Antidepressant Drug Action," *Br J Psychiatry* 195 (2009): 102–8.

162 *Botox:* Finzi, E., Rosenthal, N. E., "Treatment of Depression with Onabotulinumtoxin A: A Randomized, Double-Blind, Placebo Controlled Trial," *J Psychiatr Res* 52 (2014): 1–6.

163 *lying:* Kirsch, I., Rosadino, M. J., "Do Double-Blind Studies with Informed Consent Yield Externally Valid Results? An Empirical Test," *Psychopharmacology (Berl)* 110 (1993): 437–42; and Kirsch, I., Weixel, L. J., "Double-Blind Versus Deceptive Administration of a Placebo," *Behav Neurosci* 102 (1988): 319–23. See also Zwyghuizen-Doorenbos, A., Roehrs, T. A., et al., "Effects of Caffeine on Alertness," *Psychopharmacology (Berl)* 100 (1990): 36–39.

163 *coinage lessebo:* Sinyor, M., Levitt, A. J., et al., "Does Inclusion of a Placebo Arm Influence Response to Active Antidepressant Treatment in Randomized Controlled Trials? Results from Pooled and Meta-analyses," *J Clin Psychiatry* 71 (2010): 270–79. Contrasting the lessebo findings with the data from two- and three-armed antidepressant trials in the FDA files, I am tempted to speculate that the introduction of doubt, through the instruction that real treatment may be withheld, is a strong impediment to elaboration, while awareness of the precise odds of receiving sham treatment exerts at most a weak influence.

163 *first made note:* Trivedi, M. H., Rush, H., "Does a Placebo Run-In or a Placebo Treatment Cell Affect the Efficacy of Antidepressant Medications?," *Neuropsychopharmacology* 11 (1994): 33–43. The confirmatory study is Sinyor, Levitt, et al. 2010.

163 *Parkinson's disease:* Mestre, T. A., Shah, P., et al., "Another Face of Placebo: The Lessebo Effect in Parkinson Disease: Meta-analyses," *Neurology* 82 (2014): 1402–9.

164 *amygdala:* Lehrer, J., "The Uncertainty Effect," *Wired* blog, December 6, 2010, http://www.wired.com/2010/12/the-uncertainty-effect/. See also Hsu, M., Bhatt, M., et al., "Neural Systems Responding to Degrees of Uncertainty in Human Decision-Making," *Science* 310 (2005): 1680–83.

164 *drugs are not drugs*: But then, the claim that antidepressants are placebos with side effects is such a suggestion. I am sometimes asked whether the antidepressant controversy impairs the effectiveness of medication. I have not seen any drop-off, but my guess is that this problem, if it exists, must be least evident in practices like mine, where in session I will tend to encourage patients to take advantage of upticks in mood, whatever their origin. Likely, patients prescribed for without prompt follow-up, as can happen in primary care settings, would experience the greatest loss of benefit. In this way, widespread lessebo effects might suppress the translation of medication use into psychic benefit that in chapter 19 I called "psychotherapy for the masses."

30. Interlude: Slogging
166 *Brown colleagues*: Zimmerman, Mattia, et al. 2002. See also Preskorn, S. H., Macaluso, M., et al., "How Commonly Used Inclusion and Exclusion Criteria in Antidepressant Registration Trials Affect Study Enrollment," *J Psychiatr Pract* 21 (2015): 267–74.

31. Lowliness
169 *subdivide depression*: I discuss this issue in *Against Depression*.
169 *best for outpatients*: Undurraga, Tondo, et al. 2013.
170 *Kirsch replied*: Moncrieff, J., Kirsch, I., "Efficacy of Antidepressants in Adults," *BMJ* 331 (2005): 155–57; Kirsch, I., Scoboria, A., et al., "Antidepressants and Placebos: Secrets, Revelations, and Unanswered Questions," *Prev Treat* 5 (2002); and Moncrieff, J., "A Comparison of Antidepressant Trials Using Active and Inert Placebos," *Int J Methods Psychiatr Res* 12 (2003): 117–27.
170 *changed his opinion*: Kirsch, Deacon, et al. 2008.
170 *same data*: Horder, Matthews, et al. 2011; and Vohringer and Ghaemi 2011.
171 *floor effects cause underestimates*: In the antidepressant controversy, floor effects play their strongest role in relation to the NICE requirement that to be considered clinically useful, treatments should outperform placebo by 3 Hamilton points on average. In a group of research subjects who begin with low Hamilton scores, each remission will produce only a modest decrease in the overall average point loss. (Statisticians say, *You can't drink a whole glass of water from a glass that's half full.*) Because of the floor effect, use of the NICE standard all but guarantees that treatments will seem to work least well for low-level depression. That apparent pattern will emerge even when by other criteria the same treatments look helpful in a broad range of illness.
171 *Europeans*: Melander, H., Salmonson, T., et al., "A Regulatory Apologia—a Review of Placebo-Controlled Studies in Regulatory Submissions of New-Generation Antidepressants," *Eur Neuropsychopharmacol* 18 (2008): 623–27.
171 *trajectories*: Gueorguieva, Mallinckrodt, et al. 2011; and personal communication, John Krystal and Ralitza Gueorguieva, June 4 and 5, 2013.

32. Washout

173 *only for severe:* Fournier, J. C., DeRubeis, R. J., et al., "Antidepressant Drug Effects and Depression Severity: A Patient-Level Meta-analysis," *JAMA* 303 (2010): 47–53. The authors used the (inflated) APA labels in which moderate depression is called severe. In the text, I follow the category choices in the Penn-Vanderbilt *JAMA* paper and its constituent trials.

173 *well for mild-to-moderate:* Stewart, J. A., Deliyannides, D. A., et al., "Can People with Nonsevere Major Depression Benefit from Antidepressant Medication?," *J Clin Psychiatry* 73 (2012): 518–25.

173 *by the Penn-Vanderbilt:* Robert DeRubeis, Steven Hollon, Jay Amsterdam, and Richard Shelton are frequent contributors.

173 *neuroticism:* Tang, DeRubeis, et al. 2009.

174 *patient-by-patient:* I will continue to use the term *meta-analysis*, but these more painstaking studies (Gibbons, Hur, et al. 2012 is another example) are often termed *mega-analyses*.

174 *off-site raters:* Kobak, K. A., Leuchter, A., et al., "Site Versus Centralized Raters in a Clinical Depression Trial: Impact on Patient Selection and Placebo Response," *J Clin Psychopharmacol* 30 (2010): 193–97.

174 *identified the pattern:* Khan, A., Schwartz, K., et al., "Relationship Between Depression Severity Entry Criteria and Antidepressant Clinical Trial Outcomes," *Biol Psychiatry* 62 (2007): 65–71.

175 *severity gradient:* Say that you have two overlapping studies, one testing mild-to-moderate depression and one, moderate-to-severe depression, and say also that the healthier half of each trial is afflicted by inflation. When you combine the studies, it will look as if medicine is highly effective in severe depression (where the scores of all the patients are real), modestly effective in moderate depression (where the scores of half the patients are real), and ineffective in mild depression (where few patients had depression to start with). That pattern will emerge even when, in doctors' offices, the medicine is equally effective throughout the depression spectrum. Washout phases are meant, among other things, to prevent researchers from stumbling into that confound.

175 *most straightforward:* Wichers, M. C., Barge-Schaapveld, D. Q., et al., "Reduced Stress-Sensitivity or Increased Reward Experience: The Psychological Mechanism of Response to Antidepressant Medication," *Neuropsychopharmacology* 34 (2009): 923–31.

175 *NIMH collaborative:* Elkin, Shea, et al. 1989.

176 *showcase Saint-John's-wort:* The remedy tested was hypericum extract, containing an active ingredient in the herb: Philipp, M., Kohnen, R., et al., "Hypericum Extract Versus Imipramine or Placebo in Patients with Moderate Depression: Randomised Multicentre Study of Treatment for Eight Weeks," *BMJ* 319 (1999): 1534–38. The study was funded by an herbal-supplement manufacturer and conducted with the participation of one of the company's senior researchers.

Regarding patients' moderate levels of depression, see also my conversation with Richard Shelton, August 3, 2015.

About the hundred-milligram dose of imipramine: It can be effective, as we saw in Roland Kuhn's treatment of Paula J.F. and D. N. Nandi's work with Bengali patients. And the German team made reference to a meta-analysis in which moderate doses of imipramine show efficacy: Bollini, P., Pampallona, S., et al., "Effectiveness of Antidepressants: Meta-analysis of Dose-Effect Relationships in Randomised Clinical Trials," *Br J Psychiaty* 174 (1999): 297–303. But they also referenced texts favoring doses more ordinarily considered adequate, 150–300 milligrams. See also Fatemi and Clayton 2008. On this point, a twenty-year study of recurrent depression treated in ordinary settings found no benefit from imipramine in doses below 200 milligrams or other antidepressants prescribed at equivalent low levels. The comparison was to no medicine at all—"no treatment." One hundred milligrams of imipramine did not even give a placebo effect: Leon, A. C., Solomon, D. A., et al., "A 20-Year Longitudinal Observational Study of Somatic Antidepressant Treatment Effectiveness," *Am J Psychiatry* 160 (2003): 727–33. Parenthetically, this result suggests that in clinical medicine, with recurrent depression, there is no pill-placebo effect, not even when the pills are real drugs with real side effects. Some research on short-term treatment of depression finds a similar pattern, much stronger likelihood of response to antidepressant doses equivalent to 200 milligrams or more of imipramine.

176 *Penn-Vanderbilt team's own:* DeRubeis, Hollon, et al. 2005 and (in collaboration with the University of Washington and other institutions) Dimidjian, S., Hollon, S. D., et al., "Randomized Trial of Behavioral Activation, Cognitive Therapy, and Antidepressant Medication in the Acute Treatment of Adults with Major Depression," *J Consult Clin Psychol* 74 (2006): 658–70.

To my way of thinking, meta-analyses that rely heavily on the authors' own prior research risk running afoul of unintended bias. The problems, beginning with design and extending to implementation, parallel failures of randomization and blinding in individual outcome studies.

In designing a meta-analysis, when teams set criteria for trials whose data will be employed, they will rarely exclude their own prior work. Perhaps because it mostly enrolled people who wanted free psychotherapy, the Dimidjian (2006) trial suffered a high dropout rate in the medication arm. (The authors wrote, "We cannot rule out the possibilities that patients in our trial were unrepresentative in their unwillingness to accept or inability to tolerate medication.") Selecting trials, another research group might, say, have disqualified ones with high attrition in any arm.

A parallel problem arises in the course of implementation. Once the data-gathering begins, researchers are much likelier to access results from their own work. The *JAMA* team contacted twenty-one research groups and received analyzable patient files from four. In terms of people: If the twenty-one studies were of equal size, and if you were a participant in a study, the odds of your finding your experience represented in the *JAMA* paper would have been about one in five—unless you were in the Penn-Vanderbilt studies, when the odds would have been one in one.

For the patients in those twenty-one studies, acceptance into the analysis was no longer random. If you arrived at the head of the line via a Penn-Vanderbilt study, you were included; if you arrived via most other studies, the triage nurse would likely set your file aside. It would be difficult for the overall result to contradict the trend that had begun to emerge in the team's own data.

I do not want to imply that the Penn-Vanderbilt team is unusual in its choices. It is common for researchers to construct meta-analyses around their own prior work. My conviction—not universally shared—is that these overviews lack the rarified objectivity that evidence-based medicine pretends to. To me, their best use is as informal contributions, not cleanly separated from incidental observation, in the ongoing discussion I call judgment-based medicine.

177 *at Dartmouth:* Barrett, J. E., Williams, J. W., Jr., et al., "Treatment of Dysthymia and Minor Depression in Primary Care: A Randomized Trial in Patients Aged 18 to 59 Years," *J Fam Pract* 50 (2001): 405–12. The trial even excluded patients with an episode of major depression in the prior six months.

177 *"minor depression":* In its effects, minor depression is not trivial. It predicts bad outcomes down the road, including major depression and suicide. If the few symptoms are intrusive enough, they can constitute substantial mood disorder. I reviewed this issue in *Against Depression*.

Including minor depression in what is otherwise a study of major depression can introduce confounds.

For example: Imagine two patients with Hamilton scores of 14, average for the Dartmouth study. One has major and one minor depression. If the patient with major depression has seven symptoms, most of those Hamilton points will attach to them. The points represent substantial impairment. If the patient with minor depression has only three symptoms, most of the Hamilton points represent scattered annoyances that do not, in the judgment of raters who made the initial diagnosis, amount to much. (She may also have forms of discomfort, such as constipation or backache, that the Hamilton rates but that do not appear on the symptom list used to diagnose both minor and major depression.)

The insubstantial or peripheral problems will fluctuate, creating apparent placebo responses. For that reason, when the mild-depression Hamilton scores run high, as they do here, mild depression will test out less well than major depression of the same "severity."

177 *between five and nine:* There are other requirements. The episode needs to last for a number of weeks and cause substantial impairment.

178 *made gains:* Psychotherapy did not give that benefit. The outcome replicated findings in a parallel trial of elderly patients: Williams, J. W., Jr., Barrett, J., et al., "Treatment of Dysthymia and Minor Depression in Primary Care: A Randomized Controlled Trial in Older Adults," *JAMA* 284 (2000): 1519–26.

33. All Comers

180 *That study exists:* Stewart, Deliyannides, et al. 2012. It was not that just anyone
who walked in might get medication; an interviewer needed to believe, based on
the clinical impression, that in some general sense the person was depressed.
But there was no minimum Hamilton score, and patients with Hamiltons of 8
were admitted regularly. One clinician recalled that someone with a Hamilton of
4 once made it through. But as Hamilton scores were not used for admission,
there was no need to inflate them.

181 *different population:* In response to my query about patients who enroll in Columbia trials, Stewart wrote that "on average they are better educated than they
are employed" (correspondence July–August 2015). The average educational at-
tainment was three years of college; half of the participants were employed.

182 Lancet: Neurology: Chollet, Tardy, et al. 2011.

183 *dead:* Morris, P. L., Robinson, R. G., et al., "Depression, Introversion and Mortality Following Stroke," *Aust N Z J Psychiatry* 27 (1993): 443–49.

183 *"daily living":* Robinson, R. G., Spalletta, G., "Poststroke Depression: A Review,"
Can J Psychiatry 55 (2010): 341–49. See also Ayerbe, L., Ayis, S., et al., "Natural
History, Predictors, and Associations of Depression 5 Years After Stroke: The
South London Stroke Register," *Stroke* 42 (2011): 1907–11.

183 *cautious:* Rampello, L., Battaglia, G., et al., "Is It Safe to Use Antidepressants
After a Stroke?," *Expert Opin Drug Saf* 4 (2005): 885–97.

184 *large literature:* A few titles, from many: Chen, Y., Patel, N. C., et al., "Antide-
pressant Prophylaxis for Poststroke Depression: A Meta-analysis," *Int Clin Psychopharmacol* 22 (2007): 159–66; Hansen, B. H., Hanash, J. A., et al., "Effects
of Escitalopram in Prevention of Depression in Patients with Acute Coronary
Syndrome (DECARD)," *J Psychosom Res* 72 (2012): 11–16; Musselman, D. L.,
Lawson, D. H., et al., "Paroxetine for the Prevention of Depression Induced by
High-Dose Interferon Alfa," *N Engl J Med* 344 (2001): 961–66; de Knegt, R. J.,
Bezemer, G., et al., "Randomised Clinical Trial: Escitalopram for the Prevention
of Psychiatric Adverse Events During Treatment with Peginterferon-Alfa-2a
and Ribavirin for Chronic Hepatitis C," *Aliment Pharmacol Ther* 34 (2011):
1306–17; Schaefer, M., Berg, T., et al., "Escitalopram for the Prevention of
Peginterferon-Alpha2a-Associated Depression," *Ann Intern Med* 159 (2012):
94–103; Kraus M. R., Schäfer, A., et al., "Therapy of Interferon-Induced
Depression in Chronic Hepatitis C with Citalopram: A Randomised, Double-
Blind, Placebo-Controlled Study," *Gut* 57 (2008): 531–36.

184 *resilience in the brain:* And, perhaps, protection from cognitive decline. See Sheline, Y. I., West, T., et al., "An Antidepressant Decreases CSF Aβ Production in
Healthy Individuals and in Transgenic AD Mice," *Sci Transl Med* 6 (2014): 236re4;
and Cirrito, J. R., Disabato, B. M., et al., "Serotonin Signaling Is Associated with
Lower Amyloid-Beta Levels and Plaques in Transgenic Mice and Humans," *Proc
Natl Acad Sci USA* 108 (2011): 14968–73. See also Wilson, R. S., Capuano, A. W.,
et al., "Clinical-Pathologic Study of Depressive Symptoms and Cognitive De-

cline in Old Age," *Neurology* 83 (2014): 702–9. In *Against Depression*, I discuss the early studies on neurogenesis.

184 *antiviral effects:* Young, K. C., Bai, C. H., et al., "Fluoxetine a Novel Anti-Hepatitis C Virus Agent via ROS-, JNK-, and PPARβ/γ-Dependent Pathways," *Antiviral Res* 110 (2014): 158–67.

34. Interlude: Cotherapy
189 *primary-care practices:* Ekselius and Von Knorring 1999.

35. How We're Doing
190 *COPES:* Davidson, K. W., Rieckmann, N., et al., "Enhanced Depression Care for Patients with Acute Coronary Syndrome and Persistent Depressive Symptoms: Coronary Psychosocial Evaluation Studies Randomized Controlled Trial," *Arch Intern Med* 170 (2010): 600–608.

191 *Comparable outcomes:* Williams, L. S., Kroenke, K., et al., "Care Management of Poststroke Depression: A Randomized, Controlled Trial," *Stroke* 38 (2007): 998–1003; Melville, J. L., Reed, S. D., et al., "Improving Care for Depression in Obstetrics and Gynecology: A Randomized Controlled Trial," *Obstet Gynecol* 123 (2014): 1237–46; Unutzer, J., Katon, W., et al., "Collaborative Care Management of Late-Life Depression in the Primary Care Setting: A Randomized Controlled Trial," *JAMA* 288 (2002): 2836–45; Richardson, L. P., Ludman, E., et al., "Collaborative Care for Adolescents with Depression in Primary Care: A Randomized Clinical Trial," *JAMA* 312 (2014): 809–16; Katon, W., Von Korff, M., et al., "Stepped Collaborative Care for Primary Care Patients with Persistent Symptoms of Depression: A Randomized Trial," *Arch Gen Psychiatry* 56 (1999): 1109–15. Much of the work is by the late Wayne Katon of the University of Washington.

191 *diabetic patients:* Katon, W. J., Von Korff, M., et al., "The Pathways Study: A Randomized Trial of Collaborative Care in Patients with Diabetes and Depression," *Arch Gen Psychiatry* 61 (2004): 1042–49; and Atlantis, E., Fahey, P., et al., "Collaborative Care for Comorbid Depression and Diabetes: A Systematic Review and Meta-analysis," *BMJ Open* 4 (2014): e004706.

192 *Sequenced Treatment:* Trivedi, M. H., Rush, A. J., et al., "Evaluation of Outcomes with Citalopram for Depression Using Measurement-Based Care in STAR*D: Implications for Clinical Practice," *Am J Psychiatry* 163 (2006): 28–40; Nelson, J. C., "The STAR*D Study: A Four-Course Meal That Leaves Us Wanting More," *Am J Psychiatry* 163 (2006): 1864–66; and many more.

192 *attract a range:* Researchers have estimated that only 18 percent of STAR*D enrollees would have qualified for a typical antidepressant outcome trial: Preskorn, S. H., Macaluso, M., et al., "How Commonly Used Inclusion and Exclusion Criteria in Antidepressant Registration Trials Affect Study Enrollment," *J Psychiatr Pract* 21 (2015): 267–74.

192 *disappointing:* Insel, T. R., "Beyond Efficacy: The STAR*D Trial," *Am J Psychiatry* 163 (2006): 5–7.

193 *vigorous prescribing*: Hollon, DeRubeis, et al. 2014; and Zajecka and Amsterdam 2014.

194 *blindered view*: Sifferlin, A., "Therapy and Antidepressants Work Better Together Than Just Pills Alone," *Time*, August 20, 2014, http://time.com/3146242 /therapy-and-antidepressants-together-work-better-than-just-pills/.

196 *better on Prozac*: Nelson, J. C., Portera, L., et al., "Are There Differences in the Symptoms That Respond to a Selective Serotonin or Norepinephrine Reuptake Inhibitor?," *Biol Psychiatry* 57 (2005): 1535–42. Craig Nelson finds that in the context of overall improvement on medication, anxiety responds to reboxetine and Prozac restores energy. The study does not attempt to answer our question whether patients with differing illness patterns are likely to respond to a particular class of drugs.

196 *University of Catania*: Rampello, L., Alvano, A., et al., "An Evaluation of Efficacy and Safety of Reboxetine in Elderly Patients Affected by 'Retarded' Post-Stroke Depression. A Random, Placebo-Controlled Study," *Arch Gerontol Geriatr* 40 (2005): 275–85. In prior papers, the Italian team had presented evidence along these lines for non-brain-injury depression: Rampello, L., Nicoletti, G., et al., "Dopaminergic Hypothesis for Retarded Depression: A Symptom Profile for Predicting Therapeutical Responses," *Acta Psychiatr Scand* 84 (1991): 552–54; and Rampello, L., Nicoletti, G., et al., "Comparative Effects of Amitriptyline and Amineptine in Patients Affected by Anxious Depression," *Neuropsychobiology* 31 (1995): 130–34.

197 *larger sample*: Rampello, L., Chiechio, S., et al., "Prediction of the Response to Citalopram and Reboxetine in Post-Stroke Depressed Patients," *Psychopharmacology (Berl)* 173 (2004): 73–78.

197 *loose replication*: Metzner, R., Ho, A. P., "Can Clinicians Improve Antidepressant Remission Rates with Better Treatment Algorithms?" (American Psychiatric Association Scientific Meeting, presentation no. 54, San Francisco, CA, 2009).

197 *genetic variant*: Schatzberg, A. F., DeBattista, C., "ABCB1 Genetic Effects on Antidepressant Outcomes: A Report from the iSPOT-D Trial," *Am J Psychiatry* 172 (2015): 751–59; and Mahon, F. J., "Clinically Useful Genetic Markers of Antidepressant Response: How Do We Get There from Here?," *Am J Psychiatry* 172 (2015): 697–99. Even though the finding constitutes a replication of prior research, the result remains preliminary; in another experiment (in the elderly), the same genetic variant did not distinguish responders to Paxil from responders to Remeron.

36. Steady As She Goes

197 *Most Americans*: Pratt, L. A., Brody, D. J., et al., "Antidepressant Use in Persons Aged 12 and Over: United States, 2005–2008," *NCHS Data Brief* 76 (2011); and Borges, S., Chen, Y. F., et al., "Review of Maintenance Trials for Major Depressive Disorder: A 25-Year Perspective from the US Food and Drug Administration," *J Clin Psychiatry* 75 (2014): 205–14.

201 *nine thousand patients:* Glue, P., Donovan, M. R., et al., "Meta-analysis of Relapse Prevention Antidepressant Trials in Depressive Disorders," *Aust N Z J Psychiatry* 44 (2010): 697–705. Short-term relapse prevention is often called continuation, rather than maintenance.

201 *FDA data:* Borges, Chen, et al. 2014.

201 *R&R:* Zajecka and Amsterdam 2014. The group's own name for this study was CPT-III.

202 *observational study:* Baldessarini, R. J., Tondo, L., et al., "Illness Risk Following Rapid Versus Gradual Discontinuation of Antidepressants," *Am J Psychiatry* 167 (2010): 934–41.

202 *"Contrary to prediction":* Viguera, A. C., Baldessarini, R. J., et al., "Discontinuing Antidepressant Treatment in Major Depression," *Harv Rev Psychiatry* 5 (1998): 293–306.

202 Lancet *study:* Geddes, J. R., Carney, S. M., et al., "Relapse Prevention with Antidepressant Drug Treatment in Depressive Disorders: A Systematic Review," *Lancet* 361 (2003): 653–61.

202 *French researchers:* Lépine, J. P., Caillard, V., et al., "A Randomized, Placebo-Controlled Trial of Sertraline for Prophylactic Treatment of Highly Recurrent Major Depressive Disorder," *Am J Psychiatry* 161 (2004): 836–42. In the text, I refer to a "Zoloft arm"; there were two, using different doses. The integrated data I present is from the original paper. Most patients had previously taken an SSRI, so the study does not answer the extreme version of the objection that if patients have been exposed to SSRIs, they will later be most stable when on them.

Through its design, the French study helped answer another contested question. Some skeptics say that antidepressants only delay *relapse*, the immediate reemergence (upon drug discontinuation) of an episode of depression that had continued in subtle fashion under the cover of medication; by this account antidepressants do not stave off *recurrence*, the appearance of a new episode. The French trial's long washout phase eliminated relapsers. Zoloft prevented recurrence.

204 differential sieve: Pies, R., "Are Antidepressants Effective in the Acute and Long-Term Treatment of Depression? *Sic et Non,*" *Innov Clin Neurosci* 9 (2012): 31–40; and extensive personal correspondence and conversation.

205 *his overview:* Viguera, Baldessarini, et al. 1998. Once over 80 percent of patients on placebo had relapsed, the remainder proved to be true invulnerables. They had no further episodes of depression. By then, the differential sieve had made the comparison to medication meaningless.

37. Interlude: Nightmare

207 *rate of falls:* Gøtzsche, P. C., "Why I Think Antidepressants Cause More Harm than Good," *Lancet Psychiatry* (2014) 1:104–6. The debate over falls serves to illustrate difficulties in the scientific assessment of seemingly straightforward

questions. A recent overview concluded that current evidence fails to demonstrate that SSRIs cause falls in the elderly: Gebara, M. A., Lipsey, K. L, et al.,
"Cause or Effect? Selective Serotonin Reuptake Inhibitors and Falls in Older
Adults: A Systematic Review," *Am J Geriat Psychiat* 23 (2015): 1016–28. On
their own, depressive symptoms have been associated with falls: Kvelde, T.,
McVeigh, C., et al., "Depressive Symptomatology as a Risk Factor for Falls
in Older People: Systematic Review and Meta-analysis," *J Am Geriatr Soc* 61
(2013): 694–706. One study found that although medication change was associated with falls in nursing home patients, the highest risk occurred (presumably
with worsening illness) four days before a new psychotherapeutic drug was
prescribed: Echt, M. A., Samelson, E. J., et al., "Psychotropic Drug Initiation or
Increased Dosage and the Acute Risk of Falls: A Prospective Cohort Study of
Nursing Home Residents," *BMC Geriatrics* 13 (2013): 19. A thoughtful review
concludes: "Given the destructive nature of late-life depression on duration and
quality of life as well as physical health, withholding treatment of a true late-life
depression for fear of antidepressant side effects is probably more harmful both
acutely and over time than antidepressant side effects, especially when doses
are low and carefully prescribed to avoid drug interactions." Salzman, C., "Late-
Life Depression and Antidepressants," *Am J Geriatr Psychiat* 23 (2015): 995–98.

39. Interlude: Practicing

215 *full doses:* Leon, Solomon, et al. 2003.

215 *high-quality:* Cuijpers, van Straten, et al. 2009. While this book was in press,
Pym Cuijpers and Erick Turner published an overview, analogous to Turner's
2008 paper on pharmacotherapies, of federally sponsored trials of psychotherapies for depression. It found publication bias—and effect sizes in the 0.2 range
(low efficacy) for the unpublished studies: Driessen, E., Hollon, S. D., et al.,
"Does Publication Bias Inflate the Apparent Efficacy of Psychological Treatment for Major Depressive Disorder? A Systematic Review and Meta-Analysis
of US National Institutes of Health–Funded Trials," *PLoS One* 10 (2015):
e0137864. Overall efficacy was higher, near 0.4, but it had not been possible (as
it had been with antidepressant research) to reanalyze published trials for possible efficacy inflation through researchers' "spinning" of the data.

215 *Bright lights:* Kripke, D. F., "A Breakthrough Treatment for Major Depression,"
J Clin Psychiatry 76 (2015): e660–e61.

216 *partly inborn:* De Moor, M. H., Boomsma, D. I., et al., "Testing Causality in the
Association Between Regular Exercise and Symptoms of Anxiety and Depression," *Arch Gen Psychiatry* 65 (2008): 897–905. In one of those quirky studies I
so enjoy, Marleen De Moor used survey methods as an alternative to controlled
trials, with their liability to dropout bias. Over an eleven-year period, researchers repeatedly asked almost 6,000 twins (interviewed along with more than
2,500 family members) to report on their mood and their exercise habits. More-
active individuals had had fewer mood problems, but the association was not

causal. Instead, mood resilience and the likelihood of exercising were linked by inheritance. To simplify: A person who increased his activity level suffered no less depression than his identical twin who did not.

216 *NICE:* Depression in adults quality standard, March 2011.

216 *no mental health benefit:* Chalder, M., Wiles, N. J., et al., "Facilitated Physical Activity as a Treatment for Depressed Adults: Randomised Controlled Trial," *BMJ* 344 (2012): e2758.

217 *Baldessarini's:* Baldessarini, Tondo, et al. 2010; and Viguera, Baldessarini, et al. 1998.

219 *used to be called:* Lieb, J., Balter, A. "Antidepressant Tachyphylaxis," *Med Hypotheses* 15 (1984): 279–91. In *Listening to Prozac,* I discuss the same phenomenon under the heading of developing tolerance to a drug. The term *tachyphylaxis* dates back a hundred years in what is now called immunology; the Greek roots of the word, meaning "rapid response," bear no relationship to the current usage in psychiatry.

220 *any relapse:* Zimmerman, M., Thongy, T., "How Often Do SSRIs and Other New-Generation Antidepressants Lose Their Effect During Continuation Treatment? Evidence Suggesting the Rate of True Tachyphylaxis During Continuation Treatment Is Low," *J Clin Psychiatry* 68 (2007): 1271–76.

220 *"Prozac poop-out":* McGrath, P. J., Stewart, J. W., et al., "Predictors of Relapse in a Prospective Study of Fluoxetine Treatment of Major Depression," *Am J Psychiatry* 163 (2006): 1542–48; see also Allen, A., "The Ups and Downs of Depression Treatment," *WebMD,* quoting Jonathan E. Alpert, http://www.webmd.com/depression/features/the-ups-and-downs-of-depression-treatment.

221 *suicidal preoccupations:* Teicher, M. H., Glod, C., et al., "Emergence of Intense Suicidal Preoccupation During Fluoxetine Treatment," *Am J Psychiatry* 147 (1990): 207–10.

221 *prevent suicides:* I review the early evidence in *Against Depression.* See also Gibbons, R. D., Hur, K., et al., "The Relationship Between Antidepressant Prescription Rates and Rate of Early Adolescent Suicide," *Am J Psychiatry* 163 (2006): 1898–904; and Barbui, C., Esposito, E., et al., "Selective Serotonin Reuptake Inhibitors and Risk of Suicide: A Systematic Review of Observational Studies," *CMAJ* 180 (2009): 291–97.

222 *controversial area:* Olfson M., Shaffer D., "Relationship Between Antidepressant Medication Treatment and Suicide in Adolescents," *Arch Gen Psychiatry* 60 (2003): 978–82; and Friedman, R. A., "Teenagers, Medication and Suicide," *New York Times,* August 3, 2015, A19.

40. We Are the 38 Percent

223 *"mother's little helpers":* Kramer, Klerman, et al. 1981.

224 *busy GPs record:* When physicians do diagnose and treat depression, the disorder tends to be substantial. While this book was in press, a team studying not-for-profit healthcare networks like Kaiser Permanente reported results from chart

research on thousands of cases in which doctors had recorded a diagnosis of depression or dysthymia and then given the patient antidepressants. In 85 percent of instances, the disorder was in the moderate or severe range. The authors commented that with the remaining 15 percent of patients, those with mild or minimal depression, "it is possible that medicine may have been prescribed primarily to address some other indication, such as co-occurring anxiety disorder." The article's title conveys the researchers' conclusion, that overprescription for low-level depression does not constitute a major public health concern. Simon, G. E., Rossom, R. C., et al., "Antidepressants Are Not Overprescribed for Mild Depression," *J Clin Psychiatry* 76 (2015): 1627–32.

224 *Baltimore:* Takayanagi, Y., Spira, A. P., et al., "Antidepressant Use and Lifetime History of Mental Disorders in a Community Sample: Results from the Baltimore Epidemiologic Catchment Area Study," *J Clin Psychiatry* 76 (2015): 40–44.

225 *Harvard:* Druss, B. G., Wang, P. S., et al., "Understanding Mental Health Treatment in Persons Without Mental Diagnoses: Results from the National Comorbidity Survey Replication," *Arch Gen Psychiatry* 64 (2007): 1196–203.

227 *trazodone as a sedative:* Stein, M. D., Kurth, M. E., et al., "Trazodone for Sleep Disturbance During Methadone Maintenance: A Double-Blind, Placebo-Controlled Trial," *Drug Alcohol Depend* 120 (2012): 65–73; and Letizia, B., Anna, C., et al., "Off-Label Trazodone Prescription: Evidence, Benefits and Risks," *Curr Pharm Des* 21 (2015): 3343–51.

228 *no medical attention:* Substance Abuse and Mental Health Services Administration, *Results from the 2012 National Survey on Drug Use and Health: Mental Health Findings,* NSDUH Series H-47, HHS publication no. (SMA) 13-4805 (Rockville, MD: Substance Abuse and Mental Health Services Administration, 2013).

41. *What We Know*

229 *signaled:* Insel, T., "Keynote Address" (Research Day, Department of Psychiatry, Brown University, May 9, 2013). However, the Veterans Administration is completing a multisite trial of medication strategies for treatment-resistant depression: Mohamed, S., Johnson, G. R., et al., "The VA Augmentation and Switching Treatments for Improving Depression Outcomes (VAST-D) Study: Rationale and Design Considerations," *Psychiatry Res* 229 (2015): 760–70.

229 *largely abandoned:* Hyman, S. E., "Psychiatric Drug Development: Diagnosing a Crisis," *Cerebrum,* April 2, 2013, 5.

230 *low doses of ketamine:* Krystal, J. H., Karper, L. P., et al., "Subanesthetic Effects of the Noncompetitive NMDA Antagonist, Ketamine, in Humans: Psychotomimetic, Perceptual, Cognitive, and Neuroendocrine Responses," *Arch Gen Psychiatry* 51 (1994): 199–214.

230 *seven depressed patients:* Berman, R. M., Cappiello, A., et al., "Antidepressant Effects of Ketamine in Depressed Patients," *Biol Psychiatry* 47 (2000): 351–54.

230 *ketamine abusers:* Narendran, R., Frankle, W. G., et al., "Altered Prefrontal Do-paminergic Function in Chronic Recreational Ketamine Users," *Am J Psychiatry* 162 (2005): 2352–59.

230 *response to ketamine:* Zarate, C. A., Jr., Singh, J. B., et al., "A Randomized Trial of an N-Methyl-D-Aspartate Antagonist in Treatment-Resistant Major Depression," *Arch Gen Psychiatry* 63 (2006): 856–64.

231 *distinctive means:* Lester, H. A., Lavis, L. D., et al., "Ketamine Inside Neurons?" *Am J Psychiatry* 172 (2015): 1064–6. While this book was in press, an American Psychiatric Association task force issued a white paper that largely confirms this assessment of ketamine: Newport, D. J., Carpenter, L. L., et al., "Ketamine and Other NMDA Antagonists: Early Clinical Trials and Possible Mechanisms in Depression," *Am J Psychiatry* 172 (2015): 950–66.

232 *"kappa-opioid":* Regarding new directions in general, see Papakostas, G. I., Ionescu, D. F., "Towards New Mechanisms: An Update on Therapeutics for Treatment-Resistant Major Depressive Disorder," *Mol Psychiatry* 10 (2015): 1142–50.

232 *make new cells:* Fava, M., Johe, K., et al., "A Phase 1B, Randomized, Double Blind, Placebo Controlled, Multiple-Dose Escalation Study of NSI-189 Phosphate, a Neurogenic Compound, in Depressed Patients," *Mol Psychiatr* (posted 2015) in advance of publication.

232 *Botox:* Finzi and Rosenthal 2014.

232 *within nerve cells:* Ferrés-Coy, A., Galofré, M., et al., "Therapeutic Antidepressant Potential of a Conjugated siRNA Silencing the Serotonin Transporter After Intranasal Administration" *Mol Psychiatry* (posted 2015) in advance of publication.

232 *pheromones:* Liebowitz, M. R., Salman, E., "Effect of an Acute Intranasal Aerosol Dose of PH94B on Social and Performance Anxiety in Women with Social Anxiety Disorder," *Am J Psychiatry* 171 (2014): 675–82.

232 *scattered findings:* Shelton, R. C., "Does Concomitant Use of NSAIDs Reduce the Effectiveness of Antidepressants?," *Am J Psychiatry* 169 (2012): 1012–15.

233 *resource bank:* Andrew A. Nierenberg conversation, June 6, 2014. See http://pfaawards.pcori.org/node/20/datavizwiz/detail/4925.

234 *weight gain:* Blumenthal, S. R., Castro, V. M., et al., "An Electronic Health Records Study of Long-Term Weight Gain Following Antidepressant Use," *JAMA Psychiatry* 71 (2014): 889–96.

234 *severity:* Perlis, R. H., Iosifescu, D. V., et al., "Using Electronic Medical Records to Enable Large-Scale Studies in Psychiatry: Treatment Resistant Depression as a Model," *Psychol Med* 42 (2012): 41–50.

234 *reasonably coherent:* For a recent failed effort at subtyping, see Arnow, B. A., Blasey, C., "Depression Subtypes in Predicting Antidepressant Response: A Report from the iSPOT-D Trial," *Am J Psychiatry* 172 (2015): 743–50.

234 *bottleneck:* Papakostas, G. I., Shelton, R., et al., "Reply to Commentary by Rothschild: 'A Blood Test for Depression?'" *J Clin Psychiatry* 76 (2015): e1038.

235 *resilience functions*: Li, Z., Zhang, C., et al., "Brain-Derived Neurotrophic Factor Levels and Bipolar Disorder in Patients in Their First Depressive Episode: 3-Year Prospective Longitudinal Study," *Br J Psychiatry* 205 (2014): 29–35; and Lee, B. H., Park, Y. M., et al., "Lower Serum Brain-Derived Neurotrophic Factor Levels Are Associated with Failure to Achieve Remission in Patients with Major Depression After Escitalopram Treatment," *Neuropsychiatr Dis Treat* 10 (2014): 1393–98.

236 *alternatives like exercise*: NICE also favored "guided self-help" modeled on cognitive behavioral therapy.

236 *"lack of high quality"*: Daley, A., Jolly, K., "Exercise to Treat Depression," *BMJ* 344 (2012): e3181.

236 *in addition*: Recent preliminary research suggests that exercise may have a role as an augmenter for SSRIs: Belvederi Murri, M., Amore, M., et al., "Physical Exercise for Late-Life Major Depression," *Br J Psychiatry* 207 (2015): 235.

237 *checklists*: Urbach, Govindarajan, et al. 2014.

237 *reach out of category*: For a recent example of out-of-category case reports, see Fawcett, J., Rush, A. J., et al., "Clinical Experience with High-Dosage Pramipexole in Treatment-Resistant Mood Disorder Patients," *Am J Psychiatry* 173 (2016): 107–11.

238 *Freud's dominance*: I discuss this issue in my brief biography, *Freud: Inventor of the Modern Mind* (NY: HarperCollins, 2006).

Glossary

What follows is not a dictionary but an aide-mémoire—a listing of terms of art that appear in more than one chapter, followed by a reminder of their use in context. In the relevant academic disciplines, many of the concepts have definitions that are more precise or that cover a larger frame of reference. My intent here is only to make it unnecessary to flip back through the book to locate the original explanation of a word or expression. In each entry, the first use of a term that has its own entry elsewhere in the glossary appears in italics.

active placebo A dummy pill with side effects, ideally ones that mimic those of an *active treatment* under test. The *tricyclics* caused immediate problems such as dry mouth, and some researchers worried that the telltale symptom would allow patients and observers to *break the blind* and then attach extra *hopeful expectancy* to the *antidepressant*. An otherwise inert dummy pill that also caused dryness of mouth would, so the thought went, allow for a fairer experiment.

active treatment/experimental treatment The psychotherapy or medication (believed likely to benefit patients through its *inherent efficacy*) being tested in a *controlled trial*, often in contrast to *placebo*.

additivity/additive A statistical property of a pair of interventions: two interventions are said to be additive if when given together their effect is the sum of the effects of each given individually.

Where additivity applies, the efficacy of one treatment (such as *minimal supportive psychotherapy*) can be subtracted from the efficacy of a combined treatment (such as an *antidepressant* plus minimal supportive psychotherapy) to arrive at a difference that accurately reflects the efficacy of the other treatment in the combination (here, the antidepressant). If additivity does not apply, then the subtraction will yield an underestimate of the efficacy of the treatment (again, here, the antidepressant) whose power is being assessed indirectly.

allegiance bias   The tendency for an active treatment to show excess efficacy in *outcome trials* or *meta-analyses* conducted by adherents of or researchers with a stake in the intervention under test. For example, trials conducted by the inventor of a psychotherapy tend to show stronger favorable results than trials (of the same therapy) conducted by neutral parties.

antidepressant controversy   The long-standing debate about whether *antidepressants* are *inherently effective* in the treatment of *major depression*. The contrary view has it that they act mostly through *hopeful expectancy* and so are little better than "*placebos* with side effects." A more restrained version of the skeptical position holds that antidepressants outperform placebo only in severe or very severe major depression. See also *active placebo* and *severity hypothesis*.

antidepressants   Medications used primarily in and for the treatment of depression. The names of most antidepressants discussed in the text appear in the *SSRIs* and *tricyclics* entries below. See also *monoamine oxidase inhibitors, reboxetine, Serzone*, and *trazodone*. I refer to some antidepressants by their brand name and others by their generic name, depending on which term is in more general use.

antipsychotics   Medicines such as Thorazine (called Largactil in Roland Kuhn's Switzerland) used primarily in the treatment of illnesses, such as schizophrenia, in which delusions and hallucinations are prominent symptoms. See also *psychotic depression*.

anxiolytics   Medicines (such as Librium, Miltown, Valium, and Xanax) used primarily to treat anxiety.

arm   A group of participants in a *controlled trial* that receive a particular treatment regimen. (Every controlled trial will have a *control arm* and at least one *active treatment* arm; some will also have a *comparator* arm.) The term also covers the protocol applied to each group.

augmenter   A secondary treatment (generally one that, at the given dose, would not elicit marked favorable responses on its own) intended to help a primary treatment to work or work better. For example, when a patient does not respond to a full dose of an *antidepressant*, doctors may add a low dose of a lithium salt—a half to a third of the amount given in lithium's most common use, stabilizing patients with bipolar disorder—as an augmenter, to jump-start the antidepressant treatment.

baseline score inflation   At the start of an *outcome trial*, the exaggeration (often by raters pushing to meet a quota) of participants' depression symptom scores, especially those near the minimum set for inclusion in the study. With inflation, a trial that requires a *Hamilton score* of 16 will include a suspiciously high number of participants with initial scores of 16 and 17. Among them will be patients who in reality have lesser levels of depression and who, in the face of subsequent accurate ratings, will appear to have improved with any intervention, including dummy pills. Baseline score inflation can act as a *confound*, causing *controlled trials* or *meta-analyses* to show a *severity gradient* when there is none.

Bech scale/HAM-D6   A slimmed-down *antidepressant* rating instrument, developed by the Danish psychiatrist Per Bech in the 1970s, that employs only six of the seventeen *Hamilton scale* factors: depressed mood, guilt, work functioning, *psychomotor retardation*, psychic anxiety, and general bodily symptoms, such as low energy. (Bech calls these six factors "core symptoms" of depression.) The shortened scale was designed to reflect clinicians' assessments of patients and to give a more coherent picture than the full scale does of the course of *major depression*.

bias   A systematic flaw in an experiment or body of evidence that will tend to push results in a certain direction and so lead to spurious findings. See also *allegiance bias*, *dropout bias*, *file-drawer bias*, and *susceptibility bias*.

blind/double-blind/break the blind   Unaware of the treatment assignment. An *outcome trial* is double-blind if neither the patient nor the treating doctors and raters know who is in which *arm*. If staff or patients can tell who is taking what (drug or *placebo*), they have "broken the blind." Blinding is a protection against *bias*—in particular against a tendency to report favorable results for subjects known to be receiving the *active treatment*.

candidate-drug trial   An *outcome trial* testing a new medication, the "candidate," being proposed for approval by the Food and Drug Administration.

categorical analysis/category/categorical   A research summary that counts people (in an *outcome trial's treatment* and *control arms*) who achieve a defined level of improvement. *Response*, *remission*, and *recovery* are categories. See also *number needed to treat*. (I do not use the expression in the text, but comparisons built around average results in groups—*effect size* is an example—are called numerical analyses.)

CBT/cognitive behavioral therapy A psychotherapy focused on correcting patients' maladaptive cognitions ("Because I failed at this task, I am worthless"), often through direct didactic means.

classic placebo effect Improvement of illness, in response to an inert intervention, that arises from the impact of pill taking, doctorly authority, the clinical setting, and so on. The term also covers similarly based progress occurring in patients receiving potentially effective treatments. For well over a century, the term *hopeful expectancy* has been used to describe the psychological state that mediates the classic placebo effect.

Cochrane Collaboration An international professional organization dedicated to *evidence-based medicine* that, among its other tasks, sponsors, approves, and publishes overviews of treatment outcome research. The group is named after Archie Cochrane, a Scottish physician and public health researcher who, in the aftermath of World War II, advanced the use of *randomized trials* in the evaluation of medical treatments.

comparator A treatment of established efficacy used, in its own *arm* of an *outcome trial*, to "validate the sample" of patients. The idea is that if the group of participants is typical of those with the target illness, those in the comparator arm should improve to the expected degree, a result that will indicate that the remainder of the experiment (say, *candidate drug* versus dummy pill) is trustworthy. A trial in which the comparator does not outperform *placebo* is said to be "failed," meaning that the rest of the experiment cannot be expected to yield valid results.

completer analysis A statistical summary (of results of an *outcome trial*) that ignores patients who drop out and bases calculations on scores from participants who show up for rating sessions through the end of the experiment. If patients in a *placebo arm*, more than those in a drug arm, quit for "inefficacy"—that is, failure to improve—completer analyses will overstate the benefits of dummy pills. One alternative is an intention-to-treat analysis, which includes results from all patients who attend the first rating session of a trial. See also *differential dropout*.

confound An extraneous factor in an experiment that is liable to distort the results. Most commonly, in our discussions, we encounter confounds such as *differential dropout* that leave patients in one *arm* of a trial relatively susceptible to ongoing illness while patients in the other arm remain, on average, more resilient—after which point the trial will suffer from *susceptibility bias*. Confounds can lead to spurious conclusions.

   Confound, as a noun, is a term of art in statistics; in recent years, some authors have begun replacing it with the less felicitous (to my ear) noun *confounder*.

control arm See *control condition*.

control condition An intervention (such as administration of a *placebo* or *comparator*) included in an *outcome trial* for purposes of comparison. When the control condition involves a placebo, the *control arm* of a trial is meant to duplicate the circumstances in the *treatment arm*—the same passage of time, the same contact with raters, and so on—in the absence of the *inherently effective* element of the intervention under test. In this case, the control arm results represent the *hypothetical counterfactual*, what would have happened to patients in the treatment arm had they not received the benefits (and side effects) of the *active treatment*, via its inherent efficacy.

controlled trial A trial in which an *active treatment* is compared to a *control condition*.

core symptoms of depression See *Bech scale*.

curse of Roland Kuhn/Kuhn's curse My shorthand for the historical tendency, which Kuhn recognized, for patient samples in drug trials to become progressively less representative of depressed people in general as (with effective *antidepressants* widely available) run-of-the-mill cases are treated in doctors' offices.

demand characteristic A *confound* arising from the tendency of patients to offer symptom reports that reflect what they believe their caregivers prefer or implicitly "demand." The "hello effect" (exaggerating the level of suffering early on) and "goodbye effect" (in the late going, reporting more progress than actually occurred) are demand characteristics.

differential dropout A *confound* that can arise when patients exit different *arms* (of an *outcome trial*) for different reasons. If, in the extreme case, patients drop out of the *placebo* arm because they are floundering while patients leave the *treatment arm* when they feel all better, then the placebo arm will be left with naturally resilient patients while the treatment arm will be left with partly responsive (that is, somewhat treatment-resistant) patients. Thereafter, the trial will suffer from *susceptibility bias*. See also *dropout bias*.

differential sieve A cause of *confounds* that arise in a *controlled trial* when the interventions in the contrasting *arms* leave them with patient populations whose risk of further illness differs. For instance, over time, treatment with dummy pills may, through its lack of efficacy, act as a narrow-gauge sieve, causing vulnerable patients to exit a trial so that only naturally resilient participants pass through and remain available for further study. In the same interval, *antidepressant* treatment may act as a broad-gauge sieve, sustaining patients with chronic and recurrent depression and allowing them to pass through to the next phase of the research. From that point on, the experiment will suffer from *susceptibility bias*.

double-blind   See *blind*.

dropout bias   *Susceptibility* bias arising from *differential dropout*. If differential dropout leaves patients in one *arm* of an *outcome trial* more liable to continued illness than patients in another arm, thereafter the trial results are likely to be distorted.

dysthymia   Chronic low-level depression. The official definition in use for much of the last half century required depressed mood on most days for at least two years with at least two accompanying depressive symptoms, such as feelings of hopelessness. Other requirements concerned the relationship to *major depression* (episodes in the distant past and episodes occurring late in the course of dysthymia were permitted) and intervals (brief ones were allowed) without depressive symptoms. Some of the *meta-analyses* we have encountered used looser criteria.

effect size   A measure, developed by the statistician Jacob Cohen, of the average advantage of an *active treatment* over a *placebo* condition. Cohen provided a guide whose overuse he then warned against: an effect size of 0.2 is small; 0.5 is medium; and 0.8 is large. An effect size of 0.5 says that the average treated subject will do better than 69 percent of untreated subjects. The effect size goes beyond *statistical significance* to attempt to answer our *How much?* question—how well a treatment works. Like the *number needed to treat*, effect size provides a means of comparing the efficacy of treatments in disparate medical specialties.

Ekselius   Repeatedly I reference a study by the Swedish researcher Lisa Ekselius that showed high response rates to *SSRIs* in depressed primary-care patients—substantial improvement in over three-quarters of those entering the trial and 90 percent of those who stuck with it. The point is that in ordinary use (when the *curse of Roland Kuhn* is not in effect) the medicines work well.

elaboration   In the theory of Philip Cowen, the social and psychological processes through which, over time, a person builds on the immediate change in feeling and perception provided by *antidepressants* to achieve substantial relief from mood disorder.

evidence-based medicine/EBM   A movement announced in the 1990s that aims to ground clinical decision making less in doctorly experience and more in objective research results. The extreme or narrow version of EBM demands near-exclusive reliance on the findings of *randomized, controlled, double-blind outcome trials*.

experimental treatment   See *active treatment*.

file-drawer bias/publication bias   The tendency for a scientific literature to show exaggerated efficacy for treatments as a result of the preference (on the part of researchers and editors) for publishing favorable outcomes and shelving unfavorable ones. Erick Turner's analysis of data from the FDA files (largely involving *candidate-drug trials*) demonstrated that, compared to the published research, the entire collection of evidence showed lower *antidepressant* efficacy. The published literature had suffered from file-drawer bias.

grab bag (of placebo effects)   My term for the jumble of influences (including *baseline score inflation, classic placebo effects, demand characteristics, minimal supportive psychotherapy,* and natural healing that occurs with the passage of time) that act in the *control arms* of *antidepressant outcome trials.*

Hamilton scale/Hamilton score   A rating instrument developed by Max Hamilton in the late 1950s and used ever since in *outcome trials* of depression treatment. The scale recognizes seventeen symptoms of depression, called factors: depressed mood, guilt, suicidality, early (in the night) insomnia, middle insomnia, late insomnia, inhibition of work and other interests, *psychomotor retardation*, agitation, psychic anxiety, somatic anxiety, gastrointestinal symptoms, general bodily symptoms, genital symptoms, hypochondriasis, loss of insight, and weight loss.

Each factor receives a weighting—from 1 to (for some factors) as many as 4 points—and the sum is the Hamilton score. A score of 50 points is possible, but totals above the low 30s are rare. In simple terms, a Hamilton of 30 represents severe depression; 20, moderate; and 10, mild. Although they may still consider themselves depressed, in most formal research people with Hamilton scores below 7 or 8 are judged to be in *remission.*

hopeful expectancy   See *classic placebo effect.*

How much? question   My term for the debate over (or our general interest in) the level of efficacy of *antidepressants.* Almost all overviews show that antidepressants work. The issue is, how well?

hypothetical counterfactual   See *control condition.*

inherent efficacy/inherently effective   *Inherent efficacy* refers both to the contribution that an intervention makes through its special properties and to the basis for its making that contribution. With streptomycin, its inherent efficacy arises from its power to inhibit the growth of bacteria. With *antidepressants,* their ability to alter neurotransmission in the brain is the presumed source of their inherent efficacy. "Pharmacologic potency" is an earlier term for roughly the same concept. The implicit contrast is to the *grab bag* of *placebo* effects: drugs' efficacy based on the fact of pill taking, the passage of time, and so on.

instruction effect   In an *outcome trial,* the influence on results exerted by what the tester says. For example, telling experimental subjects given caffeinated coffee that they are drinking decaf will result in decreased reports of tension. See also *lessebo effect.*

IPT/interpersonal psychotherapy   A brief, manualized psychotherapy for depression, developed in the 1960s by Gerald Klerman and others, intended as a stand-
in (in *outcome trials*) for psychoanalysis and related psychotherapies.

lessebo effect   An *instruction effect* whereby patients given active medication and
told that they may be on *placebo* show lower drug efficacy than patients told, correctly, that they are taking a real drug. The lessebo effect may arise in part from patients' failure, once they have been made uncertain about their treatment, to engage
in *elaboration* of the initial improvement they experience.

maintenance   The extended use of medication over time. A typical maintenance
trial begins with research subjects who have done well—say, on an *antidepressant*—
in a short-term *outcome trial*. In the maintenance phase, these patients will be randomly assigned to take a dummy pill or to continue taking the antidepressant, and
the time to *relapse* or *recurrence* will be measured. Other designs are possible.

major depression   For most of the last half century, the official definition of major
depression required impairment of functioning based on at least a two-week interval
of depressed mood or inability to experience pleasure, accompanied by symptoms (for
the diagnosis, five symptoms were required in all) from a group that included low energy, guilt, impaired concentration, suicidality, *psychomotor retardation* or agitation,
disturbed or excessive sleep, and change in appetite. Before the formulation of this
definition (and oftentimes, later, in parallel with its use), clinicians diagnosed depression experientially, based on their empathic assessment of a patient's level of despondency and their past observations of similar presentations of mood disorder. See also
mild major depression and *minor depression*.

meta-analysis   A study that uses statistical methods to amalgamate the results of
many small *outcome trials*. Gene Glass developed the approach, incorporating Jacob
Cohen's concept *effect size*.

mild major depression   *Major depression*—entailing substantial impairment and
at least five depressive symptoms—but with a modest score, perhaps in the 8-to-15
range, on the *Hamilton scale*. Mild major depression is distinct from *minor depression*,
which shows scores in a similar range but involves fewer symptoms.

minimal supportive psychotherapy   The aspect of participation in an *outcome
trial*—based on frequent contacts with interested, helpful staff members (and perhaps fellow participants as well)—that acts like a supportive psychotherapy. (Supportive psychotherapy works via encouragement more than insight.) The term was
coined by the designers of the *NIMH collaborative study*, who required psychiatrists
monitoring the *placebo* and medication *arms* of the trial to provide "advice and encouragement" to prevent suicides or substantial worsening in research subjects.

minor depression A mood disorder involving fewer symptoms than the number required for major depression. In the example we consider, the "Dartmouth study," the researchers required three or four depressive symptoms and a *Hamilton scale* score greater than 10. The symptoms had to include depressed mood or the inability to experience pleasure. Minor depression is not *mild major depression*; in the Dartmouth study, patients with a fifth symptom were excluded. So were patients with *dysthymia*— which means that (in this instance) minor depression was nonchronic low-level depression.

monoamine oxidase inhibitors/MAOIs Medications that affect the way that the brain handles a broad class of *neurotransmitters*, the monoamines: dopamine, norepinephrine, and serotonin. MAOIs were the first modern *antidepressants*. Because they are difficult to use—they have life-threatening side effects—the MAOIs became less popular with time, in the United States especially.

neuroticism Hans Eysenck's term for a personality trait characterized by negative thinking, uncomfortable self-consciousness, and emotional vulnerability and instability.

neurotransmitter A chemical that carries signals from one nerve cell to another. Serotonin, norepinephrine, dopamine, and glutamate are neurotransmitters.

NICE/National Institute for Clinical Excellence A semiautonomous British governmental agency, founded in 1999, tasked with improving care in the National Health Service, largely through a focus on treatment standards. In 2005, the agency (still known as NICE) changed its name to the National Institute for Health and Clinical Excellence.

NIMH collaborative study/TDCRP Supervised by the National Institute of Mental Health in the 1980s, the Treatment of Depression Collaborative Research Program was the first large-scale clinical trial of psychotherapy. The study used imipramine as a *comparator*.

nuisance variables/noise In an *outcome trial*, circumstantial factors that can impede the effort to measure the *intrinsic efficacy* of a treatment. For example, an especially upbeat set of raters might pump up response rates in all *arms* of a study and so serve as "noise" or a nuisance factor. A major function of the *control arm* is to track nuisance variables.

number needed to treat/NNT A means of summarizing *controlled trial* results as measured by *categorical* outcomes such as *response* and *remission*. The NNT estimates the number of patients who would need to take an *active treatment* to achieve one more favorable result than would occur with *placebo*.

Consider the case in which four patients are offered an *antidepressant*. Two respond—but one would have responded on dummy pills. The doctor needed to treat four patients to achieve one additional good outcome. Equally, if all four patients respond to medication but three respond to dummy pills, the number needed to treat would be 4.

Reporting results via the NNT is a hallmark of *evidence-based medicine*. Because its use is widespread, the measure allows comparisons of the efficacy of treatments in different medical specialties.

outcome trial/outcome study An experiment testing a clinical intervention, such as *antidepressants* or psychotherapy, to see how well it works in people.

placebo In an *outcome trial*, the element in a *control condition* meant to resemble the *active treatment* but lacking its *inherent efficacy*. In antidepressant trials, generally the placebo will take the form of a tablet or capsule otherwise identical to the one delivering the drug but containing only the fillers used to stabilize or add bulk to the drug's active ingredient. There are many variations. In the *TDCRP*, a dummy pill supplemented by *minimal supportive psychotherapy* served as a placebo for the two psychotherapies being evaluated, *CBT* and *IPT*.

placebo arm In a *controlled trial*, an *arm* in which patients receive *placebo* as the primary intervention.

placebo effect See *classic placebo effect* and *grab bag (of placebo effects)*.

psychomotor retardation A symptom of depression. Psychomotor retardation includes the slowing of speech, thought, and muscular motion.

psychosomatics The study of the interface between mental illness and medical illness generally treated by nonpsychiatrists.

psychotic depression An extreme form of mood disorder characterized by depression accompanied by marked delusions—that is, fixed and highly unrealistic beliefs, and/or hallucinations. Psychotic depression generally does not respond to *antidepressants* alone but requires combined treatment that includes *antipsychotics*.

publication bias See *file-drawer bias*.

quality-of-life research Studies whose outcome measures track work and social functioning along with overall health.

randomized controlled trial See *randomized trial* and *controlled trial*.

randomized trial An *outcome trial* in which participants are assigned to the different *arms* randomly. In our image of randomizing, patients approach a triage nurse who, without regard to any of their personal characteristics, such as age or health, hands them a sealed envelope consigning them to an arm. Randomization is meant to protect trials from *susceptibility bias* that can arise from other methods of allocating participants to treatment arms.

R&R My mnemonic, because of its focus on *remission* and *recovery*, for a long-term, multisite *outcome trial* (conducted by researchers at the University of Pennsylvania and elsewhere) testing the benefits of vigorous prescribing, with or without cognitive therapy, for depression.

reboxetine An *antidepressant*, not marketed in the United States, that is thought to work via its effect on the brain's use of the *neurotransmitter* norepinephrine. In experiments, often responses to reboxetine are contrasted to responses to *SSRIs*.

recovery See *remission*.

recurrence/relapse The return of depression in a patient previously in *remission* from a prior episode. I use the terms indiscriminately, as do some authors I cite. (Other authorities reserve *relapse* for a quick reemergence of depression and contrast it to *recurrence*, appearance of a new episode after a substantial interval of good health. An associated argument—often marred by analyses that fall afoul of the *differential sieve*—has it that medication is better at preventing the former than the latter.) Definitions of *relapse* and *recurrence* vary from study to study, a problem I allude to in passing in the discussion of *tachyphylaxis*.

remission Emergence from depression, and then the subsequent interval of freedom from depression. When patients' *Hamilton scores* fall below a certain number, generally 8, their depression is said to have remitted. (Some trials require continued low scores for a period of weeks.) Early studies used the term *recovery* to comparable effect, but the mental health professions later embraced *remission*, in acknowledgment of the likelihood of *recurrence*. In the *R&R* research, the term *recovery* was reserved for remissions lasting six months.

rescue The prompt administration of *antidepressants* as an episode of depression emerges. In circumstances that might otherwise call for the prophylactic use of antidepressants, clinicians may, as an alternative strategy, follow patients closely and initiate rescue when the need arises.

response A favorable reaction to treatment. From the earliest analyses, response has been defined as a 50 percent decrease in the *Hamilton score*.

Serzone An *antidepressant* believed to work via its effect on serotonin transmission in the brain but that because of its particular mechanism of action does not qualify as an *SSRI.* Serzone is related to *trazodone,* an earlier medicine used to treat depression, anxiety, and insomnia.

severity gradient A pattern of outcomes in which a treatment has greater efficacy for severe than for mild illness.

severity hypothesis The theory that *antidepressants* work best for severe or very severe *major depression* and may have no superiority over *placebo* in the treatment of *mild* (or mild-to-moderate) *major depression.* See also *antidepressant controversy* and *severity gradient.*

SSRIs *Antidepressants* (such as Prozac, Zoloft, Paxil, Celexa, and Lexapro) thought to work via their influence on the brain's handling of the *neurotransmitter* serotonin. The SSRIs are "second-generation" antidepressants, ones with a better-tolerated set of side effects than the *tricyclics,* which they have largely replaced.

STAR*D A multisite *outcome trial* (Sequenced Treatment Alternatives to Relieve Depression), conducted in the first decade of this century, meant to test treatments, principally *antidepressants*, on a broad range of depressed patients. Most participants had chronic depression complicated by other ailments. The intent was to see how patients fare when treated as they might be in clinical practice.

statistical significance, significant A statistical standard meant to indicate whether a research result—a correlation or a treatment outcome—is real, that is, unlikely to be due to chance alone. (The usual criterion for the label *significant* requires a less than one-in-twenty chance of a random association.) Findings can be statistically significant, that is, not due to chance, without being clinically significant, that is, important to patients. Statistical significance says nothing about the *How much? question.*

stimulants Medicines, such as amphetamines or Ritalin, now used principally in the treatment of attention deficits and hyperactivity—but which on occasion prove of use in the treatment of *major depression.*

susceptibility bias A distortion (due to a failure of *randomization* or an equivalent *confound* such as *differential dropout*) that arises when participants in one *arm* of an *outcome trial* are more susceptible to further illness than participants in another arm. The arm with the less vulnerable patients may show favorable outcomes even when the treatment it tests is ineffectual.

tachyphylaxis A catastrophic failure of efficacy arising during treatment with a medicine that had previously been stabilizing. Lately, the definition has been broadened to include, in the most liberal usage, any worsening of depressive symptoms (during a *maintenance* phase of treatment) that requires an adjustment in a drug regimen.

TDCRP   See *NIMH collaborative study/TDCRP*.

trajectory   A distinctive, coherent path of response to treatment, generally one shared by a cluster of patients. For example, depressed patients who enjoy an early, abrupt improvement and then stay well or improve further in each subsequent observation would be said to be on a particular (favorable) trajectory.

trazodone   A sedating drug with *antidepressant* and *anxiolytic* properties. See *Serzone*.

treatment arm   In a *controlled trial*, the *arm* in which patients receive the experimental or *active treatment*.

tricyclics   The class of *antidepressants* (named for their characteristic three-ring chemical structure) that includes imipramine, Elavil, and desipramine. Generally, tricyclics are thought to work via their effects on the brain's use of the *neurotransmitter* norepinephrine, with varying additional effects on serotonin pathways. The tricyclics were among the first modern antidepressants, dating back to Roland Kuhn's observations of imipramine in the 1950s. Effexor and (to a lesser degree) Cymbalta are recent antidepressants thought to resemble tricyclics in their mechanism of action.

Index

A NOTE ABOUT THE AUTHOR

Peter D. Kramer is a psychiatrist, writer, and Brown Medical School professor. Among his books are *Against Depression*, *Should You Leave?*, and the *New York Times* bestseller *Listening to Prozac*. His articles and book reviews have appeared in *The New York Times*, *The Washington Post*, *Slate*, and elsewhere.